The Focke-Wulf Fw 189 Uhu

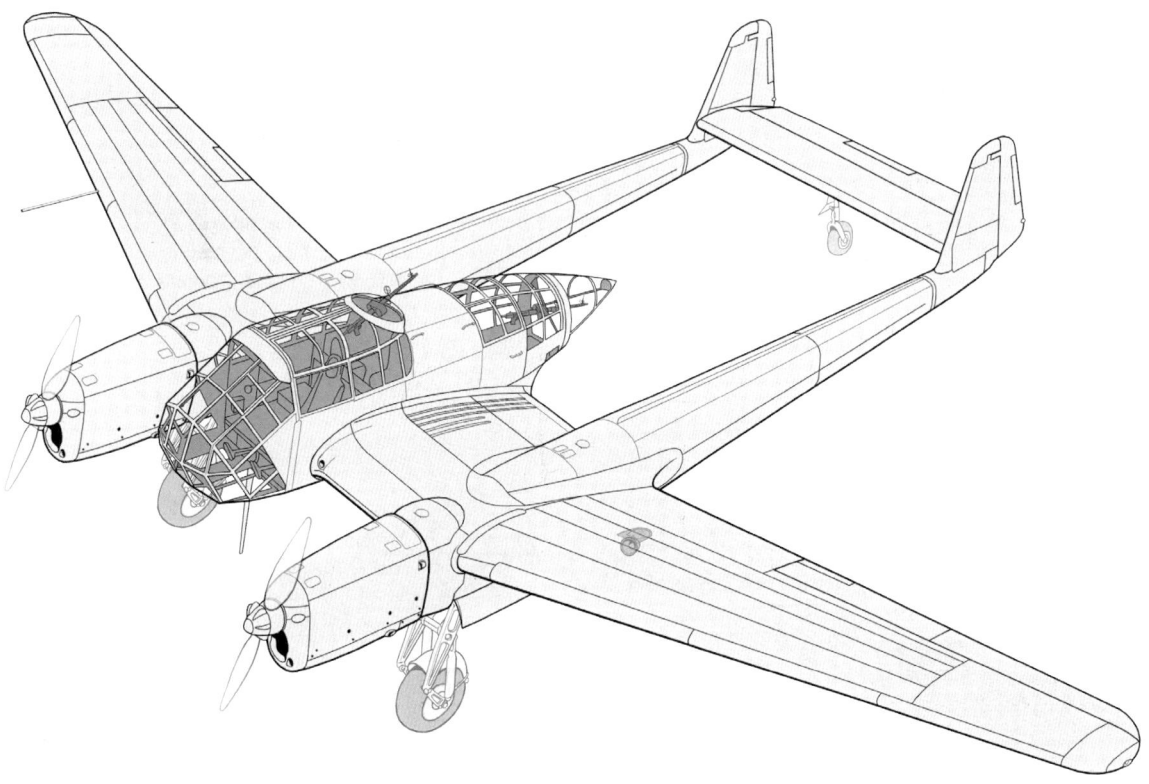

Sections

1. **Technical Description**
   Detailed coverage of construction and equipment

2. **Evolution – Prototype, Production and Projected Variants**
   3D-isometrics illustrating differences between variants

3. **Camouflage & Markings**
   Colour side profiles, notes and photographs

4. **Models**
   – 1/72nd Condor kit built by Libor Jekl
   – 1/48th Great Wall Hobby kit built by Steve A. Evans
   – 1/32nd HpH kit previewed

   Appendices
   I   Focke-Wulf Fw 189 Kit List
   II Focke-Wulf Fw 189 Accessory & Decal List
   III Bibliography

Information

Airframe Album No.6
The Focke-Wulf Fw 189 Uhu
A Detailed Guide to the Luftwaffe's 'Flying Eye'
by Richard A. Franks

First published in 2015 by
Valiant Wings Publishing Ltd
8 West Grove, Bedford, MK40 4BT, UK
+44 (0)1234 273434
valiant-wings@btconnect.com
www.valiant-wings.co.uk
◨ valiantwingspublishing

© Richard A. Franks 2015
© Richard J. Caruana – Colour Side Profiles
© Wojciech Sankowski – Side Profiles & Isometric Lineart
© Seweryn Fleischer – Cover Art

The right of Richard A. Franks to be identified as the author of this work has been asserted in accordance with sections 77 and 78 of the Copyright Designs and Patents Act, 1988.

The 'Airframe Album' brand, along with the concept of the series, are the copyright of Richard A. Franks as defined by the Copyright Designs and Patents Act, 1988 and are used by Valiant Wings Publishing Ltd by agreement with the copyright holder.

All rights reserved. No part of this publication may be reproduced or transmitted in any form or by any means, electronic or mechanical, including photocopy, recording, or any other information storage and retrieval system, without permission in writing from the publishers.

ISBN: 978-0-9575866-8-0

Acknowledgements
The author would like to give a special word of thanks to Przemyslaw Skulski & George Papadimitriou for supplying additional photographs, to Libor Jekl and Steve A. Evans for their excellent model builds and to Richard J, Caruana, Seweryn Fleischer and Wojciech Sankowski for their superb artwork.

Note
There are many different ways of writing aircraft designation, however for consistency throughout this title we have used one style, e.g. Fw 189 V1, Fw 189A-0 etc.

Cover
The cover artwork depicts Fw 189A-1, V7+IJ of 1.(H)/Aufkl. Gr. 32 over the Northern Front in 1942 (see Richard J. Caruana's alternative interpretation, with additional notes, of this scheme on the back cover). This artwork was specially commissioned for this title © Seweryn Fleischer 2015.

The mock-up of the Fw 189 V1, made from wood, wire and canvas

This starboard side view of the Fw 189 V1 mock-up does show how much longer the Hirth engine nacelles initially were, plus the envisaged pointed spinner on the propeller

Focke-Wulf Fw 189
Glossary

The Fw 189 V1 during final assembly. You can see the Hirth engines installed, as well as the rows of bolts on the wings and tail boom joints, and the centreline raised rib on each boom

Aeronautica Regala Romana	Royal Rumanian Air Force
atm	Atmosphere (= 14.696psi)
Aufklärungstaffeln	Reconnaissance Squadrons
Dipl. Ing.	*Diplom-Ingenieur* (M.S. degree)
ETC	*Elektrische Trägervorrichtung für cylinder bomben* (Electrically operated carriers for cylindrical bombs)
Fliegerführer Nord (Ost)	Aviation Leader North (East)
Funkgerät (FuG)	Radio or Radar Set
HK	*Handkamera* (Hand camera)
kg.	Kilogram (= 2.20462lb)
km/h	Kilometres per hour (= 0.621371mph)
KW	Kilowatt (= 1.34102209hp)
Lt	Litre (= 0.219969 Imperial Gallons)
Luftflotte	Air Fleet
m	Metre (3ft 3 3/8in)
Magyar Királyi Honvéd Légierö (MKHL)	Royal Hungarian Home Defence Air Force
MG	Machine Gun
Nahaufklärungsgruppen	Tactical (short-range) Reconnaissance Groups
PS	*Pferdestarkes* (Metric Horsepower)
Rb	*Reihenbilder* (shortened version of *Reihenbildmesskamera* – series-picture [topographic camera])
RLM	*Reichsluftfahrtministerium* (Reich Air Ministry)
rpm	Revolutions per minute
Slovenské vzdusné zbrane (SVZ)	Slovakian Air Force
Stammkenzeichen	Primary identification (code letters)
Versuchs or *Versuchsmuster*	Research or test aircraft (V-series)
Vozdushni Voiski	Royal Bulgarian Air Force
Werknummer (W/Nr.)	Works (construction) number
Zwilling (e.g. MG81Z)	Twin

Preface

Tactical reconnaissance was always a main part of the Luftwaffe's role, to support the *Wehrmacht* as it moved forward during operations. The Fw 189 was designed in response to an RLM specification issued in 1937 for the replacement of the Henschel Hs 126, which was, at that time, undergoing acceptance trials with the Luftwaffe. There were three designs submitted in response to the specification, the first being the Arado Ar 198, which featured a shoulder-mounted wing, radial engine and extensively glazed fuselage and ventral gondola. The second was the Blohm & Voss Bv 141 (See Airframe Detail No.1 by Valiant Wings ISBN 978-0-9575866-7-3), which was very unconventional with its asymmetric layout, a single engine mounted at the front of the tail boom assembly, and a glazed nacelle offset to starboard. The Fw 189 actually did not follow the specification, which stated the design had to be powered by a single engine, but it was more conventional looking than the Bv 141. The RLM did not really like either the Bv 141 or Fw 189, but issued production contracts for three prototypes of both the Ar 198 and Fw 189.

Construction of the prototype (V1) Fw 189 began in April 1937, under the control of *Dipl. Ing.* E. Kosel. It flew for the first time, with Kurt Tank at the controls and marked as D-OPVN, in July 1938. This prototype was powered by the Hirth HM-512 inline engine, as was the V2, which joined the V1 in the test programme (as D-OVHD) in August 1938. The V2 was the first armed airframe, having a single MG17 machine-gun in each wing root and an MG15 machine-gun in the dorsal (*B-Stand*) position. The V2 was also the first to carry bomb racks, with two ETC50 racks under each wing just outboard of the engine nacelle/tail boom; these could carry 50kg bombs of various types. The V3 (D-ORMH) first flew in September 1938 and was unarmed, but it was the first to have the Argus As 410 inline engines installed, and later, it also featured Argus-designed automatic variable-pitch airscrews operated by air pressure, which were to become standard on all future Fw 189s. With the Ar 198 proving to be unsatisfactory, the RLM ordered another four prototype Fw 189s, with the V4 (D-OCHO) completed in late 1938. This was the first true pre-production airframe and featured various revisions in relation to

Well known photo of the Fw 189 V1, D-OPVN, in flight July 1938

the V3, including the movement of the landing light from the leading edge of the port wing, to a hinged unit fitted under the port wing, inboard of the ETC racks. This machine was also the first to test the S 125 smoke-laying equipment, which could also distribute the 'Yellow Cross' group of mustard gases.

The Trainer

The V5 was the prototype for the proposed two-seat trainer version, which saw the extensively glazed nacelle of the previous prototypes replaced with a more bulbous unit that only had a small glazed panel over the aft section, and a standard canopy and windscreen over the cockpit. The RLM liked the proposed B-series and it was the first type of Fw 189 to be series-built, when three pre-production B-0s and ten production B-1s were built during mid-1939, with all of the former and three of the latter being delivered to the Luftwaffe by the end

Nice detailed image of the Fw 189 V1a viewed from the rear/port and clearly showing the initial style of armoured shell applied to the nacelle

The Fw 189 V1a, with the armoured canopy raised and no guns fitted

of the year. The B-series was unarmed, could carry five people and offered both navigational and radio operator training. The remaining seven B-1s were delivered to the Luftwaffe during January and February 1940, where they were used to familiarise crews prior to the delivery of the A-series machines.

Close-Support

The V1 was taken out of the test programme and returned to the Focke-Wulf factory in late 1938, where it was extensively revised to meet the RLM's requirement for a close-support aircraft. The nacelle was removed and replaced with a small, two-seat, heavily armoured pod that was permanently welded to the wing section (unlike the A and B-series, where the nacelle was attached in the conventional manner and could therefore be separated from the wings). The type was redesignated the V1a and initially the armoured screen installed proved to be too restrictive of the pilot's vision and the almost total lack of overall view afforded the rear gunner had a detrimental effect on his ability to protect the aircraft from attack. As a result of this, coupled with a reduction in performance that the smaller, but much heavier, armoured nacelle had on the type, it was returned to the factory for modification. These modifications saw the front windscreen enlarged with three armoured sections and the gunner's station revised with a larger armoured glass screen and smaller armoured blisters fitted above and to each side of the nacelle, in an attempt to give him better all-round vision. Numerous different layouts for the rear gunner's position were considered and the V1c, which was never actually built, used what was called a 'spherical' (*kugeliger*) mount, while the V1b, as the revised V1a now became known, had the single rear MG15 replaced with a twin MG81Z. The V1b also featured the full fixed armament of 1x MG151 20mm cannon and 2x MG17 machine-guns in each wing root. In this form the V1b went up against the other type going for the close-support role, the Hs 129. Neither type was liked by the Luftwaffe but the Hs 129 was a smaller and cheaper option, so its development continued. The V1b was eventually wrecked in a crash-landing during a demonstration flight, after the pilot nearly struck a hangar. Development of the type did not end with the V1b, as Focke-Wulf pro-

The Fw 189 V2 on its landing approach. Note the screen on the front of the canopy, which was the initial style tried to reduce glare; production machines had a curtain and screen inside the canopy/ nose cone

In this shot you can see the Fw 189 V3 now marked as TP+AW and with 9(H)LG2 at Paderborn for service trials in December 1939

The Fw 189 V3, D-ORMH, this was the first fitted with the As 410 and had the initial side-mounted oil coolers

posed a revised version in April 1940, designated the V6, which was intended as the prototype for the envisaged C-series. The Hs 129A was by this stage undergoing service trials with the Luftwaffe, so the C-series was abandoned. Before this happened, though, Focke-Wulf tried to clean up the aerodynamics of the nacelle on the V6, and this resulted in a smoother profile cover being applied to the rather angular nacelle, with a single square armoured glass panel in each side for the rear gunner.

The A-series

The first of ten A-0 series pre-production machines came off the Bremen production lines in early 1940. These were swiftly followed by twenty production A-1s, which were basically similar to the V4, but had the oil coolers removed from the side of the engine nacelles and had full armament of one MG17 machine-gun in each wing root and an MG15 in the dorsal (*B-Stand*) and aft (*C-Stand*) positions. The type also had the two ETC 50/VIII racks under each wing, outboard of the engine/booms and could carry 50kg bombs as well as the S 125 smoke (and gas) laying containers. The tactical reconnaissance role was undertaken by the fitment of an Rb 21/18, Rb 15/18, Rb 20/50 or Rb 50/30 camera in the mid-fuselage and this could be supplemented with a hand-held HK 12.5x7 or HK 19 camera operated by the observer.

Operational Use

B-0 and B-1 trainers were issued to 9.(H)/LG2 in the Spring of 1939, prior to the unit receiving its A-0s for operational trials during the Autumn of 1940. Production of the initial A-1 and revised A-2 did not get much priority, and it was not until the summer of 1942 that the type started to be used in any great numbers. The mainstay of the frontline *Aufklärungstaffeln* (H) [*Heeresgruppen*] remained the Henschel Hs 126, even throughout the invasion of Russian (Operation Barbarossa) in June 1941. In late 1941 most of these units were reorganised

The Fw 189 V5 in flight showing off its clean lines

The Fw 189 V4, D-OCHO, seen here testing the S 125 smoke (and gas) generators

Focke-Wulf Fw 189
Introduction

The two-seat Fw 189 V5, BQ+AZ, viewed from the starboard side. The aerial lead from the mast to starboard fin is for the FuG10; no lead was used for the FuG17 fitted to the recce versions (if above or below the nacelle)

into *Nahaufklärungsgruppen* [NAG {later NAGr}], tactical short-range reconnaissance groups, which were linked directly to the *Wehrmacht*. Attrition rates during operations in Russia were high and with the Kalinin offensive by the Russians in December 1941 the reconnaissance units were reorganised once again, with further reductions in the number of squadrons. The first unit to re-equip solely with the Fw 189A-1 and A-2 was 2.(F)/11, which was followed by *Aufklärungsgruppe* 10 in May 1942. By September 1942 of the 317 short-range reconnaissance aircraft listed in Russia, 174 of them were Fw 189A-1s or A-2s and eventually the type was to equip *Aufklärungsgruppen* 10, 11, 12, 13, 14, 21, 31, 32 and 41. With the failure of the *Wehrmacht* in Stalingrad, the reconnaissance units were reduced, with some units also being renumbered; 1.(10)10-1 of NAG 12 became 1.10, NAG 9 became 2.10, NAG 5 became 1.11 and NAG 1 became 5.11, whilst 1.NAG 2 re-equipped with the Bf 109 and a number of units were retrained to operate other types such as the Bf 110. In the Caucasus region 11.12 (ex-1.(H)12) and 1.21 continued to use the Fw 189, whilst NAG 2, 3, 5, 8 and 10 remained away from the frontline and started conversion training to the Bf 109 or Fw 190. From May 1943 the Fw 189 took on another role, that of anti-partisan operations behind enemy lines, seeking and destroying men and equipment. Operation Zitadelle (Citadel) started in July 1943 with Fw 189s supporting the group troops with details of all Soviet troop and tank movements, but the attack on Charkov was stopped by the Soviet counter-attack on the 12th July. By this stage

Nice shot of the Fw 189 V6 being built in which you can see the ammo boxes in the wing roots and the fact that the armoured nacelle means the wings have no follow-through spar and are thus permanently joined to the nacelle

there were no reserves of Fw 189s and the introduction of the new Soviet La-5 and Yak-3 fighters soon saw the loss rate climbing. At about this time much of the reconnaissance switched to night operations and it is said that the aircraft used in this role had special equipment for operating at night and in adverse weather conditions, although exact details of what this equipment was are elusive. By April 1944 *Luftflotte* 6 only had 42 Fw 189s left with NAGr.4 (eight), NAGr.10 (12), NAGr.15 (15)

The Fw 189 V6, D-OPVN, clearly showing the twin-leg undercarriage, bomb racks under each wing and the combination of machine-gun and cannon at each wing root

and 4(H)31 (7) plus a further two assigned to I./NJG 100 in the pure night fighter role. By the Summer of 1944 the Fw 189 could no longer be used in the tactical reconnaissance role, due to its being given high priority as a target to Soviet fighters. The type remained in use for night operations, though, often alongside Bf 109Gs, Fw 190As and Bf 110Cs.

Middle East
The only unit to use the Fw 189 in the Middle East was 4.(H)/12 *Staffel* as part of *Fliegerführer Afrika*, where they operated alongside the unit's Bf 110Cs.

Finland
Luftflotte 5's *Fliegerführer* Nord (Ost) had over 200 aircraft in Finland in which were seven Fw 189s operated by 1.(H)32, based at Kemijärvi, Alakurtti and Petsamo. These machines undertook reconnaissance missions, but also did bombing and leaflet dropping missions along the front line. By January 1944 the unit had moved to Idriza. As the Soviet forces moved forward during late 1944/45 these machines undertook missions over Poland and the 'Böhmen und Mähren Protektorat', but many were eventually destroyed on the ground by retreating German units during April and May 1945.

Final Operations
The Fw 189 remained in use by the Luftwaffe right up the end of WWII, with sixteen Fw 189s of NAGr.2 and 15 included in a group of twenty-one aircraft that undertook a night operation on the 17th April 1945. This was followed on the 19th and 20th by two Fw 189s alongside NASGr.15's Bf 109s and Bf 110s, attacking Soviet units along the front line. The last operations by the Fw 189 were probably undertaken by NAGr.2, as 1.(H)41 had been redesignated, when they operated the type right up to the armistice along the Southern Front.

Post-war
A number of Fw 189s landed in Sweden at the end of the war, claiming they had got 'lost', including W/Nr.0271, CE+PE that crash-landed at Alvestad on the 8th April 1945. An Fw 189A-1 (W/Nr.2326, U2+ZB) and A-2 (W/Nr.0215, U2+BD) landed near Bulltoft on the 8th May 1945.

At least eight intact Fw 189s were found by Allied troops in Norway, but most of these were destroyed by the RAF Air Disarmament Units during the autumn of

A closer look at the armament on the Fw 189 V6: the protruding barrels are from the MG151/20 cannon, whilst the fourth smaller hole in the starboard wing is for the gun camera

1945. One was officially taken on charge by the Royal Norwegian Air Force, who made it airworthy, but it was grounded in May 1946, probably due to a lack of spare parts, and was presumably scrapped shortly afterwards.

Foreign Service

Bulgarian Air Force
The Royal Bulgarian Air Force (*Vozdushni Voiski*) was an Axis ally during WWII, but it did not undertake operations against Russia. It did however receive a number of German aircraft, including a batch of eighteen Fw 189s. These were delivered in mid-1943 and operated by *1st Razuznavatelen Polk* (1st Reconnaissance Wing) of the *3rd Orliak* (3rd Group) that comprised two squadrons. The type was named *Tzyklon* (Cyclone) or *Oko* (Eye) in Bulgarian service and it was operated over the Black Sea. When the Bulgarian nation changed sides, from the beginning of September 1944 the air force was reorganised. The *1st Razuznavatelen Polk* was split into two *Orliaka* (Groups), comprising the 333rd and 334th *Yato* (Squadrons); the former had eight, the latter six Fw 189s. The national insignia changed from the black cross to a white roundel with a green centre and a red horizontal bar, and the units started to operate almost at once. These missions against its former allies took place over Serbia, Macedonia and, later, southern Hungary.

Fw 189A, T1+EH of 5(H)/12 in Russia, note the yellow bands under the cross and the 'E' outlined in white

The mass of glazed panels in the nose of the Fw 189A is clearly seen in this shot of KC+JN in flight

The Bulgarian Air Force Fw 189s are believed to have remained in use until the late 1940s, when they were all replaced with more modern Soviet types.

Hungarian Air Force

The Royal Hungarian Home Defence Air Force (*Magyar Királyi Honvéd Légierö* – MKHL) was formed in August 1938 and at this time operated the Heinkel He 46, WM-Fokker C.VD and WM-16 in the short-range reconnaissance role. These were supplemented by the purchase of a number of WM-21 *Sólyom* a year later. When the Soviets bombed the East Slovak town of Kosice on the 27th June 1941 (at that time Kassa, annexed by Hungary) the Hungarian nation declared war on the Soviet Union. The fast expeditionary force sent to the USSR saw action in the Ukraine, but with the entry into service of faster Soviet fighters, the need to modernise the Hungarian fleet became very apparent. The Fw 189 was chosen for the short-range reconnaissance role, however the larger crew complement per aircraft could not be met by training establishments in Hungary, so the Luftwaffe training establishment at Proskurov was used. The first unit to convert to the Fw 189 was 3/1. *közelfelderitö-század* (3/1. short-reconnaissance squadron), commanded by Capt. Imre Telbisz and they started training from the 16th April 1943 under the control of *Aufklärungsgruppe 31*. Training was completed by mid-May, when the unit received twelve Fw 189s via Kiev and the unit deployed to Kharkov airfield. Their first mission was on the 22nd and the unit had its first operational loss the next day, when the aircraft of 1st lt L. Székely failed to return; the aircraft was forced down and the pilot and gunner were taken prisoners, only to return home after five years in a Soviet POW camp. The unit continued operations and by late May it could see the build-up of Soviet forces, signifying a potential new offensive, as the Battle of Kursk was about to begin. The unit flew numerous missions in support of the German forces, but after a few days the Luftwaffe lost air superiority and these flights became more dangerous. With the failure of Operation Zitadelle (Citadel), the Soviet forces broke through on the 5th July and the unit undertook more ground-attack missions carrying SD70 bombs instead of the usual SC50 versions. On the 7th August 1943 Sgt E. Pap even managed to shoot down a Soviet La-5, but on this day the unit was ordered to retreat because the Soviet tanks were near the airfield. The unit, in the company of Luftwaffe groups, headed to Sitikovka airfield, from which flights to the

An Fw 189A being refuelling somewhere in Russia during summer 1943, whilst others of the squadron can be seen in the shelter of trees in the background

Focke-Wulf Fw 189
Introduction

One of the pre-production A-0 series, this is BQ+AU at Holzweiler in the winter of 1939-40

front line now took two hours. Operations were numerous, but Soviet fighters were becoming more aggressive, however on the 21st September Fw 189 crews managed to shoot down two La-5s. By December 1943 the unit had flown 1,000 missions, and all for the loss of three crew killed, two missing and one seriously injured. With the end of 1943 the unit was given fresh crew and relocated to Berdichev. Then in January 1944 they moved to Kalinovka alongside *5/1. fighter squadron*. With the worsening situation the unit was all but wiped out during the Soviet attack on Radzimilów airfield on the 18th March 1944, with the personnel leaving their aircraft and withdrawing to Lwów, then on to Mokre airfield near Zamoshtch.

On the 18th May 1944 a new squadron took on the short-reconnaissance role, this being *4/1. közelfelderitö-század*. Two weeks later it completed training and moved to Zamoshtch, followed ten days later by a move to Lesyatitze as part of the 1st Hungarian Army in the Central Sector. The retreats continued, though, with a move to Stanislaw on the 23rd, then twenty-five days later to Labunye. At this point the Hungarian unit came under German control and its aircraft were marked with German national insignia (*Balkenkreuz*). By the end of July 1944 the unit moved to Balice, then on the 11th August on to Ungvár (now Uzhgorod) in the Ukraine. From here the unit flew missions over Slovakia to observe the movements of the uprising in that nation and they also undertook leaflet-dropping missions. The unit retreated to Gödöllö at the end of September 1944, and there handed over their remaining Fw 189s to the Germans. In its two and a half years of operations the squadron had flown 200 missions, lost over ten machines, with 15 crew killed or missing in action, and another six wounded.

A third Hungarian unit flew tactical reconnaissance, but did so as part of a Luftwaffe unit over the Baltic Sea during mid to late-1944, when they returned their aircraft to the Luftwaffe. Some of the crews later went on to undertaken more reconnaissance missions, but this time with the Me 210D and Bf 109G-8.

Front view of an Fw 189A-0 in the firing butts at Bremen

The rear view of an Fw 189A-0 in the firing butts at Bremen

A nice close-up from a series of images taken of a line-up of Fw 189A-1s prior to delivery. Note the gaiters on the bottom of each oleo leg

Rumanian Air Force

The *Aeronautica Regala Romana* (Royal Rumanian Air Force) initially undertook all short-range reconnaissance operations with its own aircraft types, the IAR 37, 38 and 39. This situation changed in the spring of 1943 when the decision was made to create a new ground assault unit equipped with the Henschel Hs 129. The lack of a suitable twin-seat training version resulted in the RLM sending five Fw 189s to this new group (*Grupul 8 asalt*), which was based at Kirovograd. These machines remained in Luftwaffe markings and had Luftwaffe instructors, so that once the training period was completed, they all returned to Germany.

With the *coup d'état* on the 23rd August 1944, the Rumanians captured a large number of German aircraft. Most were destroyed, but some remained to be used by the Bulgarian Air Force, including two Fw 189s, which received the new red/yellow/blue roundels of the nation. These machines were never used on the front line, instead they were used for training purposes at the blind flying school at Popesti-Leordeni airfield near Bucharest. They were finally scrapped, along with all other remaining ex-Luftwaffe aircraft, in the late 1940s, when they were replaced with Soviet equipment.

Slovakian Air Force

As a Nazi ally the Slovakian Air Force's fleet during the early stages of WWII was in serious need of modernisation as highlighted numerous times by the DLM (*Deutsche Luftwaffenmission in der Slovakei*). As a result an approach was made to the RLM by the MNO (Slovakian Ministry of Defence) for the supply of modern German aircraft types. Fourteen Fw 189As were ordered in early 1943 and Aero at Prague-Vysocany was chosen as the supplier. Five A-2s (W/Nr.s 2303, 2304, 2305, 2206 and 2316) were delivered in October 1943, where they were identified by the last three of their Werke Numbers in all Slovak records. These aircraft were flown by German pilots to Trencín, where on the 6th October 1943 they were accepted by the LP-SVZ (*Letecky pluk – Slovenské vzdusné zbrane* – Aviation Regiment, Slovakian Air Force). They were all allocated to the 1st Reconnaissance Flight of the SVZ. Another ten A-2s plus two special photo-survey (Fw 189W-2) aircraft were requested, but by March 1944 only seven A-2s and a single W-2 had been delivered. By this stage production at Prague had ceased, so these machines were either all refurbished ex-Luftwaffe, or had come out of storage. All of these machines were flown from Prague to Piestany and were accompanied by eight

A nice staged image of newly built Fw 189A-1, SI+EM, out on the airfield prior to delivery; the markings and camouflage is typical of all production A-series machines

Focke-Wulf Fw 189
Introduction

The B-series nacelle is quite bulbous due to the redesigned canopy etc., as seen here on B-0, W/Nr.0011, coded BS+AA. Note the supporting/lead-in wires on either side of the aerial mast, something that is unique to the B-series

machines destined for Bulgaria. The W-2 was allocated to the *Photogrammetrical Institute of ing. Gál* in Bratislava, while all the A-2s joined the existing machines with the 1st Reconnaissance Flight at Zilina. Three machines were lost in quick succession, the first two due to landing accidents, but the third in a fatal crash near Domaniza, south east of Rajec, when all on board were killed. Accounts then state that the 'remaining' six aircraft (should be nine?) [W/Nrs.2310. 2315, 2316, 2327, 2328 & 2340] were sent to Isla airfield near Presov on the 27th June 1944, where they were incorporated into the aircraft group of *mjr.* Trnka, as part of the East Slovakian army of *gen.* Malár. The W-2 undertook photo-reconnaissance flights over central Slovakia from Piestany airfield prior to the SNP (Slovakian Nationalist Uprising). It then went to Trencin for repairs, but a return flight was banned, so the crew went back to the *Photogrammetrical Institute of ing. Gál* at Bratislava by train. However the W-2 did not remain at Trencin, because pilot J. Setvák and mechanic Kurpel took the aircraft and defected with it to Poland. Six Fw 189s (W/Nrs.2310, 2315, 2316, 2327, 2328 and 2340) were flown from Isla to the Soviets on the 31st August 1944. Once the uprising broke out, one machine, W/Nr.2316, was flown back to Tri Duby (now Sliac) airfield by *rtm.* Slivka and *slob.* Mesko on the 6th September 1944. On board this aircraft was a Soviet liaison officer, I.I. Skripka-Studensky and the aircraft was subsequently used to co-ordinate the Combined Flight of the uprising forces, thanks to the FuG 17 radio equipment it carried. On the 11th September 1944 another machine, landed at Tri Duby airfield flown by *stotn.* P. Gasparovic and *slob.* J. Mej. It too flew with the insurgent Slovak Air Force and once the uprising was over, returned to the Soviets on the 24th October 1944.

A nicely posed propaganda shot of an Fw 189A-1 with the crew in front, that was taken on the Eastern Front. Note the location of the starting handle in the port nacelle

Fw 189A-2, 5D+FH of 1(H)/31, showing the yellow band around the boom underneath both of the aft codes, plus the application of a unit badge on the outer face of the engine cowling

Specification

Engines
- Fw 189 V1 and V2: 2x Hirth HM-512 inverted V-12, rated at 395 PS each
- Fw 189 V3 onwards: 2x Argus As 410A-1 inverted 60° V-12, rated at a maximum of 465 PS at 3,100rpm each (415PS/3,100 rpm @ 2,400m climbing or 325PS/2,820rpm @ 2,400m continuous)
- Fw 189 V14: 2x Gnôme-Rhône 14M 7-cylinder radial rated at 522Kw (700hp) each
- Fw 189 V15: 2x Argus As 411MA-1 inverted 60° V-12 rated at 600PS (441kW) @ 3.300rpm

Propellers
- Fw 189 V1 and V2: Initially Schäfer two-blade, wooden, later replaced with VDM variable-pitch, two-blade metal
- Fw 189 V3: Initially VDM, variable-pitch, two-blade, metal, later replaced with Argus, two-blade, air-adjusted (automatically), wooden
- Fw 189 V4 onwards: Argus, two-blade, wooden with automatic air-adjusting pitch mechanism of 2.6m diameter, running at a ratio of 2:3 in relation to engine speed

Wings
- Span 18.4m
- Length 12.03m
- Height 3.1m

Undercarriage Prototypes & Pre-production
- Main: Single oleo leg, single wheel, rearwards retracting with oleo-pneumatic shock-absorber and shrouded spring actuator arm. Wheel – Elektron alloy hubs with independent hydraulic brakes operated by separate accumulator pumps directly connected to each rudder pedal. Tyres inflated at 3.80 atm
- Tailwheel: Retractable 'Y' yoke, which swivels through 360° and oleo-pneumatic shock-absorber. Fitted with electrical-conductive tyre and inflated to 2.75atm

Undercarriage A-1 onwards
- Main: Double oleo leg, single wheel, rearwards retracting with oleo-pneumatic shock-absorber and shrouded spring actuator arm. Wheel – Elektron alloy hubs with independent hydraulic brakes operated by separate accumulator pumps directly connected to each rudder pedal. Hubs fitted with 770x270mm diameter tyres inflated at 5.75 atm
- Tailwheel: Retractable 'Y' yoke, which swivels through 360° and oleo-pneumatic shock-absorber. Fitted with electrical-conductive tyre of 350x135mm diameter and inflated to 3.00atm

Weight
- Empty (A-1): 2,830kg
- Take-off [normal] (A-1): 3,950kg
- Take-off [maximum] (A-1): 4,170kg

Performance
- Maximum speed, climbing power @ 2,400m: 350km/h (A-1 onwards)
- Speed for sustained power @2,400m: 325km/h
- Maximum permitted diving speed: 502km/h

Fuel
- 200lt per hour (A-1 onwards)

Ceiling
- 7,300m (2,700m on one engine) (A-1 onwards)

Range
- 670km (A-1 onwards)

Armament
- V1 – None
- V1a – Fixed MG17 and MG15 in each wing root, firing forward, plus an MG81Z in the mock-up 'vertical' rear gun position
- V1b – Fixed MG17 and MG15 plus MG 151/20 cannon in each wing root, firing forward, plus an MG81Z in the armoured rear gun position
- V2 onwards – 2x MG17 fixed machine-guns, one in each wing root firing forward, plus 1x MG15 in a flexible mount above the fuselage centre-section (B-Stand) and in the rear cupola (C-Stand)

Ordnance
- V1 – None
- V2 onwards – 4x ETC 50/VIII electrically operated racks, two under each wing panel, outboard of the nacelle with the capacity to carry one 50kg or 70kg bomb each. Both racks could also be used to carry one S 125 smoke (and gas) generator under each wing

Note: Please note that as the Focke-Wulf was built and tested using Metric measurements we have refrained from offering Imperial conversions in the above data.

An Fw 189B-0 of the training school at Brandenburg-Briest seen in the winter of 1941-2 with a prominent unit badge and large '1' applied in yellow

For many years it was said no C-series machines were built, but that is not true and here you can see Fw 189C-0, W/Nr.0017, NA+WA being towed around the factory site. No rear armament is fitted at this time

Technical Description

What follows is an extensive selection of images and diagrams that will help you understand the physical nature of the Focke-Wulf Fw 189.

Group 1 – Fuselage
1 – Cockpit Interior
2 – Canopy
3 – Main Fuselage
4 – Fuel, Pneumatic, Undercarriage, Oil & Oxygen systems
5 – Electrical & Radio systems

Group 2 – Undercarriage
1 – Main
2 – Tailwheel

Group 3 – Booms & Tail
1 – Booms
2 – Tail

Group 4 – Wings
1- Wings
2 – Ailerons, Flaps & Control Linkage

Group 5 – Engines, Cowling, Propellers
1 – Engine & Propeller
2 – Exhausts & Cowlings

Group 6 – Weapons
1 – Armament
2 – Ordnance
3 – Sighting & Release
4 – Camera

Group 7 – Miscellaneous
1 – Access Panels & Ribs
2 – Miscellaneous Equipment

All photos © the author unless otherwise noted

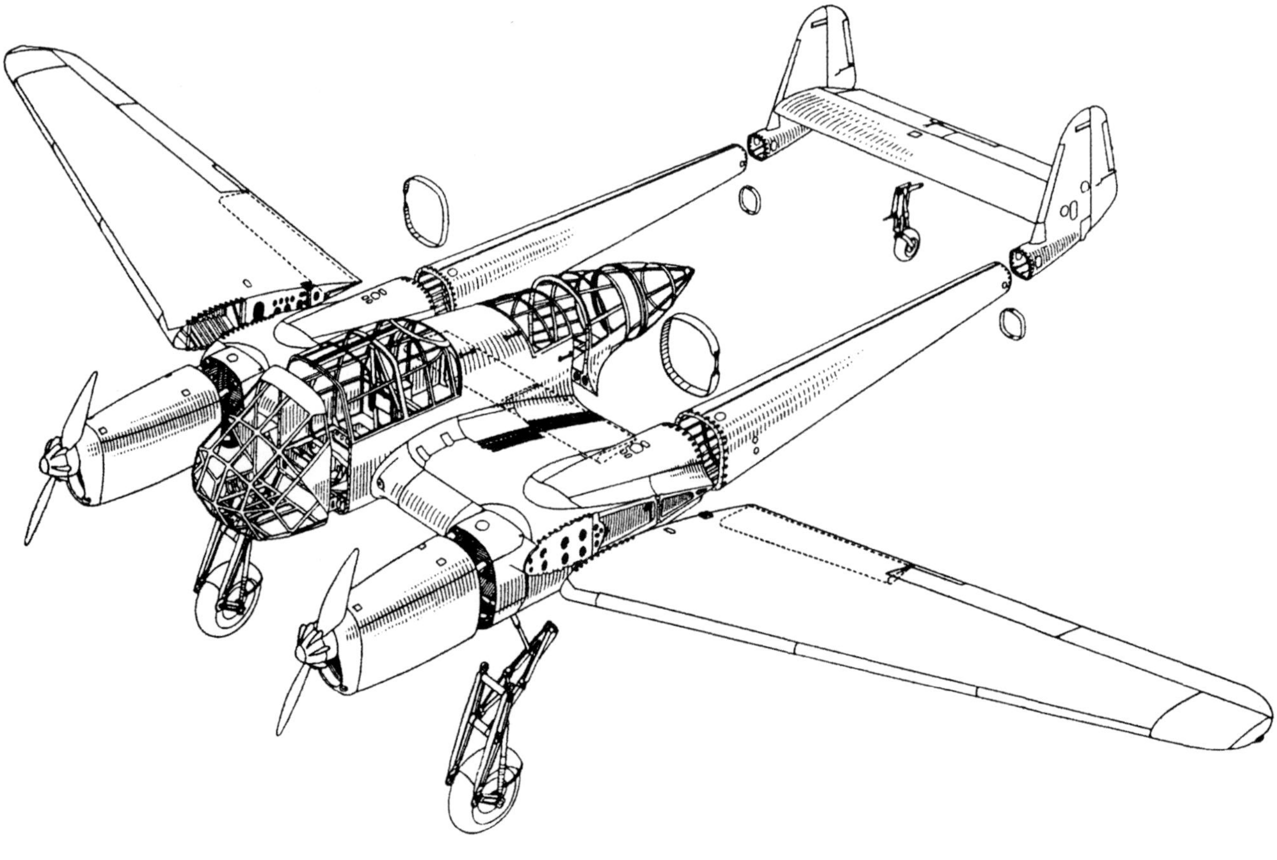

Fuselage
Cockpit Interior – V

Nice period photo, probably the V1 or V2, showing the port side of the cockpit areas, the seat, control column, sidewall and rudder pedals. You can tell this is a prototype due to the lack of any of the bomb aiming equipment that is usually in the area alongside the control column on the cockpit floor ahead of the observer's sliding seat

A view from the mid-section of the wooden mock-up looking aft, with the camera in the foreground to port, the spar box running from side to side and the single MG15 visible in the background

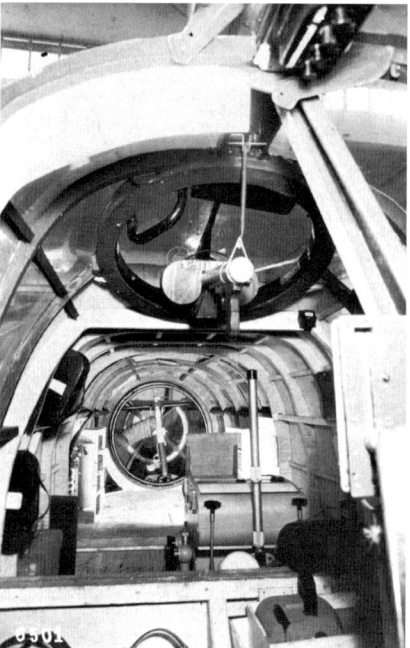

This shot of the same mid-section of the V1 wooden mock-up does allow you to see more clearly the dorsal gun mount. The black items seen on the starboard wall etc., are MG15 (saddle-type) ammunition drums

Another view inside the V1 wooden mock-up, this is looking forward from the mid-section, with the front spar in the lower foreground and the pilot's seat to port and observer's sliding seat to starboard. The item in the very top (middle) of the photo is a wooden mock-up of the dorsal MG15, as you can just make out the handgrip and trigger

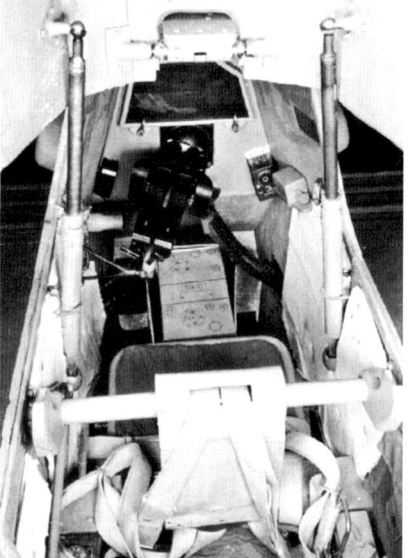

An overall view from the front looking aft, of the V1b nacelle mock-up, this is the later revised layout, defined by the MG81Z, large armoured glass panel with smaller ones in either side (and, unseen, on top); the first layout had a smaller rear glazing and no side/top ones

Another view of the V1b mock-up, looking from the port side across, you can see the basic seat, harness, side console and the Revi gunsight and clock that are mounted outside of the cockpit

The V1b mock-up again, looking from the starboard side across, here you can see the limited controls in this area and the map case; the white material was probably padding, intended to reduce splinters flying off inside when bullets etc. hit the outer armoured nacelle

Group 1 – Side 2
Fuselage 1
18 Cockpit Interior – A

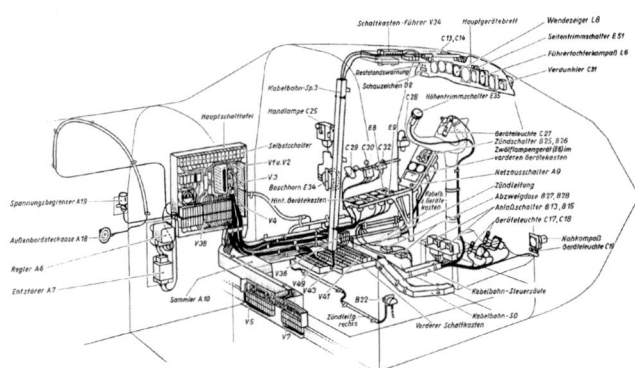

This diagram shows the layout of all the main electrical components in the A-series nacelle, but also illustrates the overall interior fixtures

A view out of the nose of an A-series, the anti-glare curtains can be seen tied back to the right, note also the production style rudder pedals in comparison with the V1 and the tiny Focke-Wulf company logo mounted in the middle of the control yoke

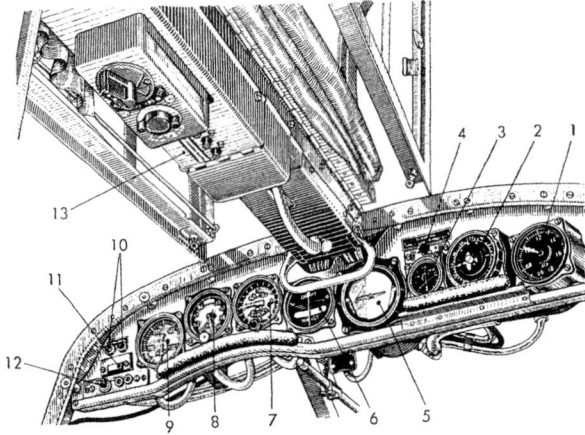

This diagram shows the main and secondary instrument panels in the cockpit roof

Key

1. Doppeldosen-Ladedruckmesser (Dual-dose Boost Meter)
2. Führertochterkompaß (Pilot's master compass)
3. Anzeigegerät für Funknavigation (Radio navigation display)
4. Verstellschalter für Seitentrimm (Adjusting switch for trim)
5. Horizont (Artificial Horizon)
6. Elt. Wendezeiger (Turn Indicator – electrical)
7. Variometer (Variometer)
8. Fein- und Grobhöhenmesser (Fine and Coarse Altimeter)
9. Fahrtmesser (Airspeed Indicator)
10. Merkleuchte für Reststandswarnung (Warning lights for fuel levels)
11. Gitterschauzeichen für Staurohrheizung (Indicator (grid) for Pitot head heater)
12. Schalt- und Kontrollkasten für starre Schußwaffen (Switching and control box for fixed armament)
13. Schaltkasten für den Flugzeugführer (Control panel for the pilot)

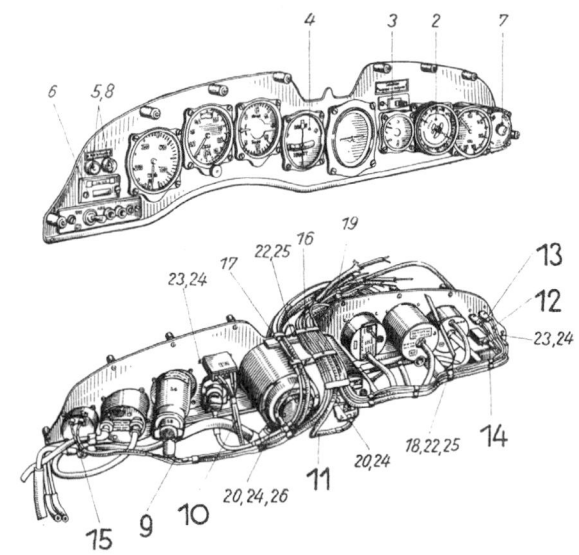

This diagram shows the instrument panel from the front and rear

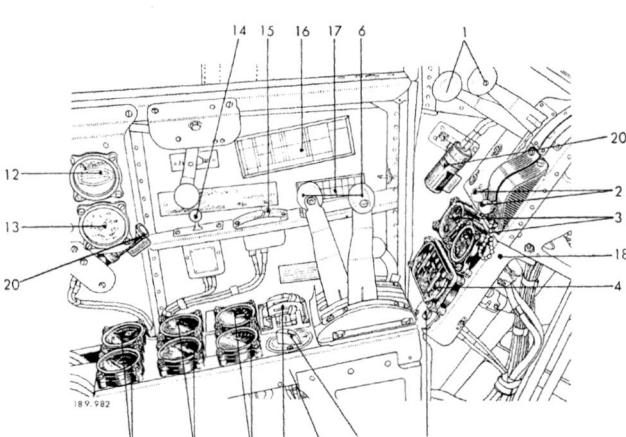

This diagram shows the port side console

Key

1. Brandhahnhebel (Fuel cock control levers)
2. Zündschalter (Ignition switch)
3. Elt. Temperaturanzeiger für Schmierstoff (Oil temperature indicator (electrical))
4. 12-Lampen-gerät für Fahrwerks- und Landeklappenüberwachung (12-lamp landing gear and flaps position indicator)
5. Netzausschalter (Power control switch)
6. Gashebel (Throttle)
7. Drehschalter für Landeklappenverstellung (Rotary switch for flap adjustment)
8. Kommandoschalter für Luftschrauben-verstellung (Command switch for propeller adjustment)
9. Stellungsanzeiger für Seiten- und Höhentrimm (Position indicator for rudder and elevator trim)
10. Doppeldruckmesser für Kraftstoff und Schmierstoff (Double pressure gauge for fuel and oil)
11. Elt. Vorratsanzeiger für Kraftstoff (Electrical supply gauges for fuel)
12. O2-Wächter (Flugzeugführer) (Oxygen flow indicator – pilot)
13. Sauerstoffdruckmesser (Flugzeugführer) (Oxygen pressure gauge – pilot)
14. Bedienschalter für Scheinwerfer (Control switch for landing lights)
15. Schalter für Scheinwerferleuchte (Landing light 'on' switch)
16. Betriebsdatentafel (Operating data chart)
17. Deviationstabelle ([Compass] Deviation table)
18. Vorderes Gerätbrett (Front equipment board)
19. Hinteres Gerätebrett (Rear equipment board)
20. Geräteleuchte (Cockpit light)

Group 1 – Side 3	
Fuselage	**1**
Cockpit Interior – A	19

This period photo looks down from the port side onto the pilot's seat, control column, observer's sliding seat (which is in the fully forward position) and the bomb aiming related equipment mounted ahead of it. Up above on the starboard side you can see the anti-glare curtain tied back and to the left if it, the Morse key etc

A nice period photo taken from the starboard side looking across the cockpit area and showing the pilot's seat, control column and port side console

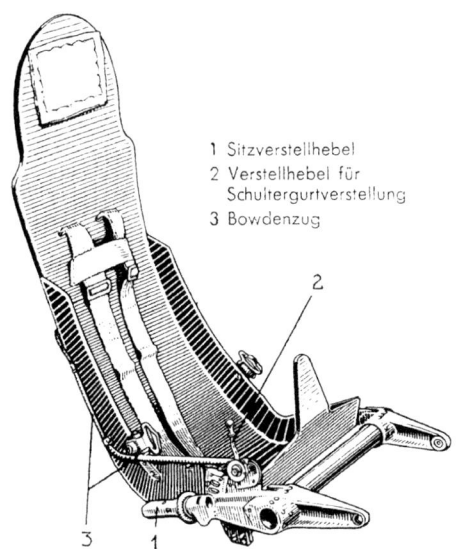

This diagram from the manual shows the pilot's seat in detail

In this period photo you can see, in the foreground, the observer's seat in the fully back position

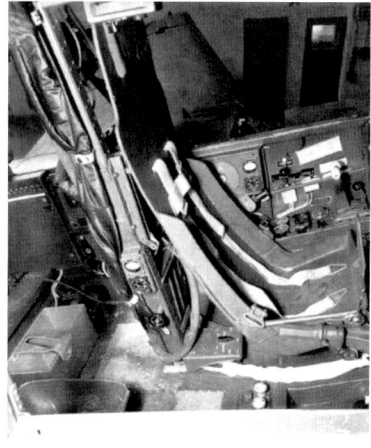

An overall shot of the pilot's seat and the area immediately around it

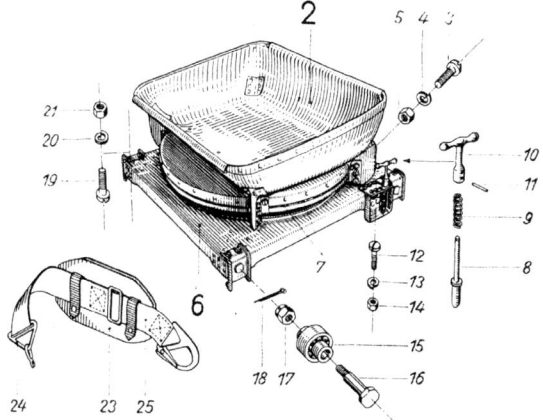

This diagram from the manual shows the observer's seat, as well as the strap assembly ('22')

The observer has a sliding seat, as seen here in this image from the manual

Group 1 – Side 4
Fuselage 1
20 | Cockpit Interior – A

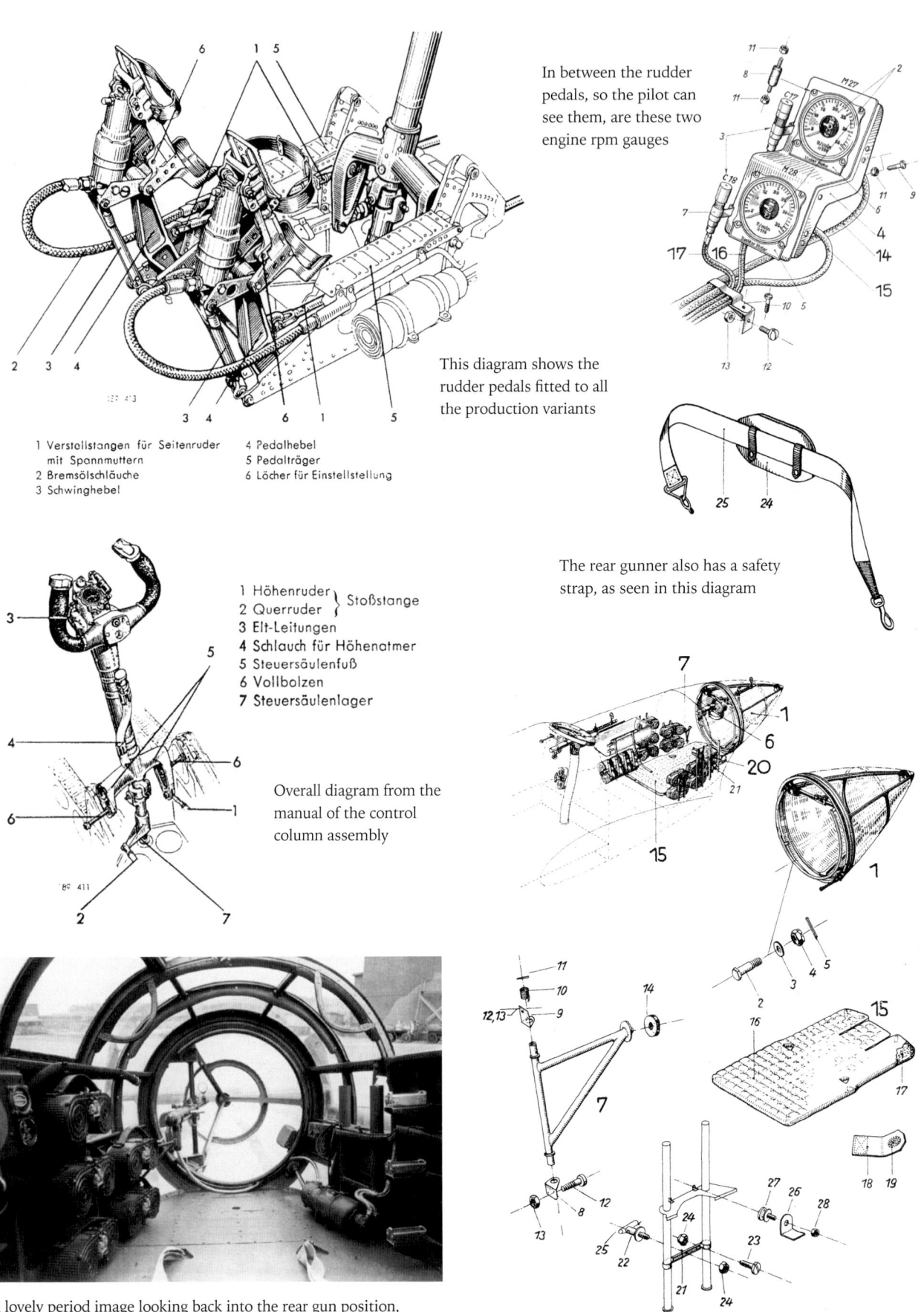

In between the rudder pedals, so the pilot can see them, are these two engine rpm gauges

This diagram shows the rudder pedals fitted to all the production variants

1 Verstellstangen für Seitenruder mit Spannmuttern
2 Bremsölschläuche
3 Schwinghebel
4 Pedalhebel
5 Pedalträger
6 Löcher für Einstellstellung

1 Höhenruder ⎱ Stoßstange
2 Querruder ⎰
3 Elt-Leitungen
4 Schlauch für Höhenatmer
5 Steuersäulenfuß
6 Vollbolzen
7 Steuersäulenlager

Overall diagram from the manual of the control column assembly

The rear gunner also has a safety strap, as seen in this diagram

A lovely period image looking back into the rear gun position, you can see the motor that powers the gun ring in the lower right corner, plus the large number of saddle-type ammunition drums mounted on the starboard side. The two gauges visible by the ammo drums are for the gunner's oxygen system flow and levels

This diagrams shows the rear gun support stay ('7'), the padded floor panel ('15') that the gunner lies on and the two tubes that project up into the area that contain the rear access ladder

AA06/11/20 Valiant Wings Publishing Issued: February 2015

Group 1 – Side 5
Fuselage
Cockpit Interior – B

Period photo looking from the starboard side across the instrument panel towards the port side in the B-series, you can see the dual control columns, side-by-side seats and the large direction finding compass mounted in the centre of the instrument panel

This is the view of the starboard side of the B-series front cockpit area, again the revised layout of the controls, seats and control columns are evident

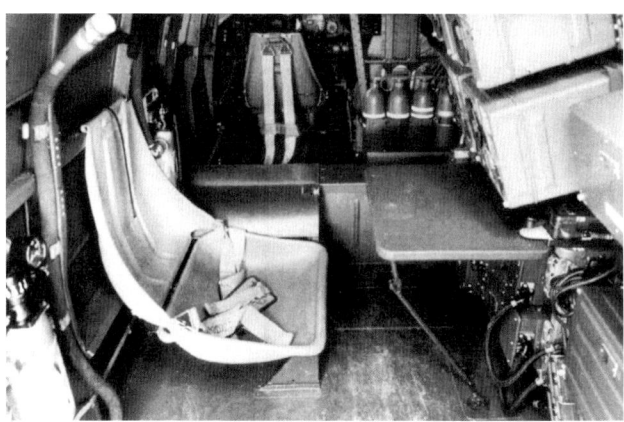

This is the pupil's seat, viewed from the back looking forward, the spar box is evident, as are the various oxygen bottles mounted on the walls for the crew and pupils

Moving forward and turning to look fully aft, now you can see the radio equipment on the starboard side, the seat on the port side and the two additional seats right at the back in the B-series

A closer look at the radio equipment mounted on the starboard side of the B-series interior

Still looking from the front, here you can see the pupil's seat on the port side of the mid-section in the B-series

At the rear of the B-series nacelle are these seats, you can see the nearest one is folded down revealing the First Aid box and oxygen distribution valves. The items behind the mesh screen are oxygen bottles

Group 1 – Side 6
Fuselage
Cockpit Interior – B/C

An overall view from the rear of the B-series looking forward; in this shot the pilot's seat (on the left) has been folded down, whilst the canvas item draped over the unit in the middle is part of the screens (the other set of curtains can just be made out tied back to the vertical member) to shut off the rear area for 'night navigation' training

Nice overall shot of the controls and instrument panel in the V6, the overall claustrophobic environment is evident!

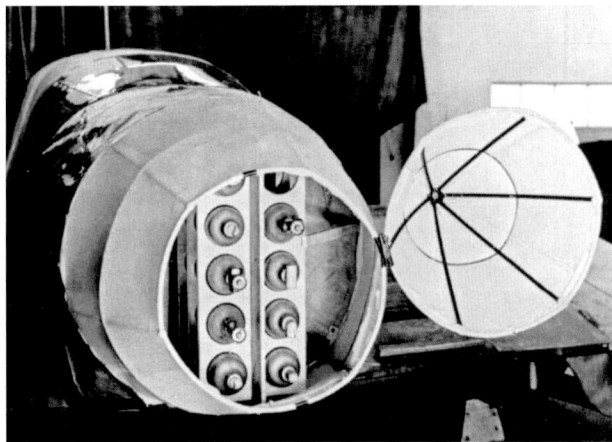

This is the V5 mock-up, but it shows the extreme tip of the nacelle hinged back to show the stack of oxygen bottles housed in this area

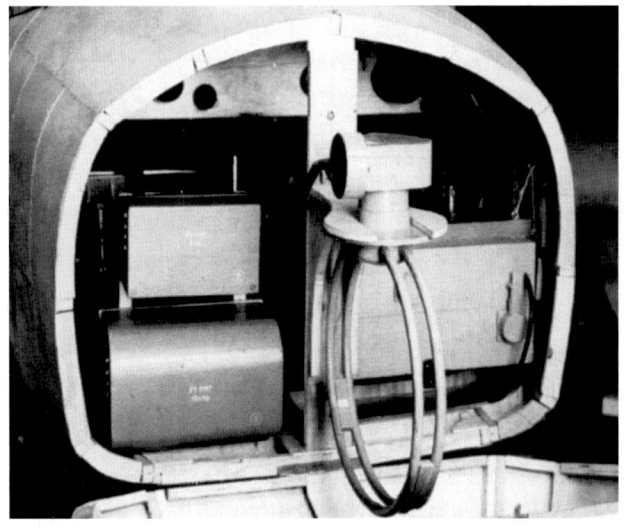

An overall shot of the instrument panel etc. in the pre-production C-0 series, the externally-mounted Revi gunsight lacks the clock seen mounted at its base on the V1b. The vertical columns on the top of the instrument panel are ammunition counters for the machine-guns and cannon fitted

None of the B-series have any DF loop visible outside, this is because it is relocated here, inside the nose cone, as seen here on the V5 wooden mock-up

Fuselage
Canopy & Forward

Nice overall shot of A-1, KD+RU with all the access panels open in the front and rear sections of the nacelle

An overall view, taken in the factory, of the starboard side of the nose on the A-series

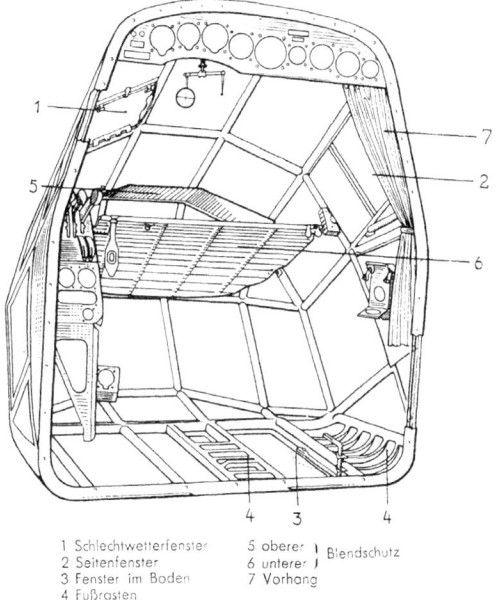

1 Schlechtwetterfenster
2 Seitenfenster
3 Fenster im Boden
4 Fußrasten
5 oberer ⎫ Blendschutz
6 unterer ⎭
7 Vorhang

A drawing from the manual showing the equipment fitted inside the front nose cone, including the gunsight in the top/centre, the anti-glare curtains tied back on the starboard side ('7') and the anti-glare panel ('6') in the fully extended position; the items listed as 'Fußrusten' mean 'foot rests' because this is where the observer puts his feet when sighting for bombs or the camera

This photo shows how the front canopy framework is made, including the 'ladder' frames visible in the bottom sections to reinforce where the observer's feet go

This period image shows the 'bad weather window' viewed from the inside of the cockpit

Although small, this is a lovely period shot showing how good the view was out the front of the Fw 189, but also therefore how exposed the crew were

Fuselage
Canopy & Forward

Group 1 – Side 8

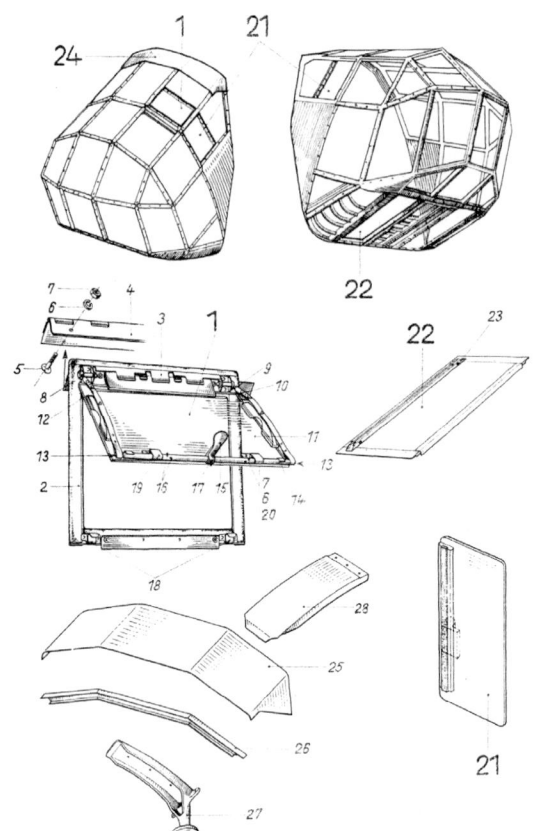

This diagram shows what is often termed the 'bad weather window', a hinged panel on the upper, port side of the nose glazing

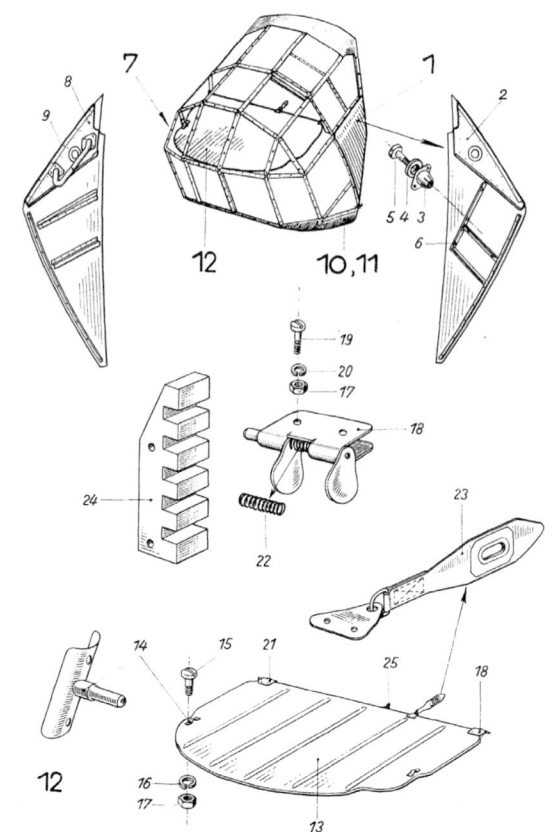

This diagram shows the anti-glare shield ('12') that was often fitted into the nose of the Fw 189A-series

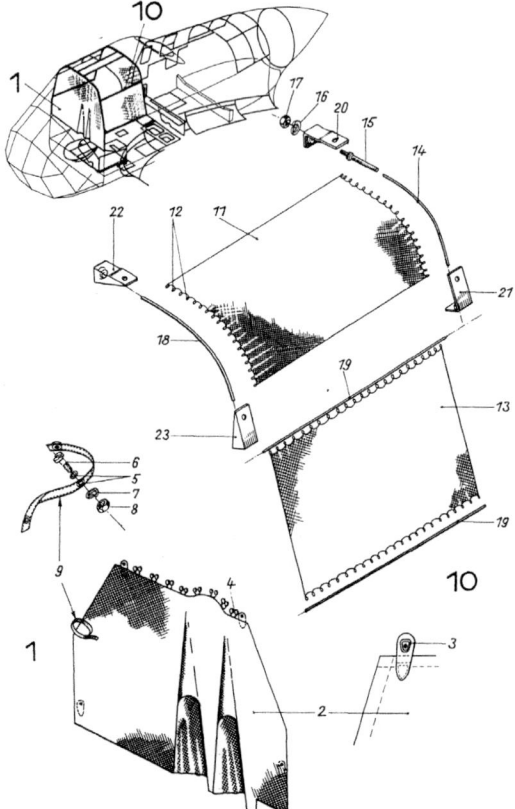

Sun shields, made of canvas, were fitted into the remaining glazings and this diagram shows those in the panels around the pilot as well as those to go across in front of him

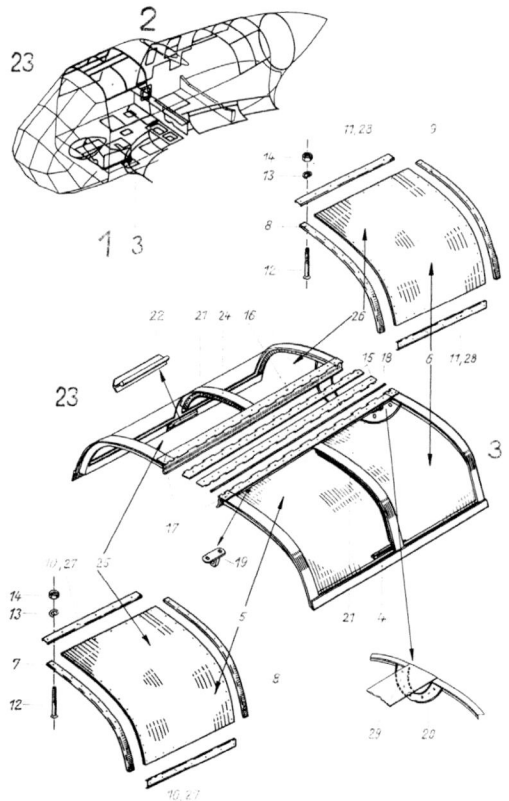

This diagram shows the construction and hinges of the two upper panels in the forward section of the A-series canopy

Group 1 – Side 9
Fuselage
Canopy & Forward

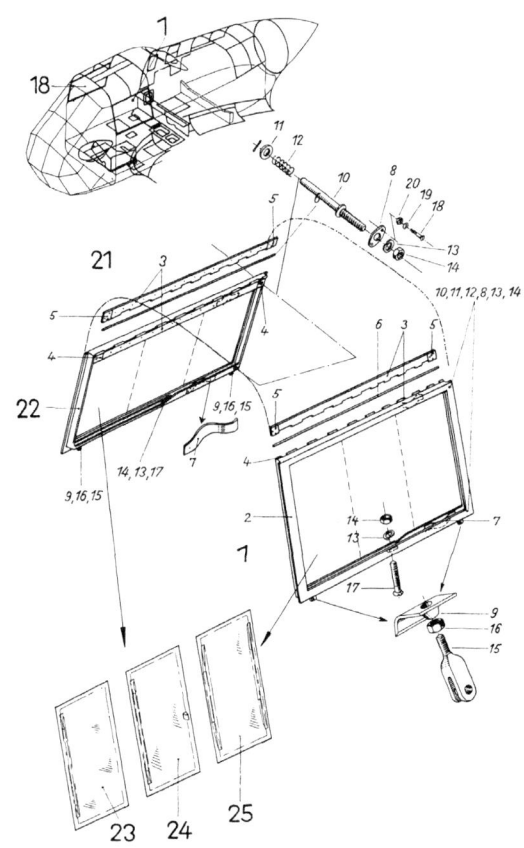

Here you can see the construction of the lower sections of the panels in the forward canopy of the A-series

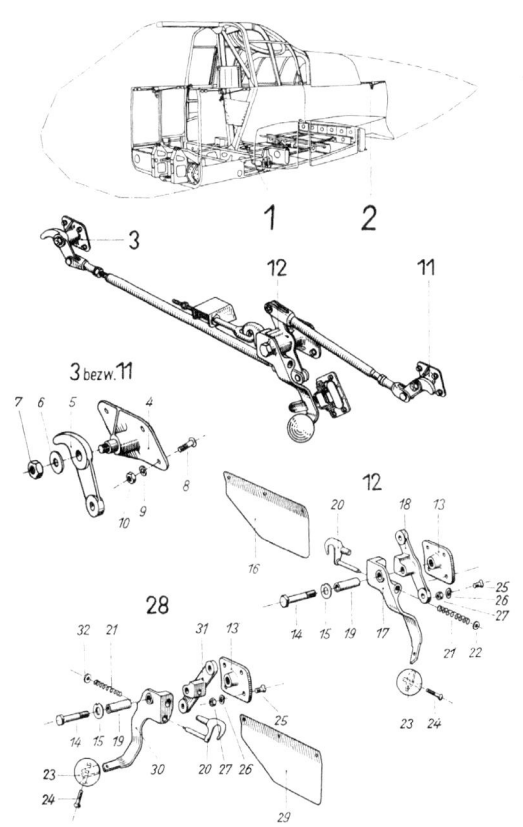

The front and rear sections can be unlocked by pushing release buttons mounted into the port side nacelle sides, as seen in this diagram

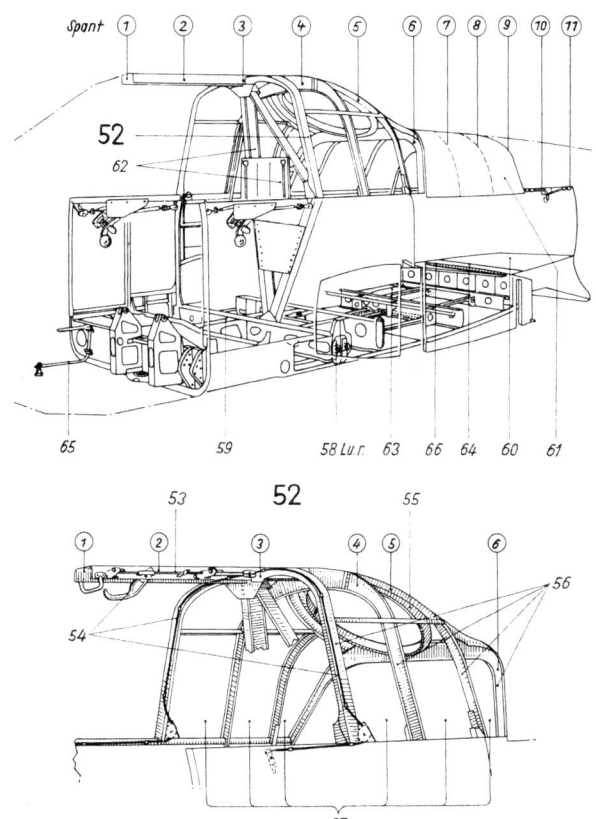

This diagram shows the construction of the mid-upper sections, but you can also see (unmarked) the locations of the two canopy release levers for the front sections [the starboard side one being just below the number '62']

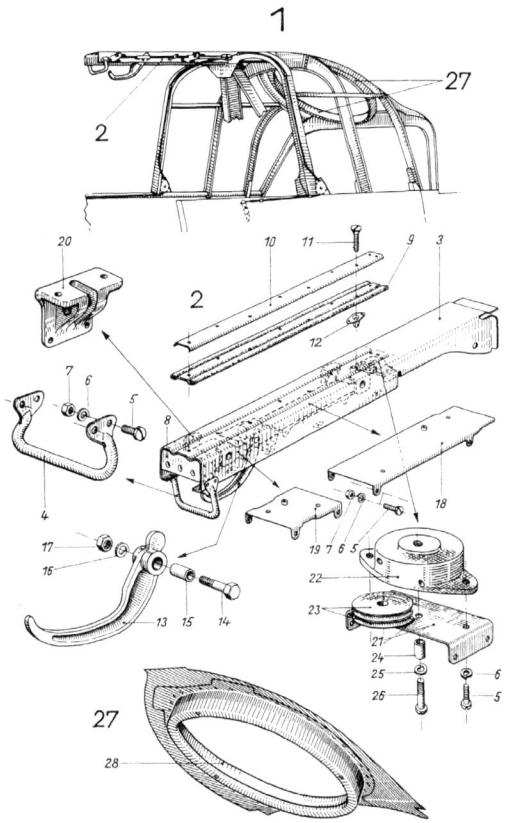

An interesting diagram showing the construction of the mid-section upper framework, which also includes a detailed diagram of the mount for the gun ring ('27')

Group 1 – Side 10
Fuselage
Canopy & Forward

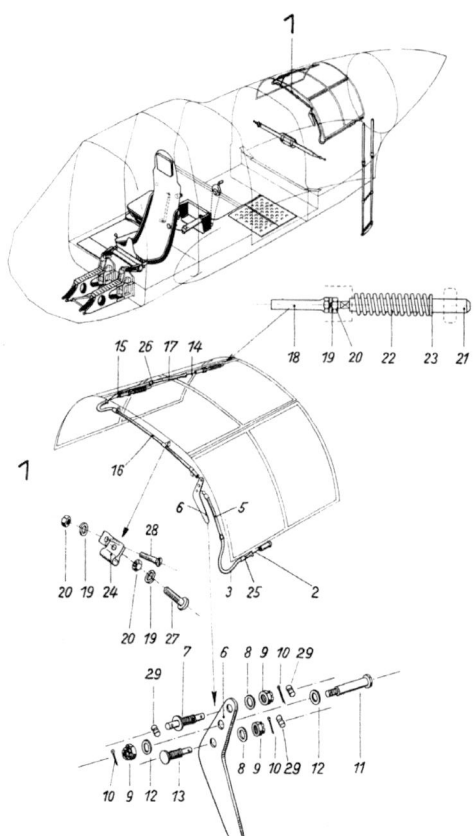

This diagram shows how the rear upper panels are locked in place from the inside using arm '6' and released from the outside via the pull-cord '2'

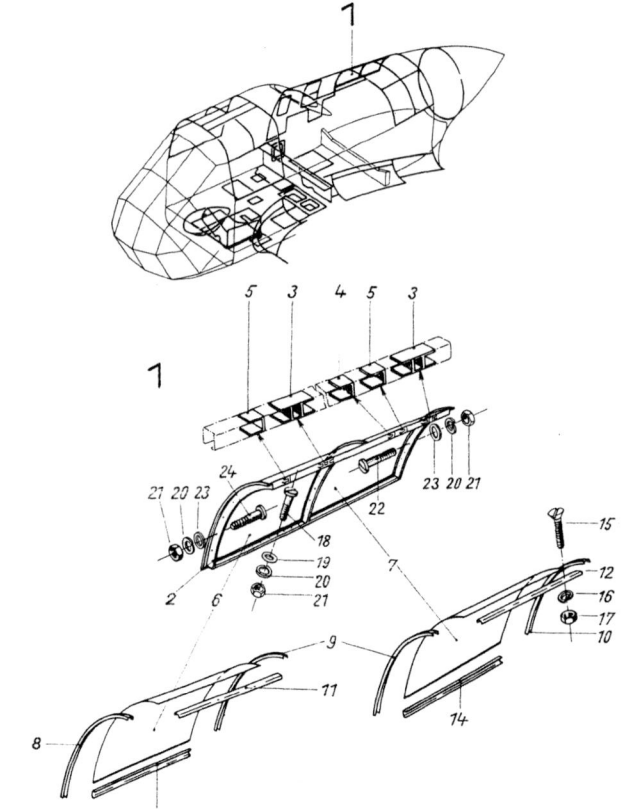

Construction of the aft/upper glazed panels on the starboard side, which are fixed in place

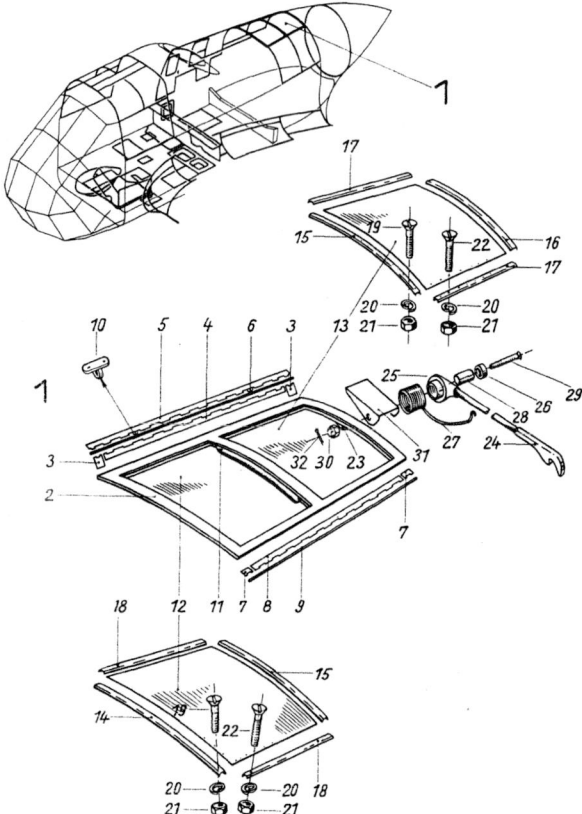

Here is the aft/upper panel, which is hinged (to starboard) along with the panel below it on the port side

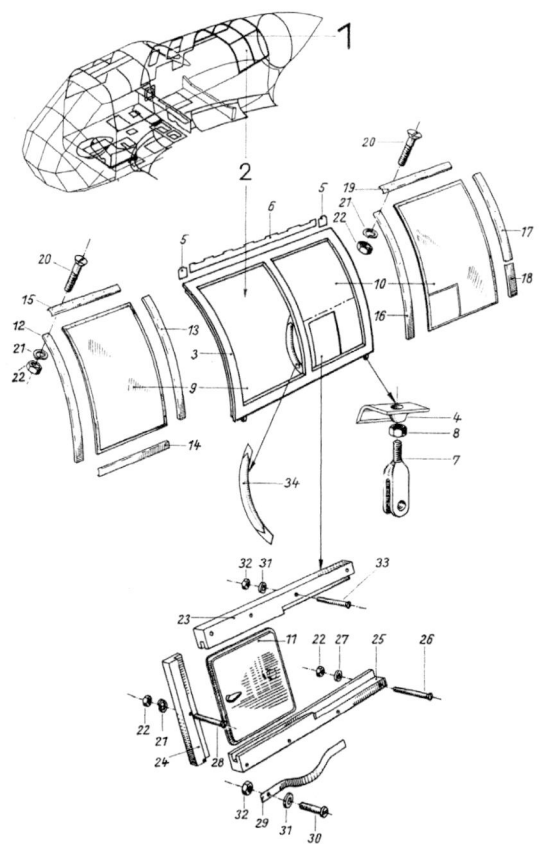

Finally, the lower aft panel, which is joined to the upper one and hinges with it as it opens to starboard for crew access

Group 1 – Side 11
Fuselage
Main & Aft – V

This is a nice overall view of the main fuselage on the V1, the T-shaped grips you can see were replaced on production machines with the more usual 'loop' style hand-holds. You can also see the initial layout of the rear glazing panels, which changed on later prototypes and for the production machines both in size, location and layout

A period photo of the V1a armoured crew pod, which in this unpainted state allows you to see the heavy weld lines for the various panels used to make its complex shape. The tiny pilot's glazing, high profile of the pod and the lack of any bulges for armoured glass panels in the rear identify this as the V1a in its initial (built) form

This is the rear armament layout proposed for the V1b, shown here in wooden mock-up form

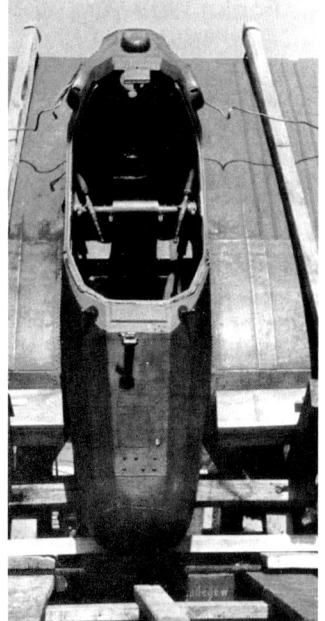

Much is written about the V1b, but no photos exist of it; this image often claims to be it, but this is the V1a after modification, the rear gun position is now for the MG81Z, the profile has been lowered and the armoured glass in the rear is bigger and supplemented by the three blisters you can see on the top and sides, which also contain small armoured glass panels

This period photo shows the wooden mock-up of the initial style of armoured pod for the V1a, which was never actually built

This is the overall pod of the V1b wooden mock-up, it has three windscreen panels, that are larger than the V1a but not as large as the V6, plus it has the three blisters on the rear section (again these are not as large as those fitted to the V6)

Group 1 – Side 12
Fuselage 1
Main & Aft – V

These two images show the revised pod of the V6, you can clearly see the much larger windscreen panels in relation to the revised V1a or the V1b layout

Just to prove the difference between the V1b rear layout and the V6, here is a photo of that area on the V1b mock-up…

…and here is the same area on the V6, note the different shape of the armoured glass and the side/top blisters

Attempts were made with the rear gunner's position for the proposed revised ground-attack version, the V1c, this shows the 'vertical' first version

The angular shape of the nacelle on the V6 was such that it caused turbulence and drag, so this image shows the attempt to smooth out the lines of the pod; it made little difference to performance

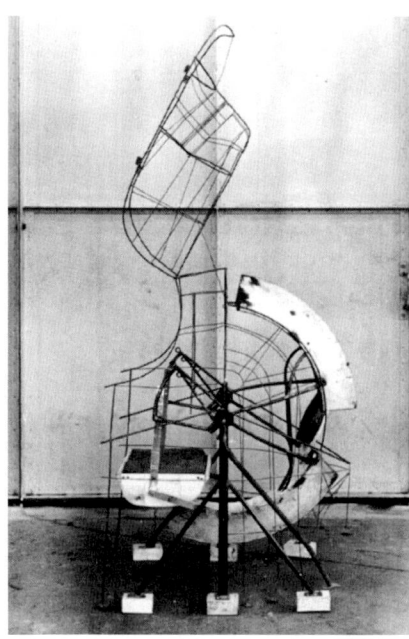

This is a mock-up of the second 'spherical' gun position considered for the V1c

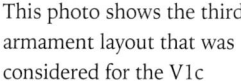

This photo shows the third armament layout that was considered for the V1c

Group 1 – Side 13
Fuselage
Main & Aft – A

This period photo shows the nacelle assembly, viewed from the port side

A lovely factory shot showing the fuselage of A-0, W/Nr.0008, which was retained by Focke-Wulf for use as a courier aircraft. It was unarmed, but you can clearly see the 'loop' style grab handles added, along with the revisions to the rear glazed panels in relation to the V-series

A shot of an A-series on the final assembly lines clearly showing that the canopy framework was pre-painted before assembly. The opening on the mid-upper decking was a temporary item to allow equipment to be installed, later a solid panel would be fitted there

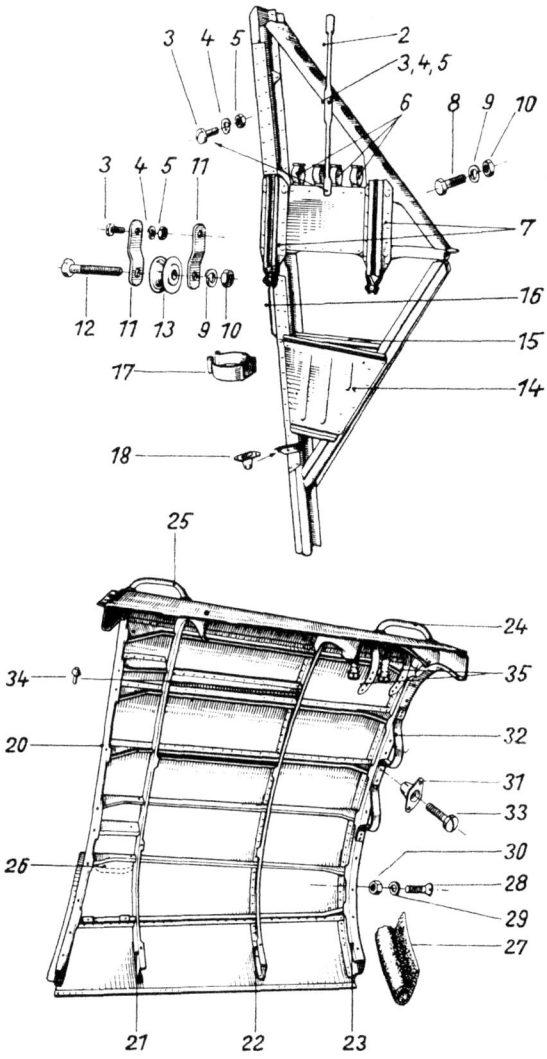

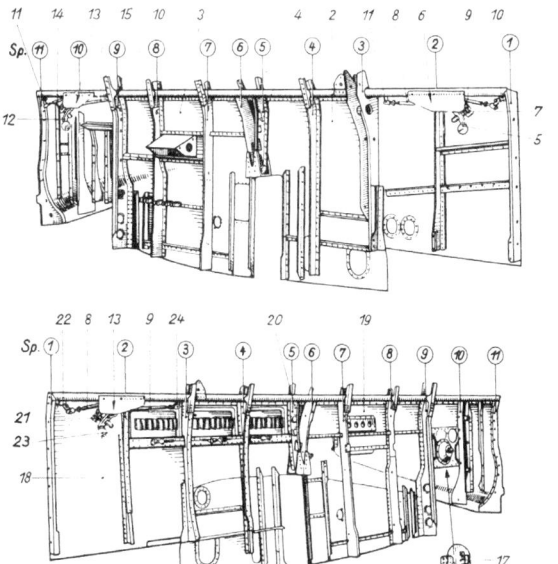

The fuselage sides were made up of these two sections, themselves built from a number of panels; item '2' on each is the canopy release mechanism

This diagram shows the roll-over frame behind the pilot (top), plus the mid-upper panel (bottom) mentioned previously

Fuselage
Main & Aft – A

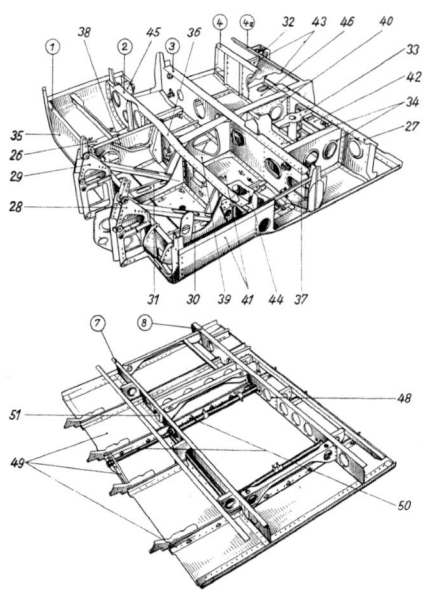
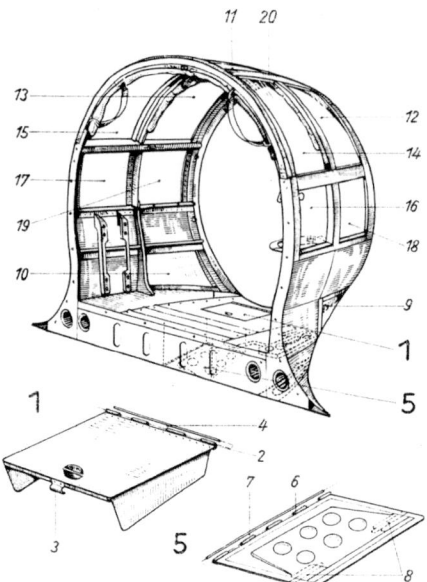
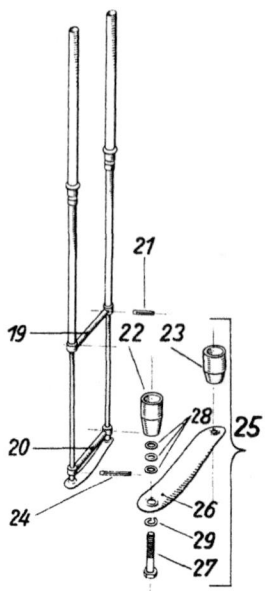

The floor was made up of two panels, placed in front (top) and in between (bottom) the spar box; the aft one contained the opening for the camera

This little diagram of the section aft of the main centre section is useful as it shows the access flap ('5') over the crew access ladder

This diagram shows the components of the crew access ladder for the A-series

This is the section aft of the main centre section element, seen here straight out of the jig

The section aft of the main centre section seen masked and after initial priming, because all the 'glazed' areas had the Perspex added and then were painted before final assembly

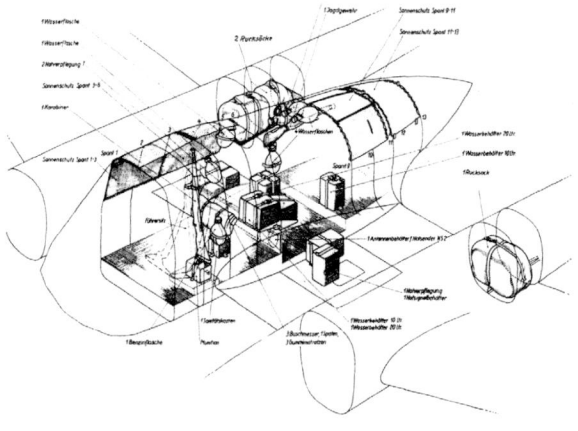

The rearmost section of the A-series nacelle was this glazed gun cone, which is seen here without the extreme tip fitted

This diagram actually shows all the various additional equipment fitted in the fuselage (and booms) for a tropical environment

Group 1 – Side 15
Fuselage
Main & Aft – B/C

This photos shows the wood, wire and canvas mock-up of the V5, the prototype for the B-series

This shot of the rear of the V5 mock-up clearly shows the paper covering the glazed panel in the aft section from a standard A-series plus the new solid tail cone, which therefore must also be of the same dimensions as that of the A-series

An in-service B-series viewed from the rear, showing the opening glazed panel in this area that is identical to the A-series; it's just the solid nature of the tail section that makes the area look different

The B-series had the Peil G.V DF loop installed inside the nose cone, as seen here with the cone removed

This shot shows the nacelle of C-0, W/Nr.0021 from the starboard side, anyone who doubted the existence of the C-series should just take moment to count the ones visible in the background! Note the additional square armoured panel, this is not fitted on the port side

A nice view from the back of the fuselage on a C-0, note the much bigger rear glass, larger armoured side blisters and the fitment of the sight and mounts for the MG81Z (the gun itself not being installed); the item sticking out the back is the bottom rung of the crew access ladder, which has not been put back into its housing full

Group 1 – Side 16
Fuselage
32 | Fuel, Undercarriage

This period image shows one of the fuel cells removed from inside the tail boom

An interesting period photo showing the fuel cell being lifted up into position within the tail boom

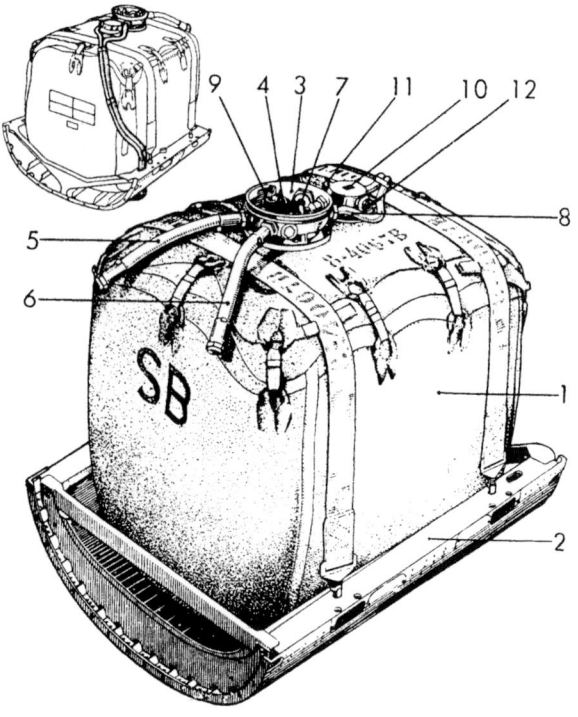

The fuel cell diagram from the manual

Key
1. Behälter (Fuel tank [literally 'Container'])
2. Behälterraumschale (Fuel tank compartment tray)
2. Kraftstoffbehälterkopf (Fuel tank head)
4. Füllanschluß mit Belüftungsventil (Filling connection with vent valve)
5. Entnahmeleitung (Fuel feed pipe [literally 'Extraction pipe'])
6. Entnahmeleitung (Fuel feed pipe [literally 'Extraction pipe'])
7. Überlaufleitung (Overflow pipe)
8. Entlüftungsleitung (Vent pipe)
9. Peilstab (Dipstick)
10. Vorratsgeber (Fuel gauge sender unit)
11. Elt. Anschluß für Vorratsgeber (Connector electrical for gauge sender unit)
12. Elt. Anschluß für Reststandswarnung (Connector electrical for fuel level warning unit)

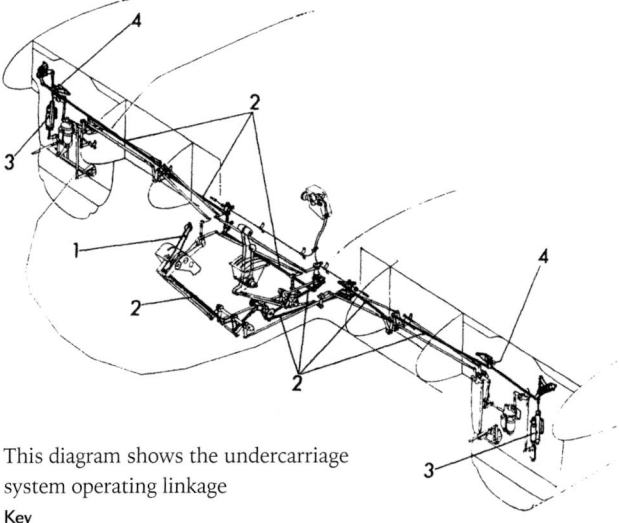

This diagram shows the undercarriage system operating linkage

Key
1. Fahrwerksschalthebel (Undercarriage shift (selection) level)
2. Gestänge (Linkage)
3. Schalter (Switch)
4. Entriegelungshebel (Release lever)

Fuselage

Group 1 – Side 17

Pneumatic, Oil, O_2 — 33

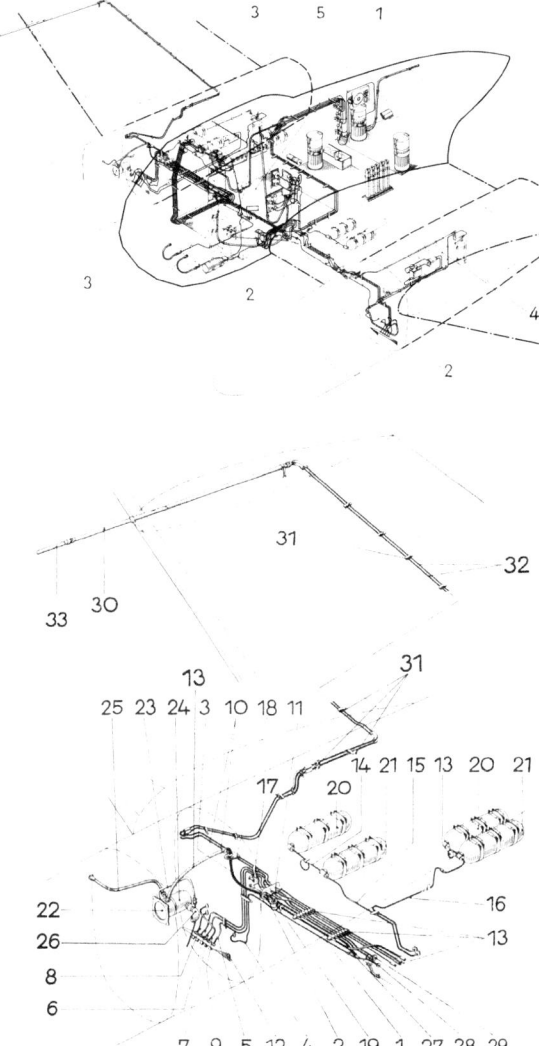

This diagram shows the overall pneumatic systems in the Fw 189

A more detailed look at the overall pneumatic equipment in the wing, including the linkage to the pitot tube

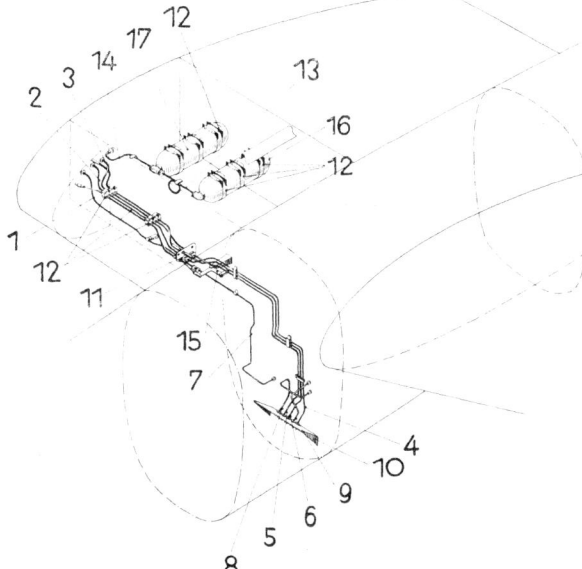

This diagram shows the two compressed air cylinders in each wing (this is starboard) and the lines to the charging point in the front of the wheel well

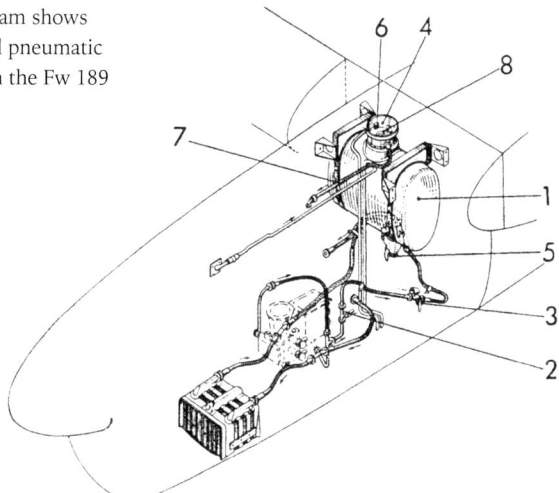

The lubrication system diagram

Key

1. Schmierstoffbehälter (Lubricant reservoir)
2. Druckmesserleitung (Pressure gauge line)
3. Absperrhahn (Stopcock)
4. Behälterkopf (Reservoir head)
5. Schmierstoffbodenentnahme (Drain plug [literally 'Lubricant soil removal'])
6. Überlaufleitung (Overflow pipe)
7. Entlüftungsleitung (Vent pipe)
8. Füllanschluß (Filler point)

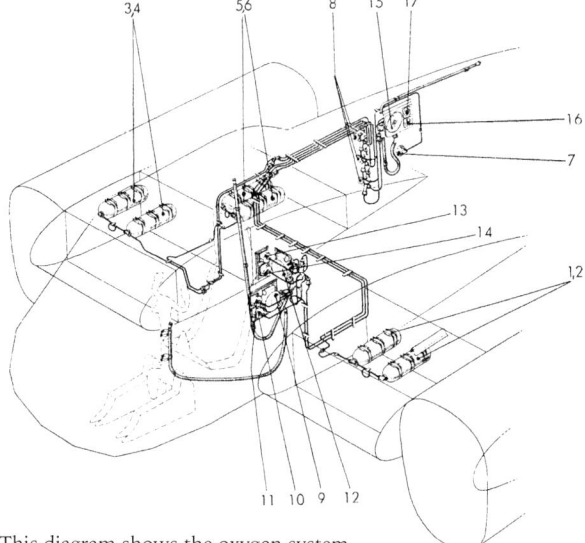

This diagram shows the oxygen system

Key

1 & 2. Sauerstofflaschen für den Flugzeugführer (Oxygen bottles for the pilot)
3 & 4. Sauerstofflaschen für den Beobachter (Oxygen bottles for the observer)
5 & 6. Sauerstofflaschen für den Schützen (Oxygen bottles for the gunner)
7. Außenbordanschluß – Outboard connection (e.g. charging/filler point)
8. Flaschenfernventile (Oxygen bottle remote valves)
9. Membranlunge für den Flugzeugführer (Oxygen regulator for the pilot [literally 'membrane lung for the pilot']
10. Druckmesser für den Flugzeugführer (Pressure gauge for the pilot)
11. O2-Wächter für den Flugzeugführer (Flow gauge for the pilot [literally 'O2 guardian/watcher for the pilot'])
12. Membranlunge für den Beobachter (Oxygen regulator for the observer)
13. Druckmesser für den Beobachter (Pressure gauge for the observer)
14. O2-Wächter für den Beobachter (Flow gauge for the observer)
15. Membranlunge für den Schützen (Oxygen regulator for the gunner)
16. Druckmesser für den Schützen (Pressure gauge for the gunner)
17. O2-Wächter für den Schützen (Flow gauge for the gunner)

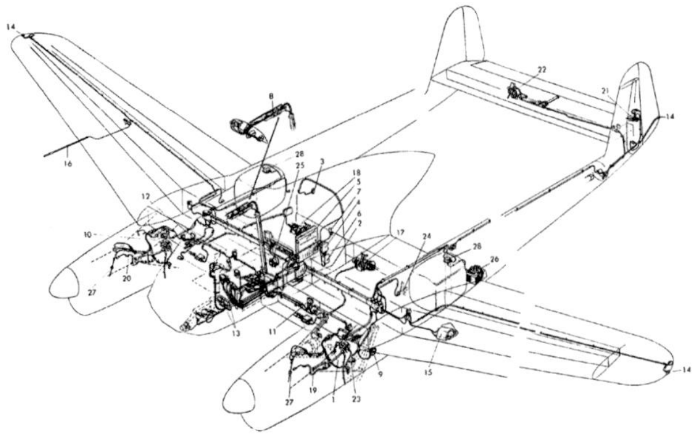

Group 1 – Side 18
Fuselage
34 Electrical & Radio

An overall diagram of the electrical systems

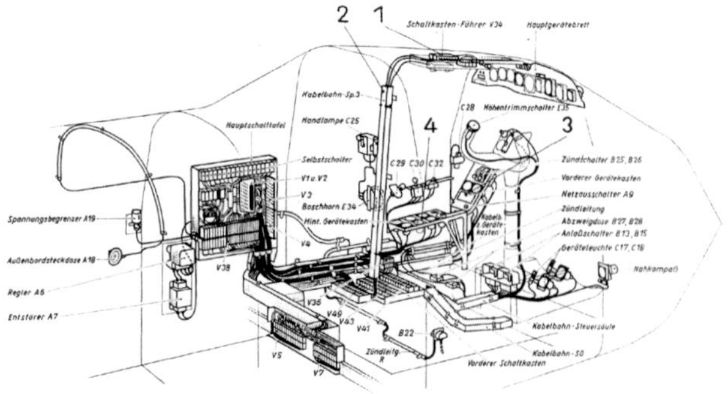

This diagram shows all the electrical systems in the main fuselage

Key

- Spannungsbegrenzer A19 (Voltage limiter A19)
- Außenbordsteckdose A18 (Outboard socket A18, e.g. external charging point)
- Regler A6 – Regulator A6
- Entstörer A7 – Suppressor A7
- Hauptschalttafel (Main switchboard)
- Kabelbahn Sp.3 (Cableway Sp.3)
- Handlampe C25 (Flashlight C25)
- Selbstschalter (Auto switch)
- Boschhorn E34 (Bosch Horn E34)
- Hinter Gerätkasten (Rear panel box)
- Schaltkasten – Führer V34 (Control box – Main V34)
- Hauptgerätebrett (Main instrument panel)
- Höhentrimmerschalter E35 (Height trimmer switch E35)
- Zündschalterr B25, B26 (Ignition switch B25, B26)
- Vorderer Gerätkasten (Front equipment/instrument box [literally 'tackle box'])
- Netzausschalter A9 (Power control switch A9)
- Zünderleitung (Igniter line)
- Abzweigdose B27, B28 (Junction box B27, B28)
- Anlaßschalter B13, B15 (Starter switch B13, B15)
- Gerätleuchte C17, C18 (Light unit C17, C18)
- Nahkompaß (Close compass)
- Kabel. z. Gerätekasten (Cables from equipment/instrument box0
- Kabelbahn- Steuersäule (Cableway – control column)
- Kabelbahn – SO (Cableway – SO)
- Vorderer Schaltkasten (Front control panel)
- Zündleitung – Ignition Cable

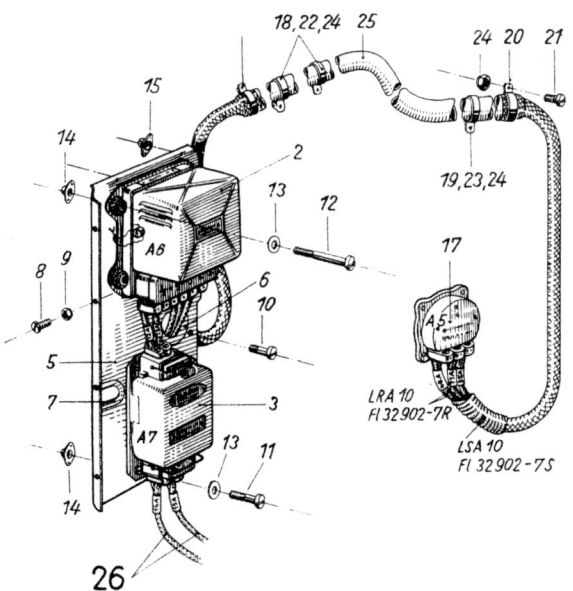

This is the secondary electrical panel aft of the main switchboard, containing the regulator (top) and suppressor (bottom)

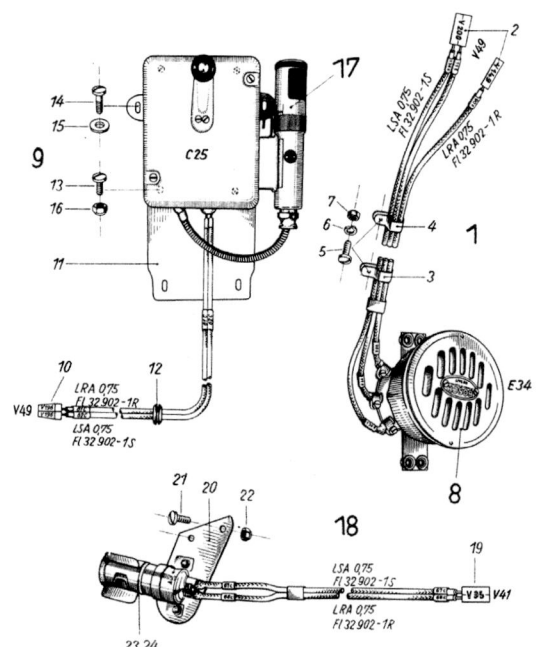

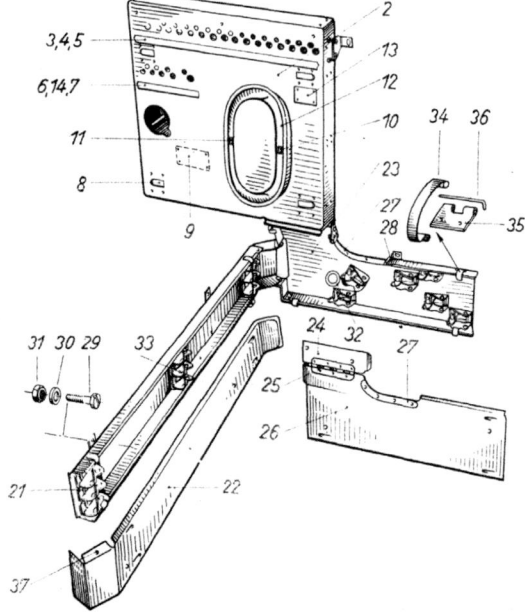

This diagram shows the main wiring conduits from the main switchboard

This diagram shows the two cockpit lights (17 & 18) and the undercarriage warning horn (1)

Group 1 – Side 19
Fuselage
Electrical & Radio

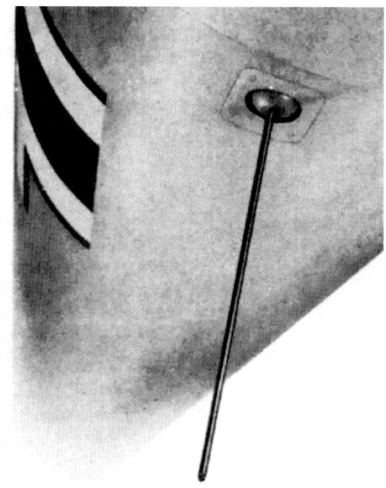

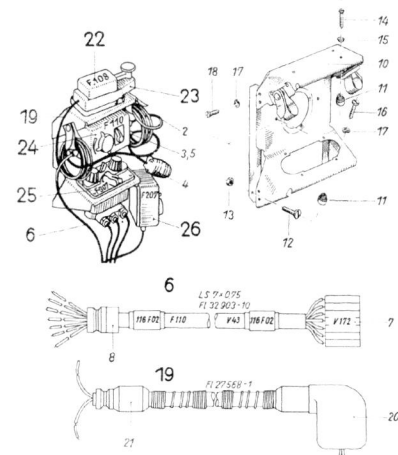

This is the 30cm long flat rod antenna for the FuG 25 IFF below the starboard tail boom

A Morse key was mounted in the front cockpit area, on the starboard sidewall, as shown here

The FuG 17 radio aerial mast was on the centreline under the fuselage, with the Peil G.IV DF loop mounted in a clear blister to port of it, as shown in this period photo

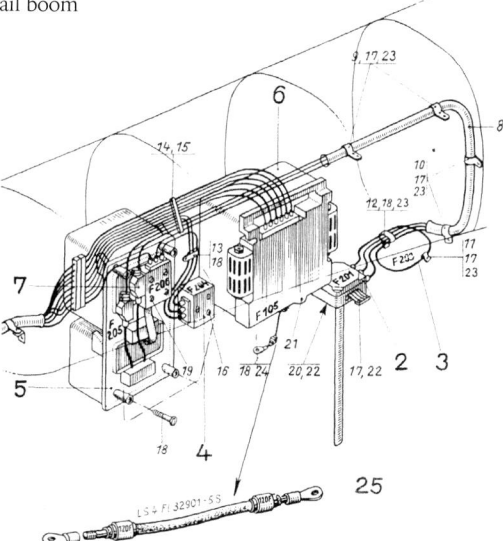

This diagram shows the radio equipment (front) and IFF FuG 25 (rear) mounted in the starboard tail boom

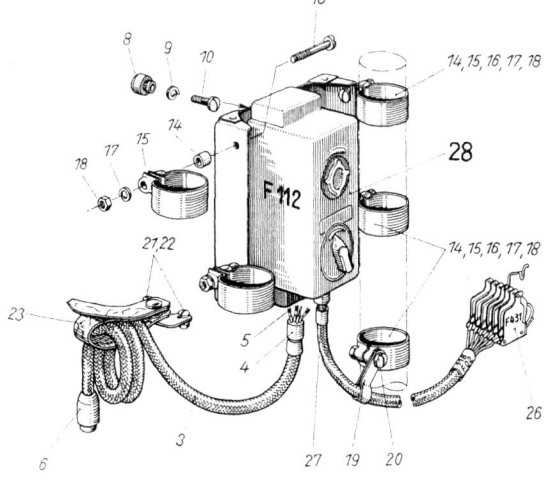

The intercom inside the aircraft was linked via this type of unit, seen here for the rear gunner and mounted between the tubes for the rear access ladder (marked as '14, 15, 16, 17, 18')

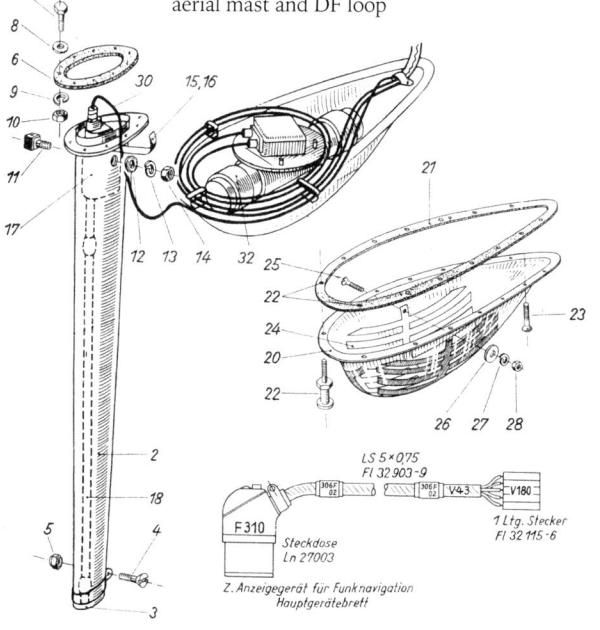

This diagram shows the components of the aerial mast and DF loop

This period image from the manual shows the Peil G.IV DF unit from the side; the bars are metallic and mounted into the clear cover, whilst the DF unit itself is made of a sort of plastic material that is a medium brown colour

For some of the proposed developments of the Fw 189 the Peil G.IV DF loop was to be replaced with this, the Peil G.VI version, which would have been mounted under a clear panel aft of the dorsal gun position (as per the Ju 87 or Ju 88 etc.)

Group 2 – Side 1
Undercarriage 1
36 Main

Many of the prototypes and pre-production machines adopted a single leg oleo unit, as seen in this period photo, which shows the unit fitted to the V2

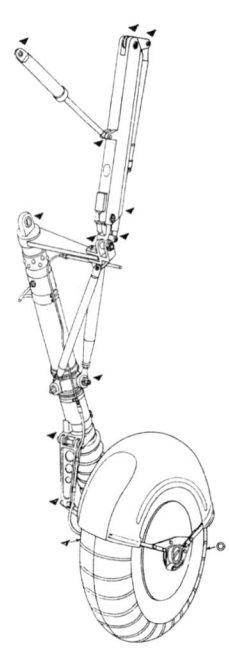

This diagram shows the construction of the early undercarriage unit, along with the mudguard

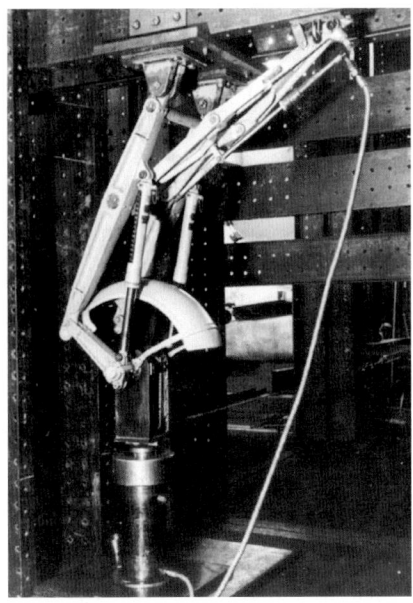

The unit adopted for service use was this twin leg unit, seen here on the test rig; in service the moving parts of the hydraulic rams were covered with gaiters

A useful period image looking up and aft into the main undercarriage bay; this is the port side

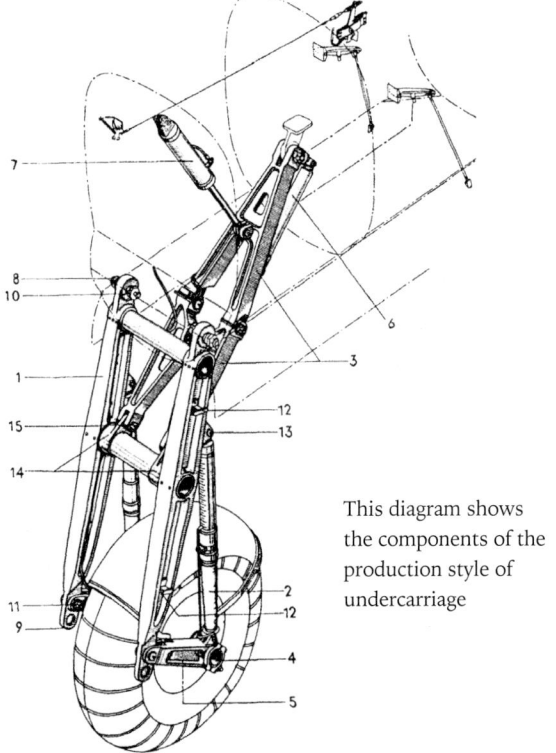

This diagram shows the components of the production style of undercarriage

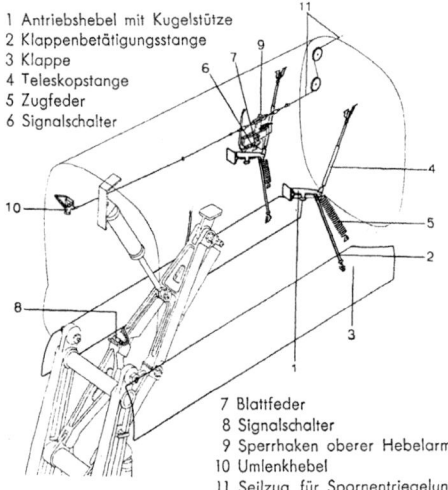

1 Antriebshebel mit Kugelstütze
2 Klappenbetätigungsstange
3 Klappe
4 Teleskopstange
5 Zugfeder
6 Signalschalter
7 Blattfeder
8 Signalschalter
9 Sperrhaken oberer Hebelarm
10 Umlenkhebel
11 Seilzug für Spornentriegelung

This diagram shows how the undercarriage and doors are retracted

Key
1. Fahrwerksverband (Landing gear main leg)
2. Federstrebe (Spring strut)
3. Knickverband (Hinged linkage [literally 'buckling union'])
4. Radachse (Wheel axle)
5. Schwinghebel (Rocker arm)
6. Kraftspeicher (Retraction unit [literally 'power storage'])
7. Einziehzylinder (Retracting cylinder)
8. Oberes Anschlußauge (Upper connecting eye)
9. Unteres Anschlußauge (Bottom connecting eye)
10. Rändelbuchse (Knurled bush)
11. Schmierbolzen (Lubricating bolts)
12. Beschlag (Mounting)
13. Schmierbolzen (Lubricating bolts)
14. Knickstrebenanschluß (Connecting strut)
15. Schmierbolzen (Lubricating bolts)

Group 2 – Side 2
Undercarriage
Main

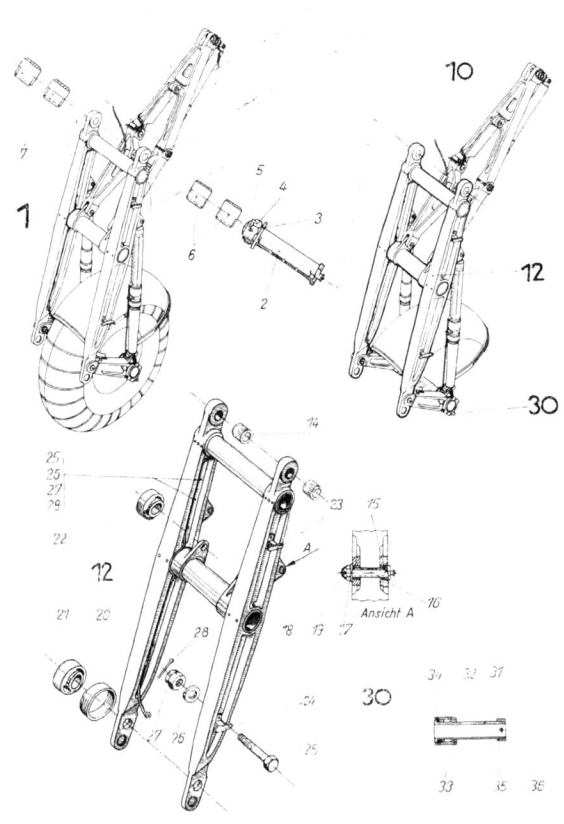

A component diagram showing the main pressed alloy undercarriage legs

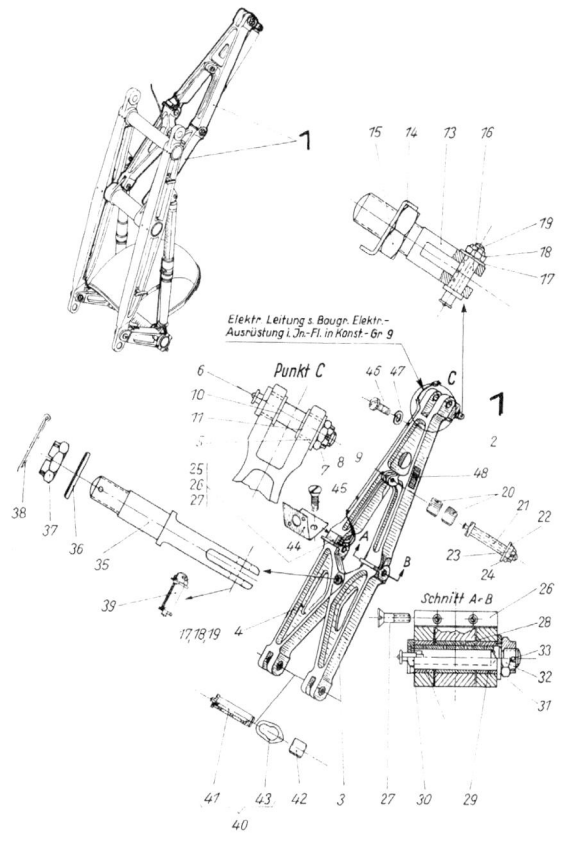

A detailed diagram shows the retraction (hinged) unit at the rear of the undercarriage

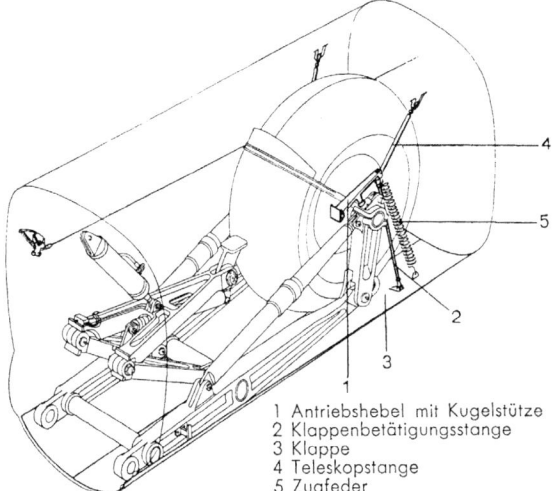

1 Antriebshebel mit Kugelstütze
2 Klappenbetätigungsstange
3 Klappe
4 Teleskopstange
5 Zugfeder

This diagram shows the undercarriage and doors in the fully retracted positions

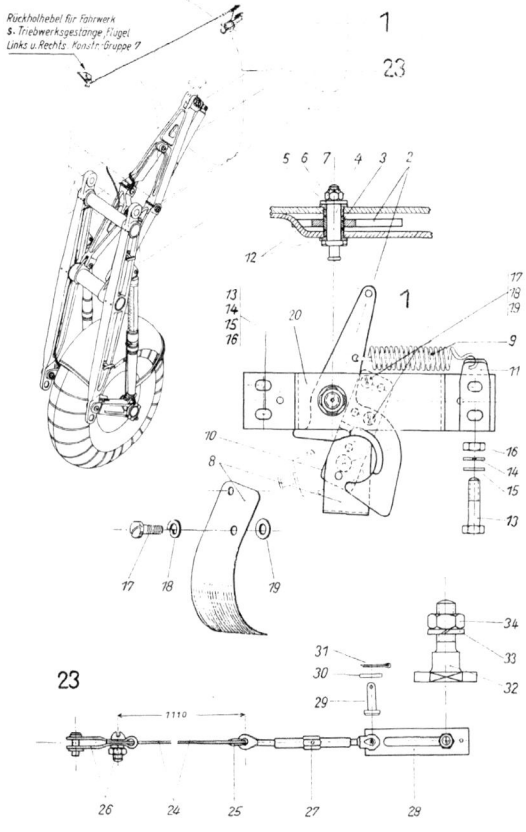

This diagram shows the 'up lock' situated in the top of each wheel well

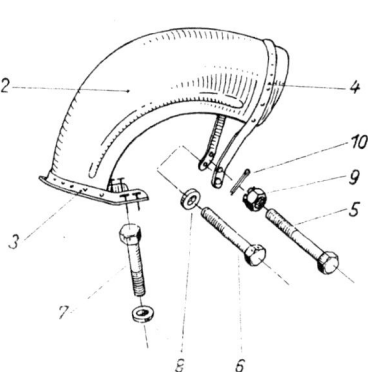

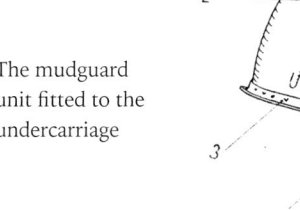

The mudguard unit fitted to the undercarriage

Group 2 – Side 3
Undercarriage 1
38 | Main/Ski

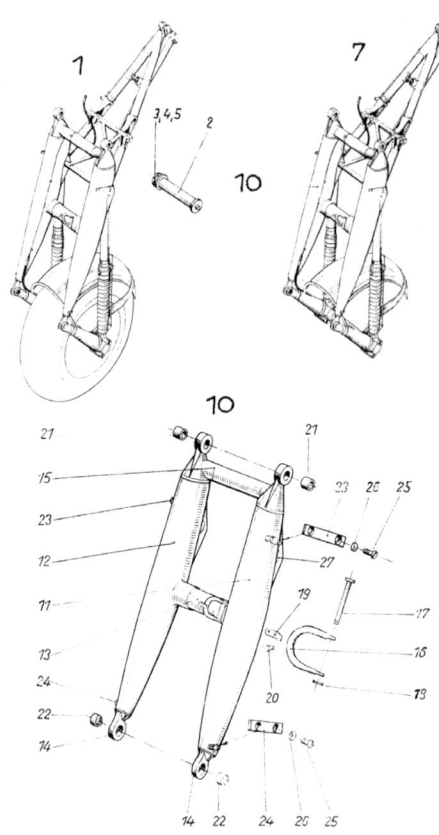

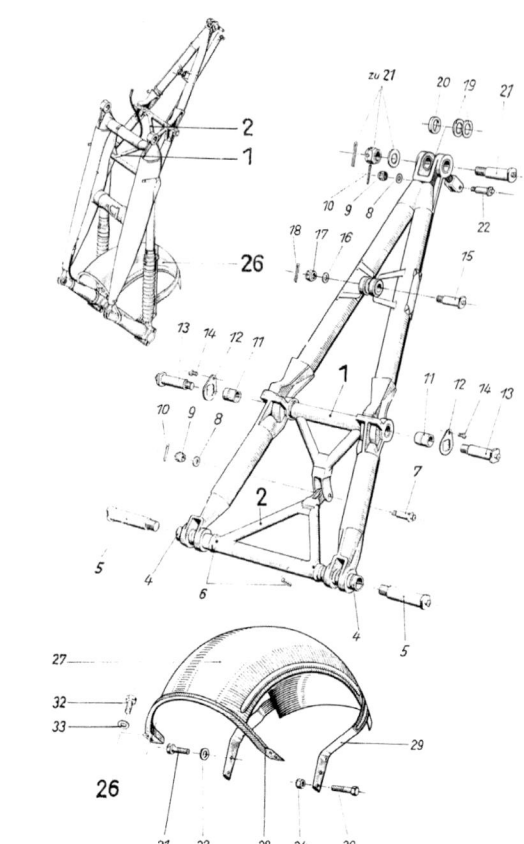

Oddly the manual also carries details of this style of undercarriage for the Fw 189, it is welded steel, but we can find no period images showing a machine with them fitted?

This is the retracting arm on the welded steel version

The Fw 189A-series could also be fitted with skis, which replaced the standard undercarriage and which were locked in the 'down' position all the time

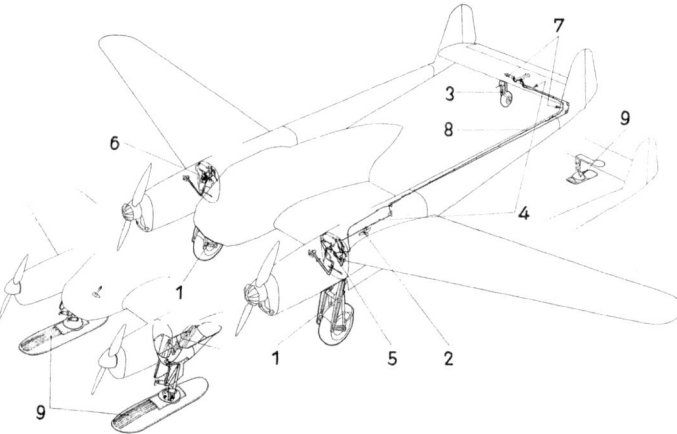

A nice period photo, taken from the Elektra catalogue, showing the hubs made by that firm for use on the Fw 189

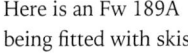

Here is an Fw 189A being fitted with skis

AA06/12/38 — Valiant Wings Publishing — Issued: February 2015

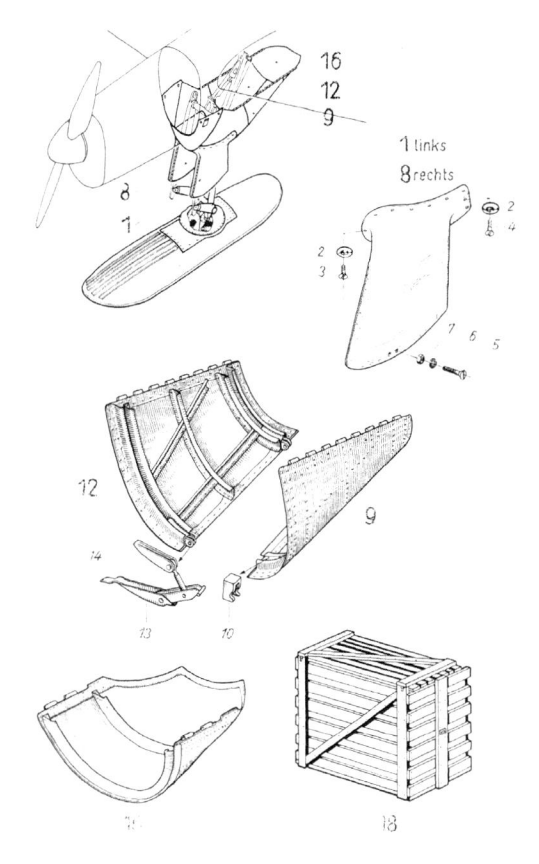

Group 2 – Side 4
Undercarriage
Ski/Tailwheel

This diagram shows the rear element of the fixed cover/fairing and those for the undercarriage legs themselves

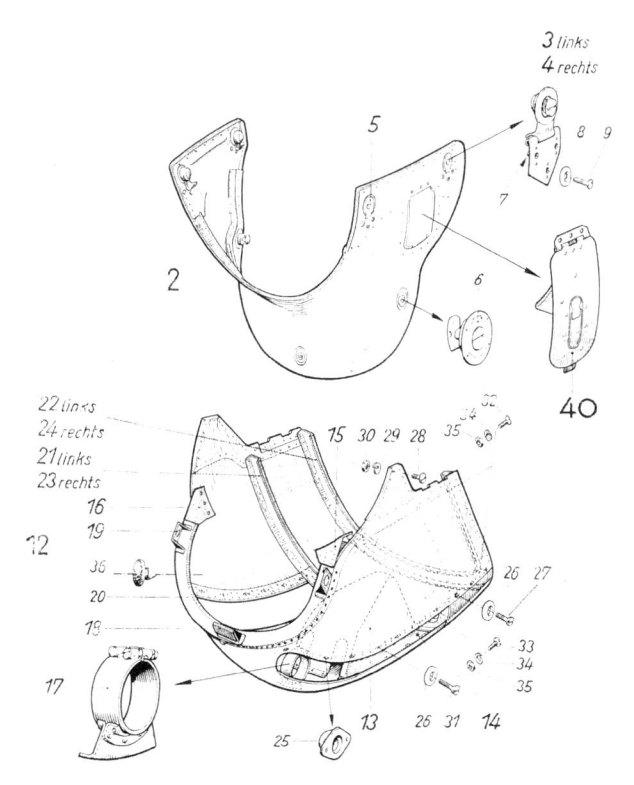

The upper area received this fixed cover/fairing for the front and main leg

Had the V7 or V8 been built, along with the proposed floatplane version of the B-series, this is the type of float that would have been installed

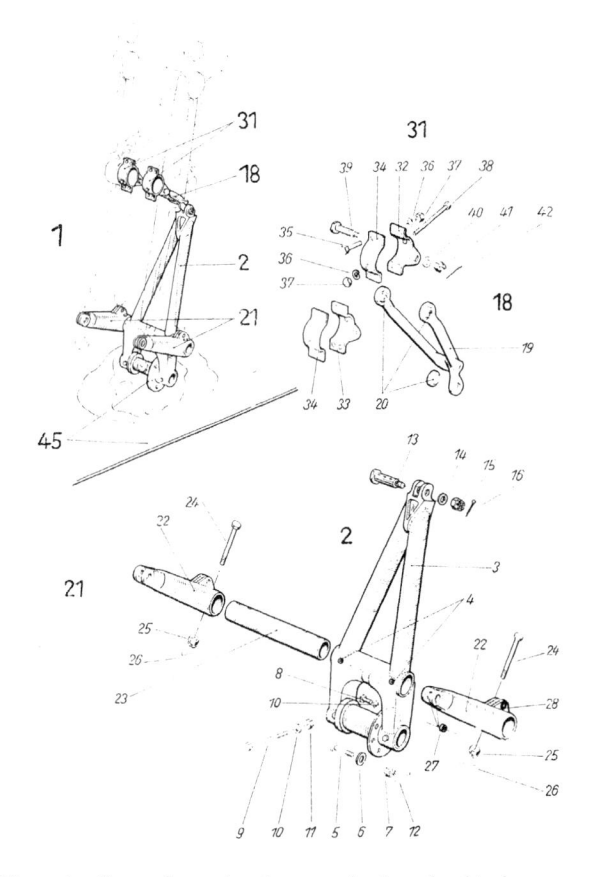

The main alloy undercarriage legs remained on the skis, however the bottom linkage etc. was replaced with this assembly

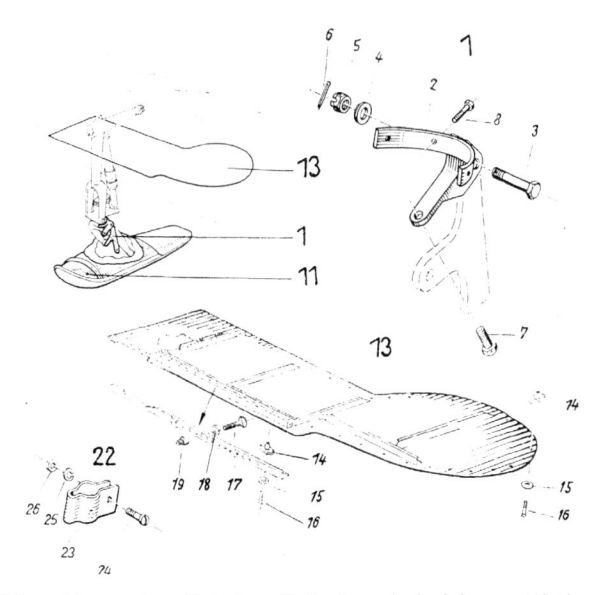

When skis were installed, the tailwheel was locked down, with the well covered over and a ski in place of the wheel

Group 2 – Side 5
Undercarriage
Tailwheel

The early solid tyre unit and wheel well, showing that these early machines featured a different shape to the well and two separate undercarriage doors

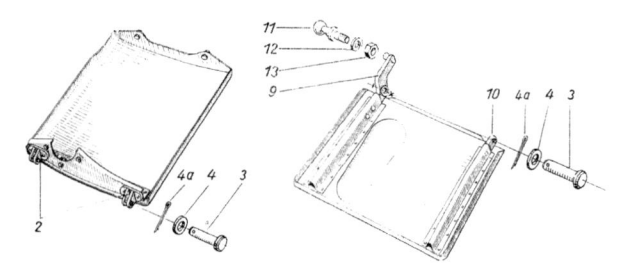

A useful diagram showing the two undercarriage doors for the tailwheel of the production versions

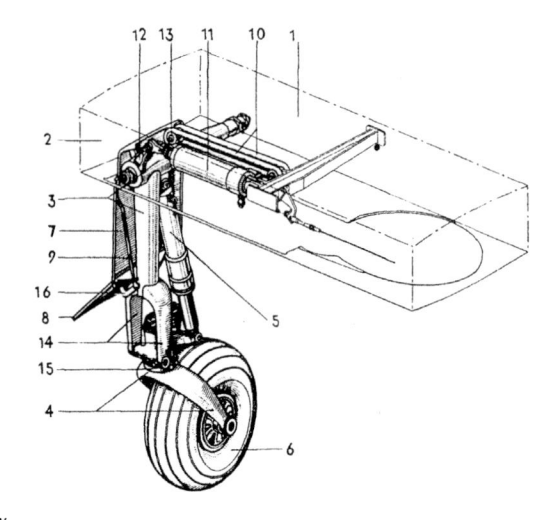

This is the solid rubber tyre unit used for many of the prototypes and pre-production series

The production series adopted a pneumatic wheel of 350mm x 150mm diameter and a revised oleo leg, wheel well and door arrangement as seen in this diagram

Key
1. Hauptholm (Main spar)
2. Hilfsholm (Auxiliary spar)
3. Spornbrücke (Spur bridge)
4. Spornradlagerung (Tailwheel well [literally 'storage'])
5. Federstrebe (Spring strut)
6. Spornrad (Tailwheel)
7. Spornverkleidung (Undercarriage door [literally 'spur trim']
8. Spornklappe (Undercarriage door, lower [literally 'spur flap'])
9. Stoßstange (Bumper)
10. Kraftspeicher (Power storage [e.g. elastic cords])
11. Einziehzylinder (Retracting cylinder)
12. Lagerhebel (Bearing lever)
13. Träger (Support bracket [literally 'carrier'])
14. Gabel (Fork)
15. Rolle (Roller tube)
16. Klappenhebel (Door linkage [literally 'flap lever'])

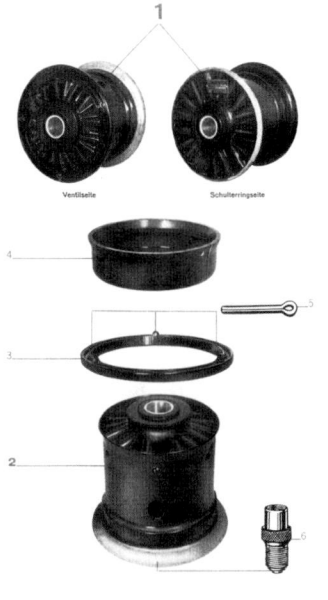

A photo from the Elektra catalogue showing the tailwheel hub assembly they made for the Fw 189

A period photo showing the tailwheel unit and well of a production machine, viewed from the rear, port side

Although not as good a quality, this photo is included because it shows the front aspect of the tailwheel assembly and thus includes areas not seen in the previous image

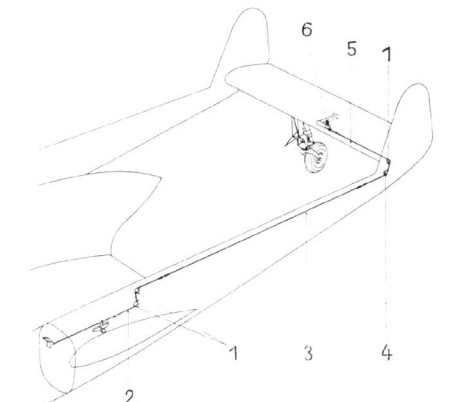

Group 3 – Side 1
Booms & Tail

Booms

41

This diagram shows the 'up lock' control lines for the tailwheel

An interesting period photo from Focke-Wulf, showing the inside of each half of the tail boom

Each boom is mounted onto this sub-assembly, which contains the fuel cell at the back (left) and the undercarriage at the front (right); the boom attaches to the far left

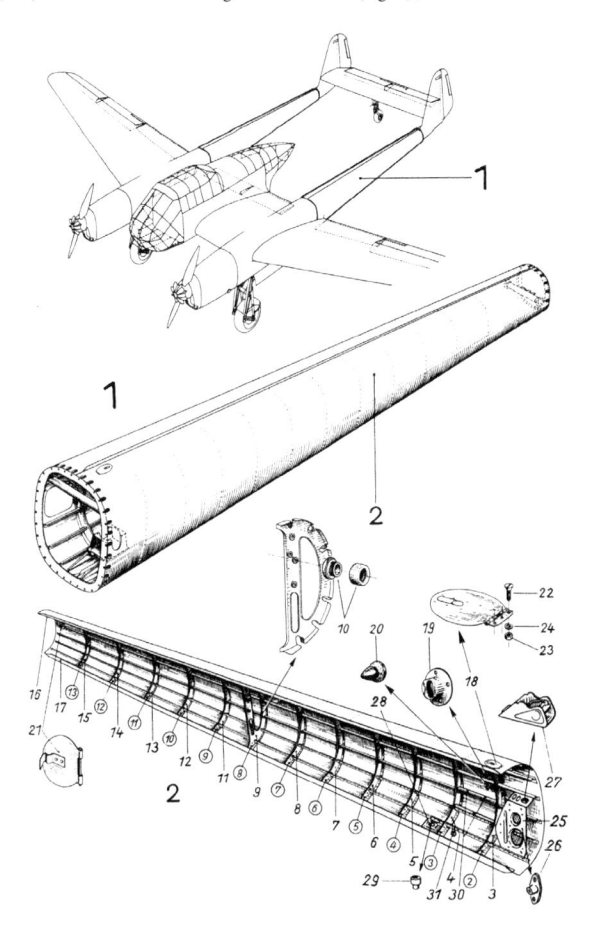

This diagram shows the port half of either boom

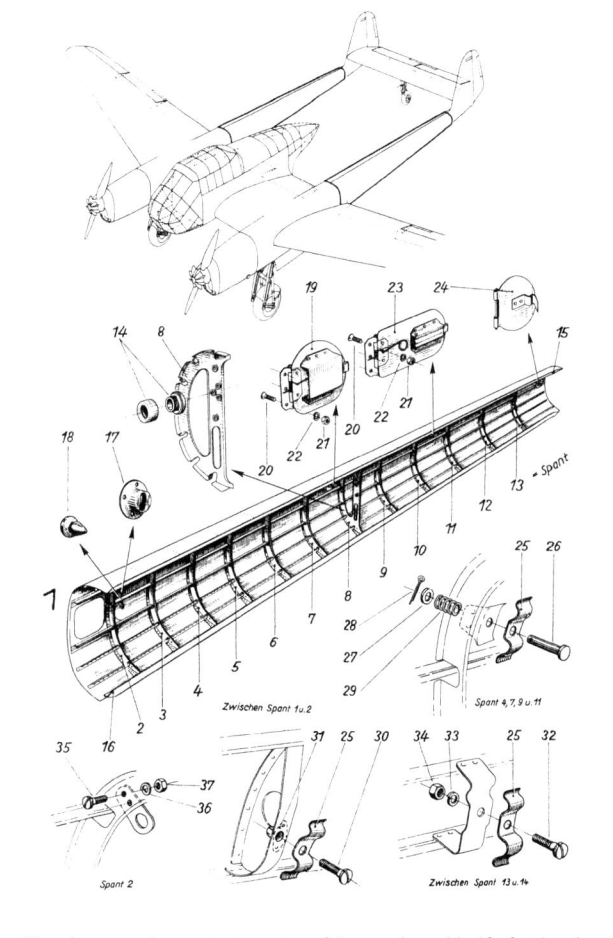

This diagram shows the interior of the starboard half of either boom

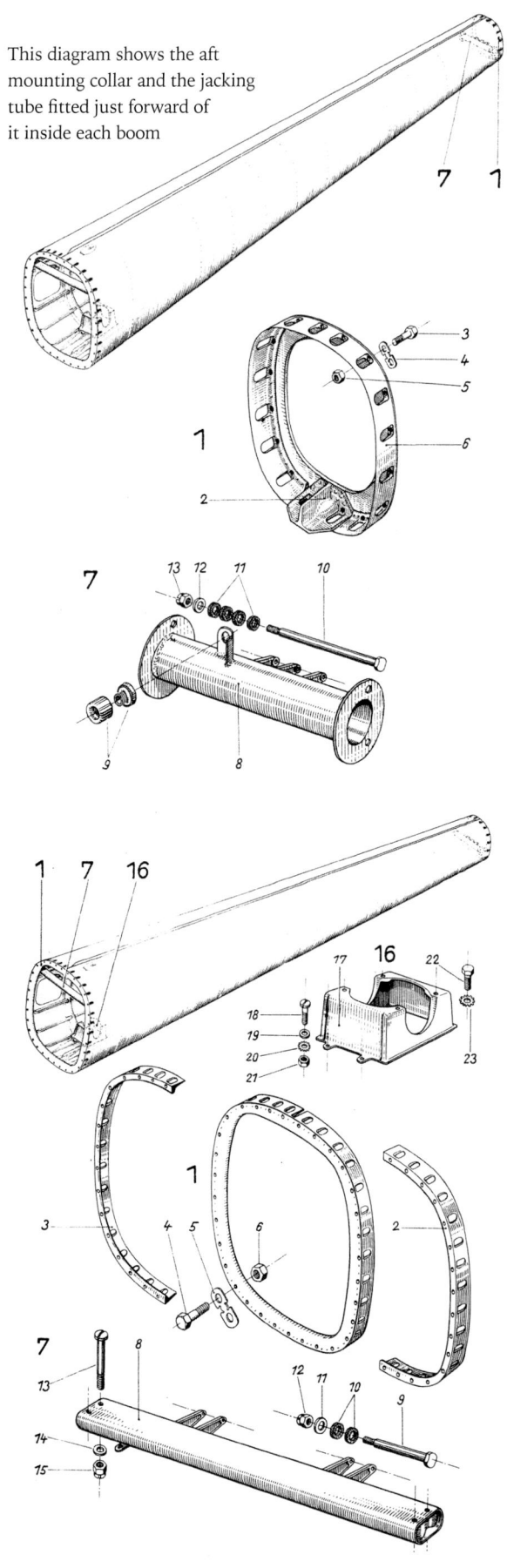

Group 3 – Side 2
Booms & Tail — 1
42 | Booms

This diagram shows the aft mounting collar and the jacking tube fitted just forward of it inside each boom

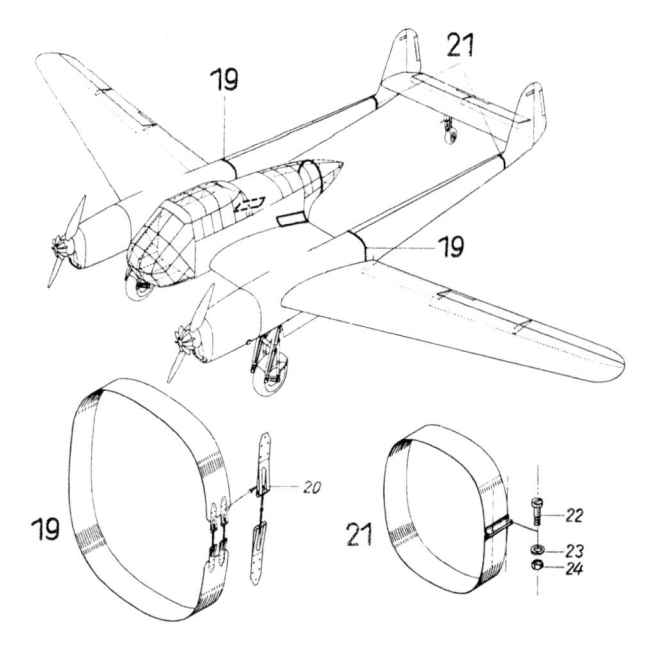

The fore and aft joints are covered with these collars

This Focke-Wulf photo shows a completed tail boom assembly

The front connection is done via this internal flanged collar unit with the jury strut ('7') to add strength above the access panel on the starboard side

This period image shows the access point for the 110lt tank in the forward boom/undercarriage area, you can also see in the bottom right the front/mid boom joint because the collar (cover) is not fitted

Group 3 – Side 3	**1**
Booms & Tail	
Tail	43

This period image shows completed tail units on shipping stands ready to be installed on the final assembly line

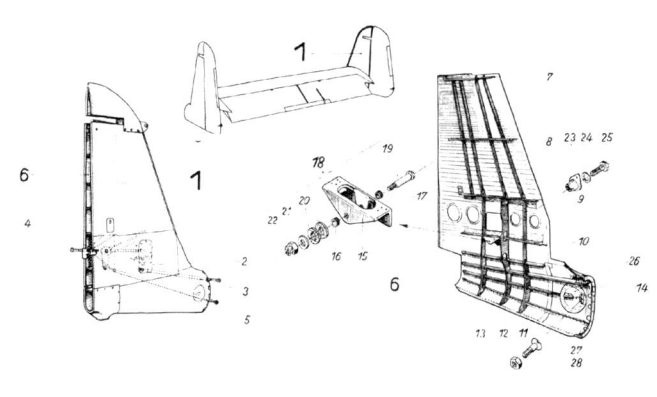

This diagram shows the main elements of the inboard side of the vertical fin for the starboard side, although the port one is identical

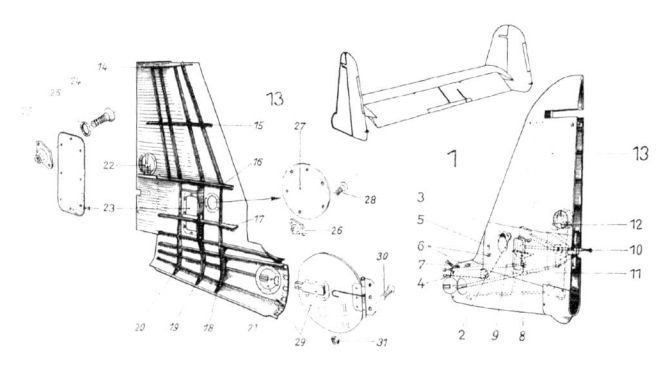

This diagram shows the main elements of the outer face of the vertical fin for the port side, although the starboard one is identical

A period image of the vertical fin and rudder on W/Nr.0155, which also happens to have a kill marking (dated 29th June 1941) on it

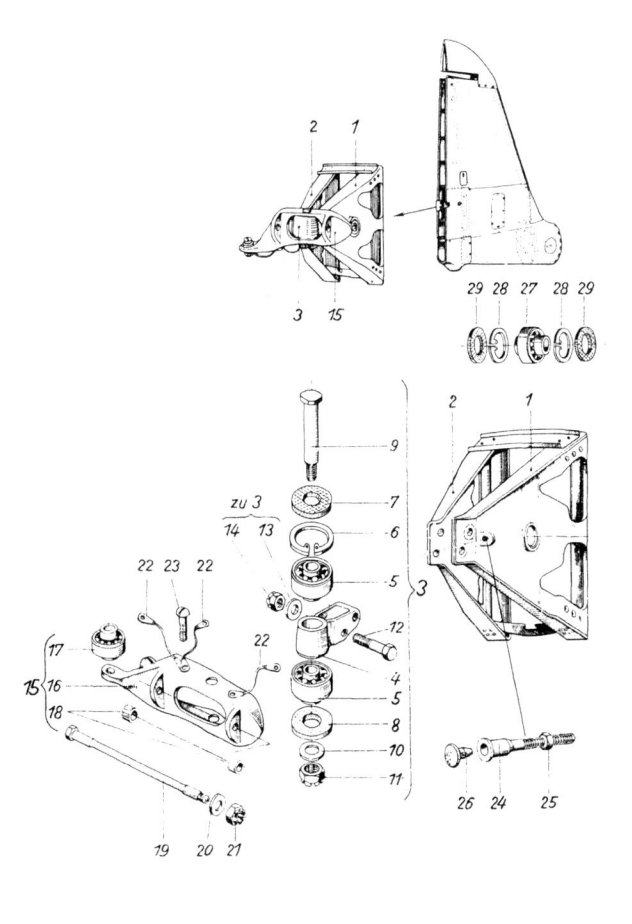

The leading edge and top cap for the starboard vertical fin, the port one is identical

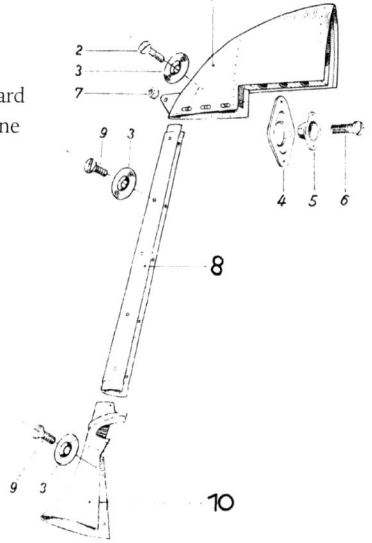

This is the main, lower, mounting point for the rudder and again it is identical for port or starboard sides

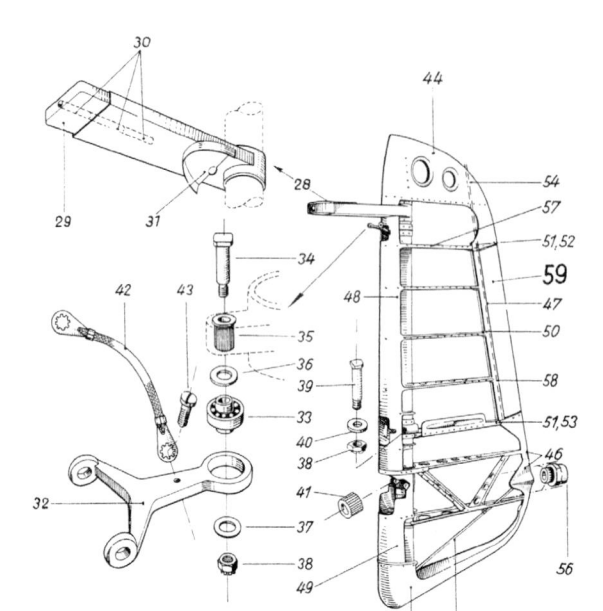

Group 3 – Side 4
Booms & Tail 1
44 Tail

Here is the corresponding upper rudder bracket, which is part of the rudder itself and is again identical for port or starboard sides

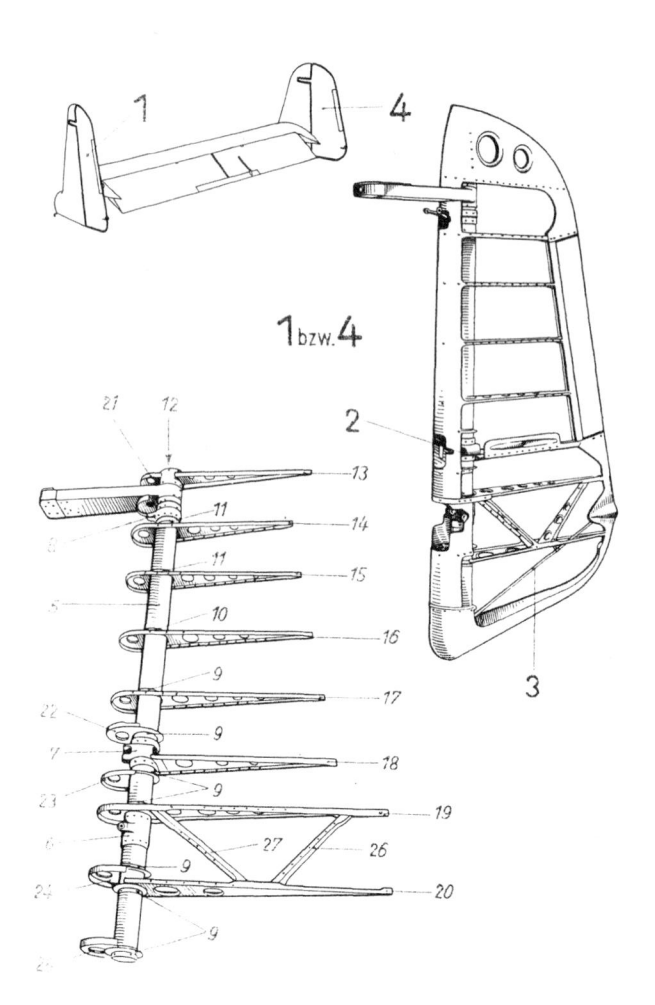

This diagram shows the ribs etc. within the rudder

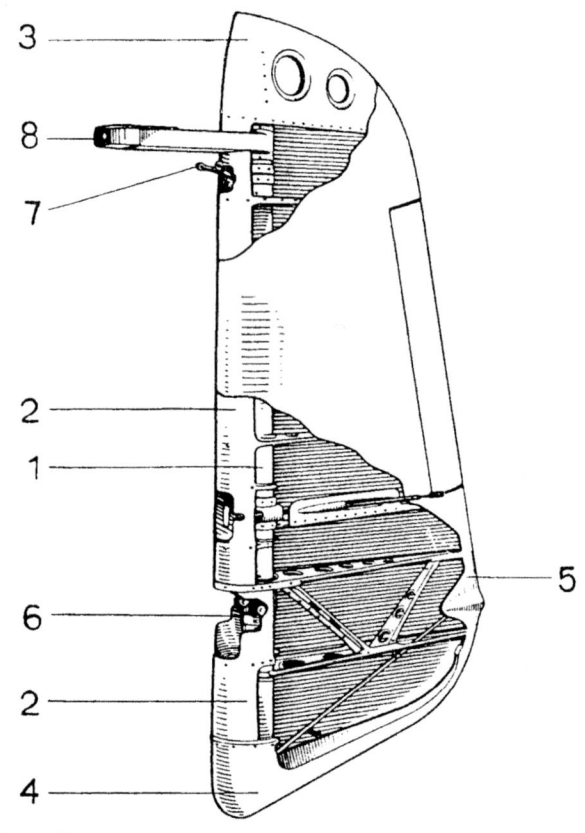

The rudder components

Key

1. Holm (Vertical tube)
2. Nasenformblech (Leading edge metal sheet [literally 'nose shaped sheet'])
3. Randklappe (Top cap [literally 'edge cap'])
4. Randbogen (Bottom cap [literally 'border bow'])
5. Randblech (Trailing edge profile [literally 'edge plate'])
6. untere Lagerstelle (Lower bearing)
7. obere Lagerstelle (Upper bearing)
8. Ausgleichgewicht (Balance weight)

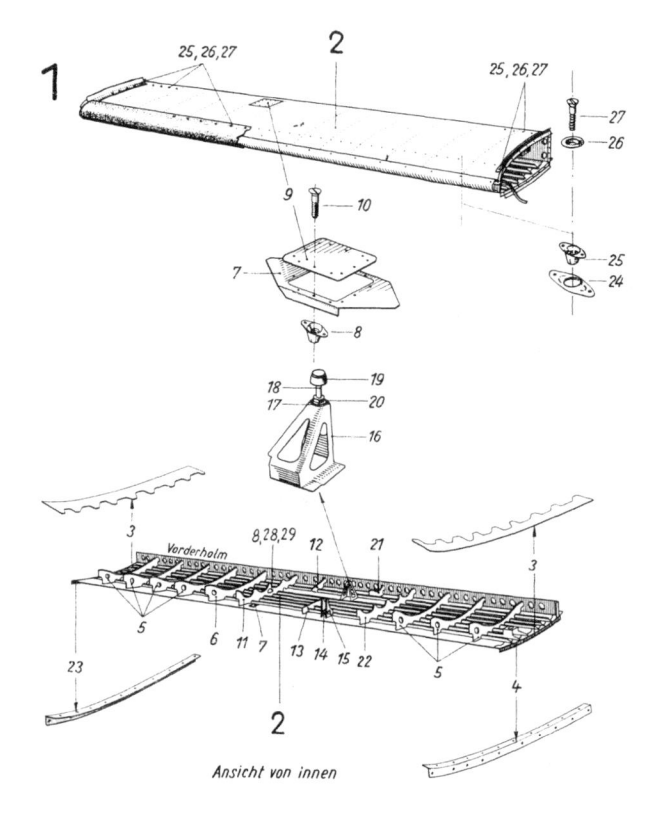

This diagram shows the upper skin of the tailplane

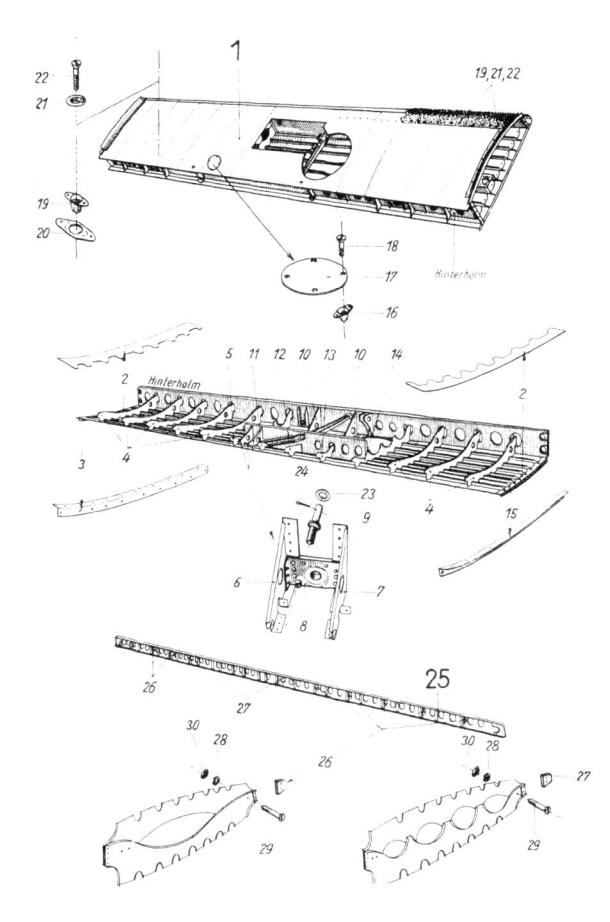

Group 3 – Side 5
Booms & Tail
Tail

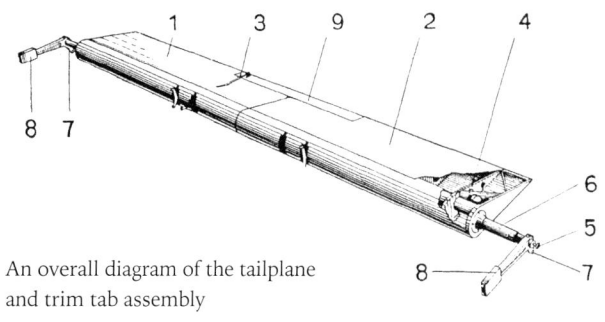

An overall diagram of the tailplane and trim tab assembly

Key
1. Höhenruderhälfte (Elevator half)
2. Höhenruderhälfte (Elevator half)
3. Höhenhilfsrudergestänge (Trim tab linkage)
4. Holm (Tube)
5. Äußere Lagerzapfen (Outer bearing pins)
6. Wellenstummel (Shaft end)
7. Ruderantriebshebel (Rudder actuator lever)
8. Ausgleichsgewichte (Balance weights)
9. Trimm- und Ausgleichsruder (Rudder trim balance)

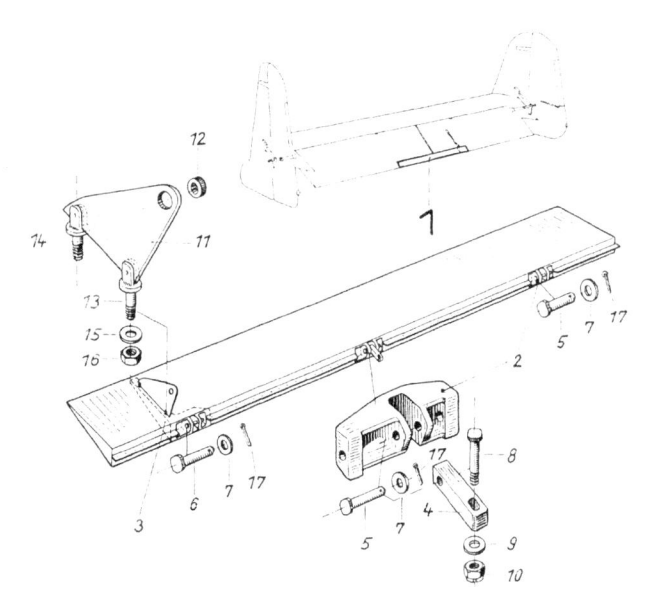

This is the lower skin of the tailplane with the wheel well in it

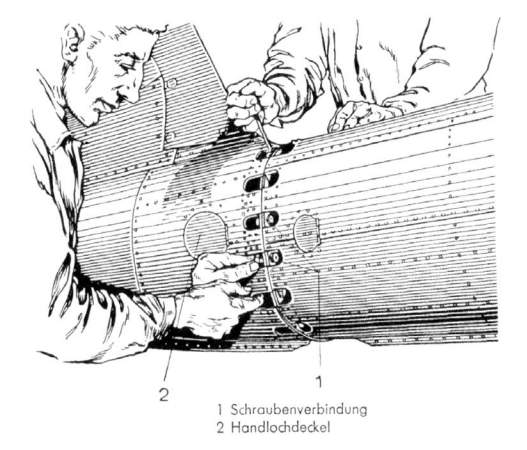

1 Schraubenverbindung
2 Handlochdeckel

Here you can see how the tail was bolted to the tail boom

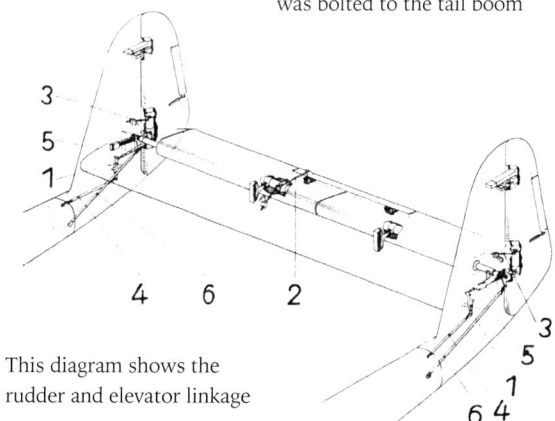

A detailed component diagram for the trim tab

This diagram shows the rudder and elevator linkage

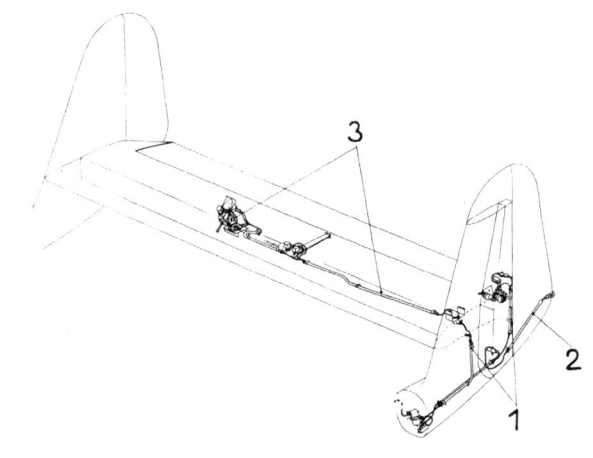

This diagram shows the electrics in the fin and tailplane including the servomotor for the tailwheel retraction (3) and the rear formation light (2)

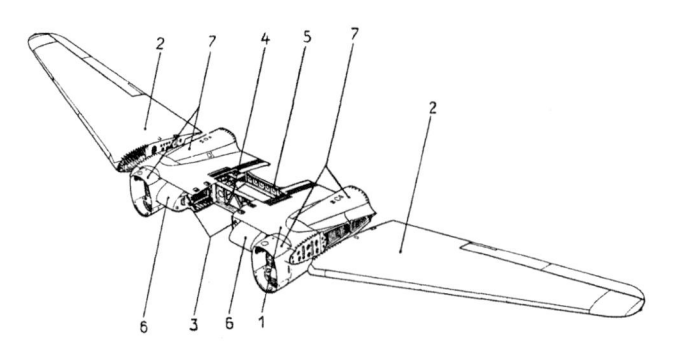

Group 4 – Side 1
Wings

This diagram shows the overall construction of the wings

Key
1. Innerflügel (Inner wing)
2. Außenflügel (Outer wing)
3. Nasenholm (Nose spar)
4. Hauptholm (Main spar)
5. Hinterholm (Rear spar)
6. Nasenklappe (Leading edge flap)
7. Motorgondel (Engine nacelle)

This period photos shows the centre section of the wing on the jig; you are looking at the underside here and the oblong hole in the centre is for the camera

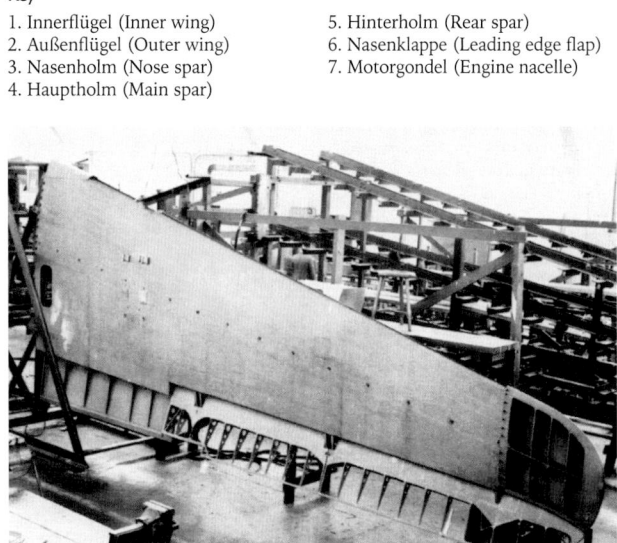

This is an outboard wing panel on the jig, you are looking at the underside and the step in the front is caused by the leading edge fillet not being fitted at this stage

A port outer mainplane having work done on the assembly line; you can see, especially in the wing ahead, how the aileron is split in two

A nice view of the underside of the port outer mainplane, showing the ETC racks to the right and the hinged landing light to the left (this retracted with the undercarriage)

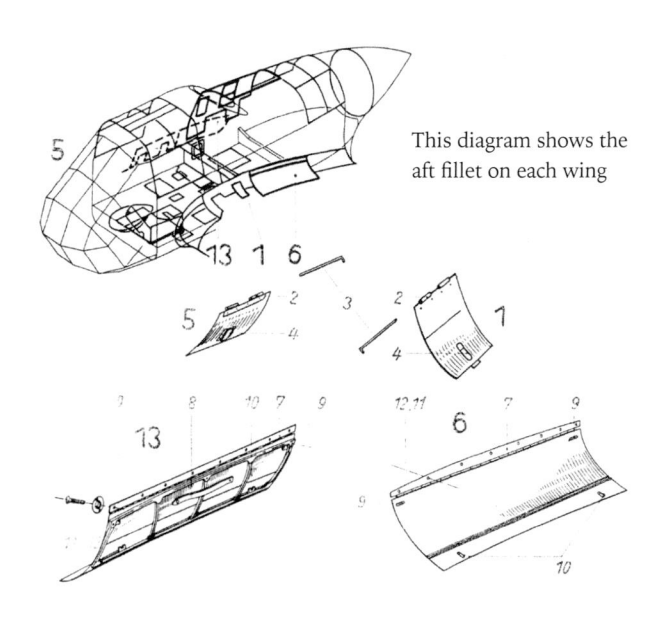

This diagram shows the aft fillet on each wing

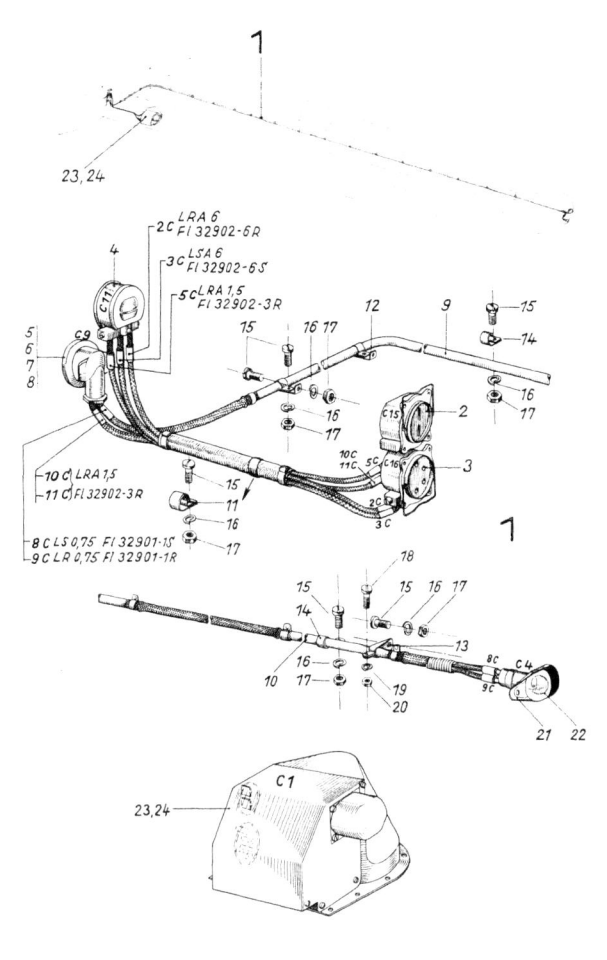

Wings

Group 4 – Side 2

Cockpit Interior

This diagram shows the wiring in the port wing to the landing light (23 & 24) and the tip light (1)

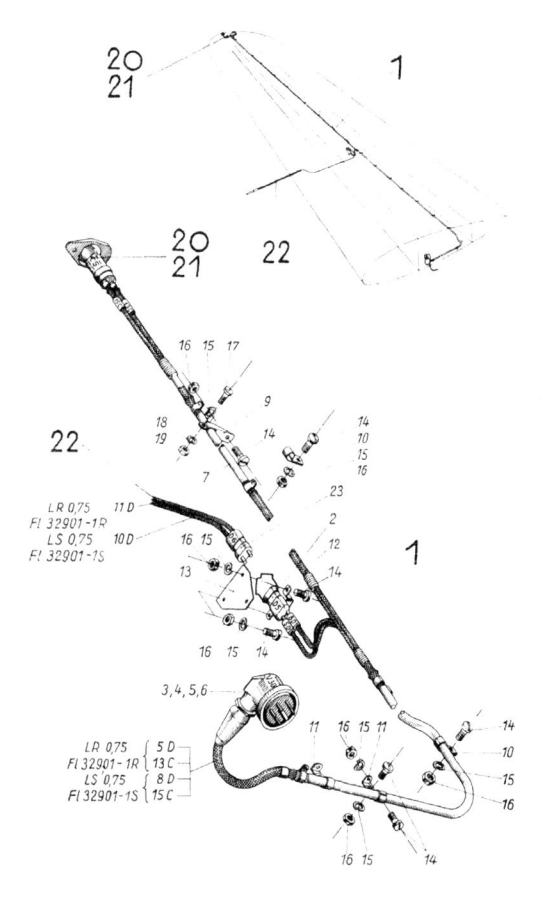

The wiring diagram for the starboard wing, again showing the tip light (20 & 21) but on this side also the heating to the pitot head (22)

This diagram shows the mid fillet on each wing

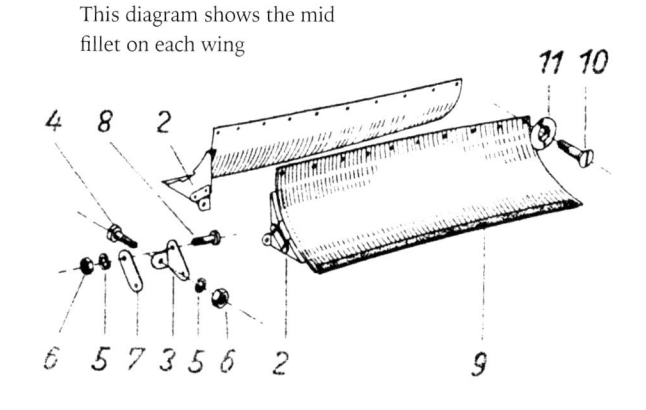

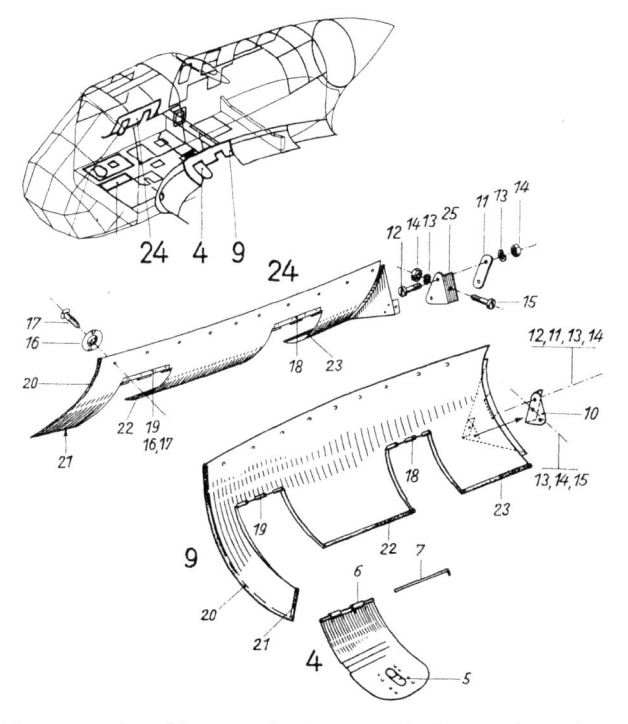

There are various fillets at each wing root, this diagram shows the front ones

The only exception to the manner in which the wing was installed on the Fw 189 was on the V6 and the C-series, which had no centre section as such, with the revised wings being permanently attached to the armoured nacelle, as seen here on W/Nr.0021 (Fw 189C-1, NA+WE)

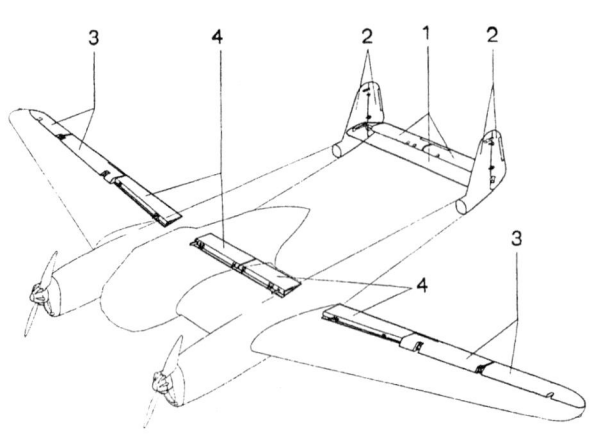

Group 4 – Side 3
Wings
48 | Ailerons & Flaps

This diagram shows the control surfaces

Key
1. Höhenleitwerk (Tailplane)
2. Seitenleitwerk (Fin)
3. Querruder (Ailerons)
4. Landklappe (Landing flaps)

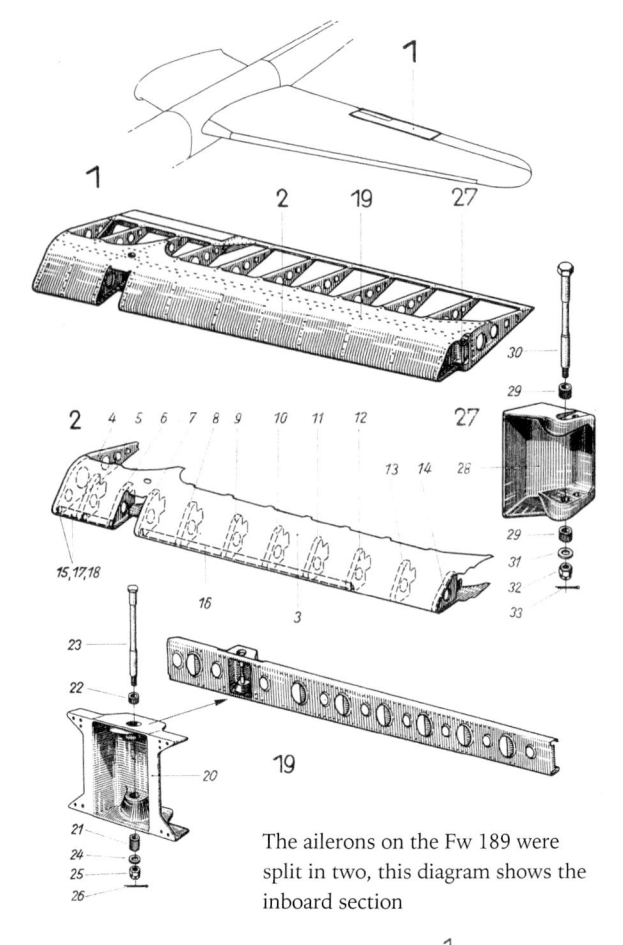

The ailerons on the Fw 189 were split in two, this diagram shows the inboard section

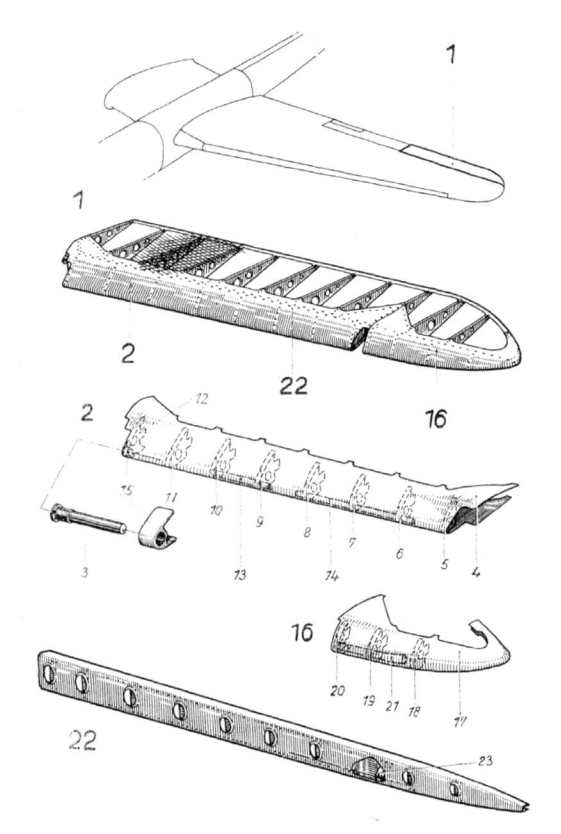

This diagram shows the outboard element of the aileron

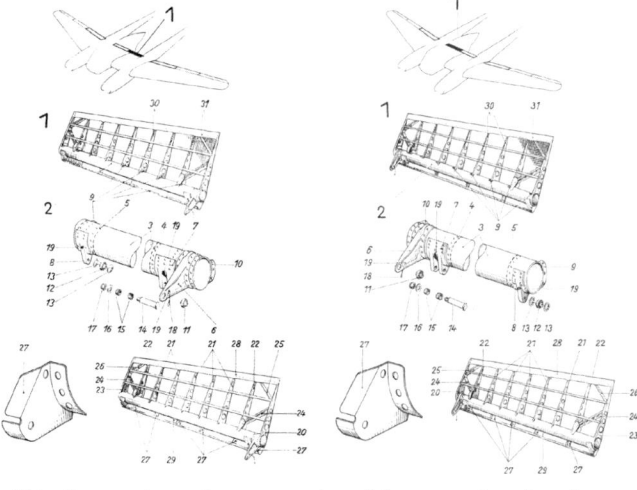

This diagram shows the construction of the port and starboard inner flaps

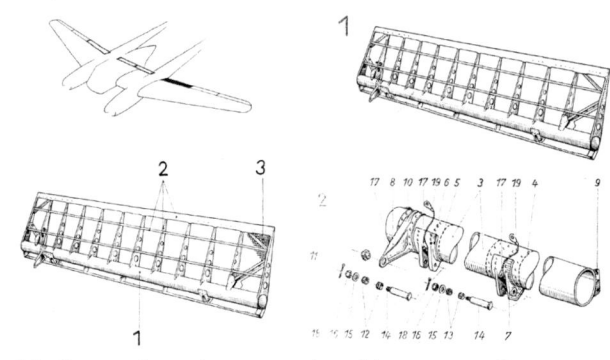

This diagram shows the construction of the port outer flap

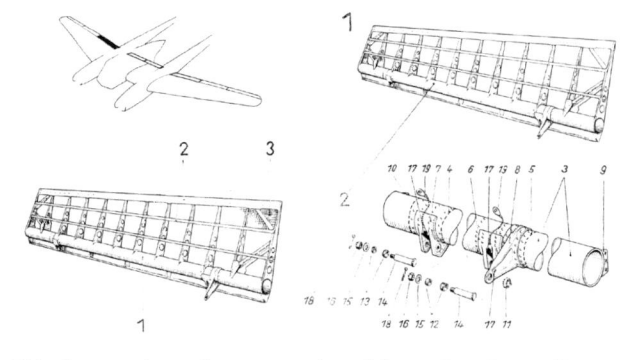

This diagram shows the construction of the starboard outer flap

AA06/14/48 — Valiant Wings Publishing — Issued: February 2015

Engines

Engine & Propeller

The initial powerplant for the V1 and V2 was the Hirth HM512

Here you can see the Hirth HM512 installation in the wooden mock-up of the V1

A number of the early V-series machines such as the V3, V4 and V5 adopted the As 410 engine but had the oil cooler mounted on the outer face, as seen here on the port engine of the W/Nr.0004

A nice period photo of a complete As 410 engine unit on the hoist prior to installation in which you can see all the oil tank and engine bearers as well as the cowlings

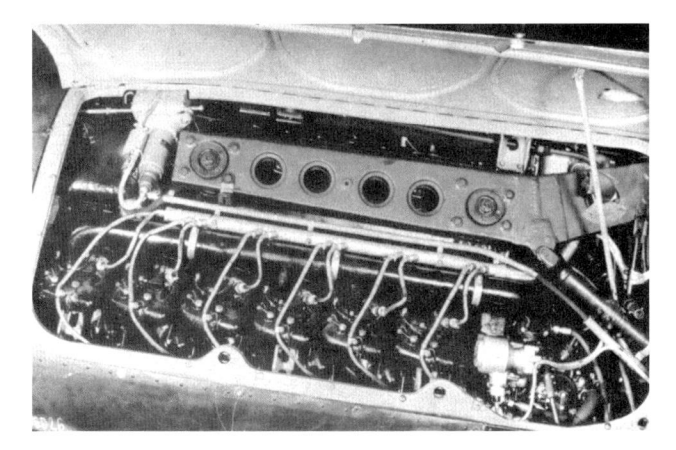

A nice period image of the port side of the As 410 with the cowl open

A view of the starboard side of an installed As 410 with the cowl open

Group 5 – Side 2
Engines
50 | Engine & Propeller

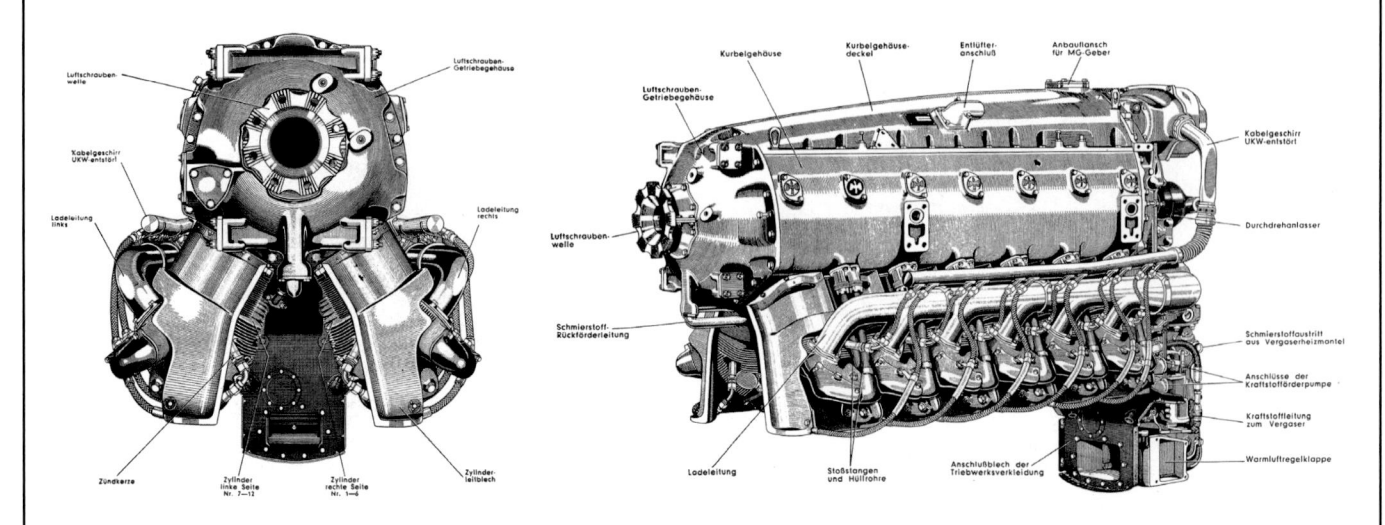

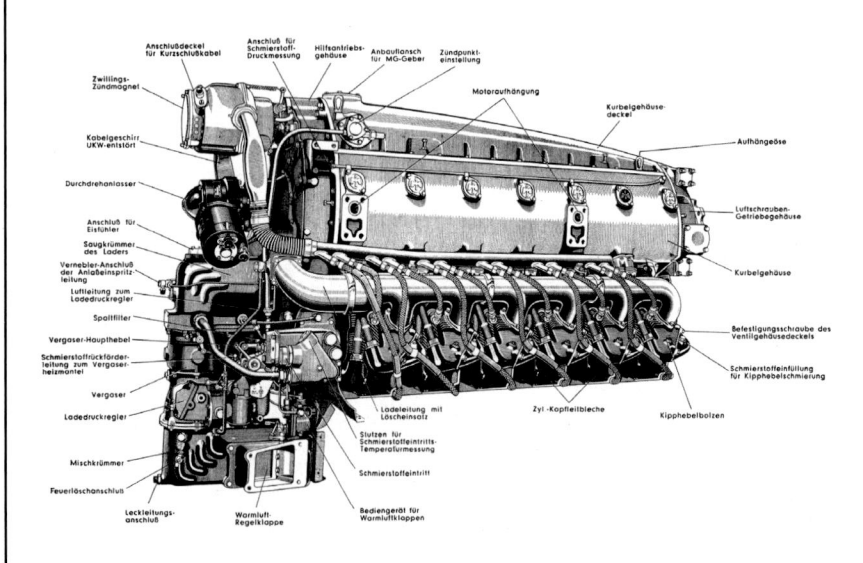

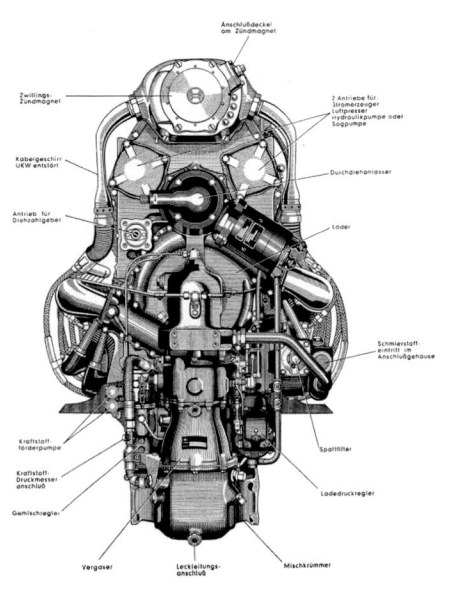

Line drawings from the manual of the of the As 410

- Antriebe für Stromerzeuger Luftpresser Hydraulikpumpe oder Saugpumpe (Two drives for the power generators, air compressor, hydraulic pump or suction pump)
- Anbauflansch fr MG-Geber (Mounting flange for MG-timer)
- Anschluß für Eisfühler (Connection for ice sensor)
- Anschluß für Schmierstoff-Druckmessung (Connection for oil pressure measurement)
- Anschlußblech der Triebwerksverkleidung (Connecting plate for the engine cowling/air intake)
- Anschlußblech für Kurzschlußkabel (Connecting plate for short cable)
- Anschlußdeckel am Zündmagnet (Access covers on magneto)
- Anschlüsse der Kraftstofförderpumpe (Connections of the fuel pump)
- Antried für Drehzahlgeber (Drive for rev counter)
- Aufhängeöse (suspension eyelet [literally 'hanging loop'])
- Bediengerät für Warmluftregelklappe (Control unit for hot air control flap)
- Befestigungsschraube des Ventilgehäusedeckels (Screw securing the valve housing cover)
- Durchdrehanlasser (Starter motor)
- Entlüfter-anschluß (Breather pipe connection)
- Feuerlöschanschluß (Fire extinguisher terminal)
- Gemischregler (Mixture control)
- Hilfsantriebs-gehäuse (Auxiliary drive enclosure)
- Kabelgesschirr UKW-entstört (Cable (covered) VHF interference suppression)
- Kipphebelbolzen (Rocker arm shaft)
- Kraftstoff-Druckmess-anschluß (Fuel pressure measurement connection)
- Kraftstoff-förderpumpe (Fuel feed pump)
- Kraftstoffleitung zum Vergaser (Fuel line to the carburettor)
- Kurbelgehäuse (Crankcase)
- Kurbelgehäuse-deckel (Crankcase cover)
- Ladedruckregler (Boost pressure regulator)
- Ladeleitung (Induction pipe [literally 'charging tube'])
- Ladeleitung links (Induction pipe, left [literally 'charging tube'])
- Ladeleitung mit Löscheinsatz (Induction pipe, with fire extinguisher [literally 'charging tube with fire fighting procedure'])
- Ladeleitung rechts (Induction pipe, right [literally 'charging tube'])
- Lader (Inlet [literally 'loader'])
- Leckleitungs-anschluß (Drain plug [literally 'leakage line connection'])
- Luftleitung zum Ladedruckregler (Air line to the waste-gate)
- Luftschrauben-Getriebegehäuse (Propeller gearbox)
- Luftschraubenwelle (Propeller shaft)
- Mischkrümmer (Inlet manifold)
- Motoraufhängung (Engine mounting)
- Saugkrümmer des Laders (Supercharger inlet manifold)
- Schmierstoff-Rückförderleitung (Oil return line)
- Schmierstoffaustritt aus Vergaserheizmantel (Lubricant drain from the carburettor heating jacket)
- Schmierstoffeinfüllung für Kipphebelschmierung (Rocker shaft lubricant point [literally 'Lubricants for filling rocker shaft'])
- Schmierstoffeintritt (Lubricant inlet)
- Schmierstoffrückförder-leitung zum Vergaser-heizmantel (Lubricant feed-line to the carburettor heating jacket)
- Spaltfilter (Split filters)
- Stoßstangen und Hüllrohre (Pushrods and tubes [literally 'Bumpers and cladding tubes'])
- Stutzen für Schmierstoff Eintritts-Temperaturmessung (Spigot for lubricant inlet temperature measurement)
- Vergaser (Carburettor)
- Vergaser-Haupthebel (Carburettor main control/actuation lever)
- Vernebler-Anschluß der Anlaßeinspritz-leitung (Air drain plug from the injection line)
- Warmluft-Regelklappe (Warm air control flap)
- Zündpunkt-einstellung (Ignition point-setting)
- Zwillings-Zündmagnet (Twin magneto)
- Zyl.- Kopfleitbleche (Cylinder head baffles)
- Zylinder linke Seite Nr.7-12 (Cylinder, left, numbers 7 to 12)
- Zylinder rechte Seite Nr.1-6 (Cylinder, right, numbers 1 to 6)
- Zylinder-leitblech (Cylinder baffle)

Group 5 – Side 3
Engines
Engine & Propeller

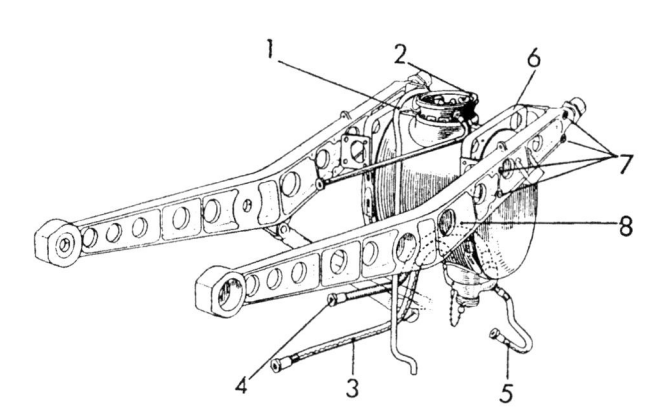

This diagram shows the oil tank installation within the engine bearers

Key
1. Überlaufleitung (Overflow pipe)
2. Entlüftungsleitung (Vent pipe)
3. Schlauchleitung zum Schmierstoffkühler (Hose for oil cooler)
4. Schlauchleitung zur Schmierstoffpumpe (Hose line to the oil pump)
5. Kaltstartleitung (Cold start line)
6. Träger (Carrier)
7. Befestigungsschrauben (Mounting screws)
8. Motorträger (Engine bearers)

For some of the later (never to be built) series, the Argus As 411 engine was to be installed

Colour images of the As 411 can be seen on page 101

It had been intended to use stocks of the Gnome-Rhône 14M captured in France in some of the projected variants

Only one machine actually tested the Gnome-Rhône installation, the V14, seen here at Villacoublay

With the late V-series and for all production machines the As 410 engine came in revised cowls with the exhaust as one outlet low on the outer side; this montage of shots shows the installation of an engine on the production line

Engines
Exhausts & Cowlings

Group 5 – Side 4 – 1

52

Initially the V1 and V2 used the Hirth engine, so the cowling was longer and had individual exhaust stacks, as seen here on the V1 not long after its initial roll-out. The type also used a different type of two-blade propeller

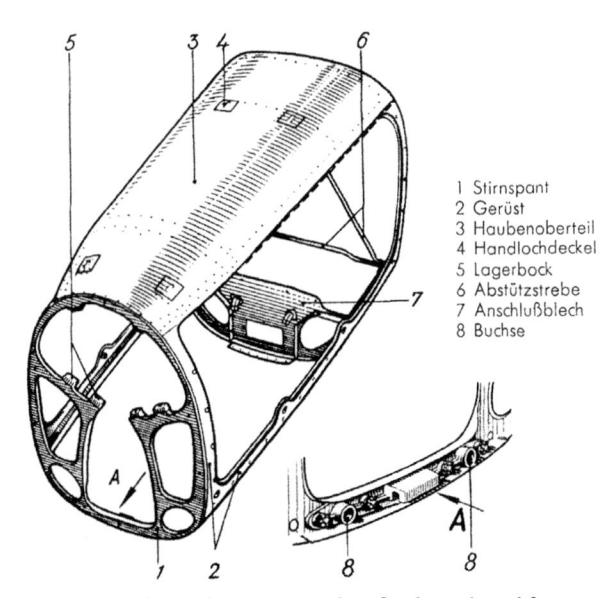

1 Stirnspant
2 Gerüst
3 Haubenoberteil
4 Handlochdeckel
5 Lagerbock
6 Abstützstrebe
7 Anschlußblech
8 Buchse

This diagram shows the engine cowling fixed panels and framework for the As 410

With the V3, V4 and V5 the engine changed to the Argus As 410, but these machines had the oil cooler outer on the outer face of each cowling, as shown here on the V3. The propeller by this time is a VDM two-blade metal unit

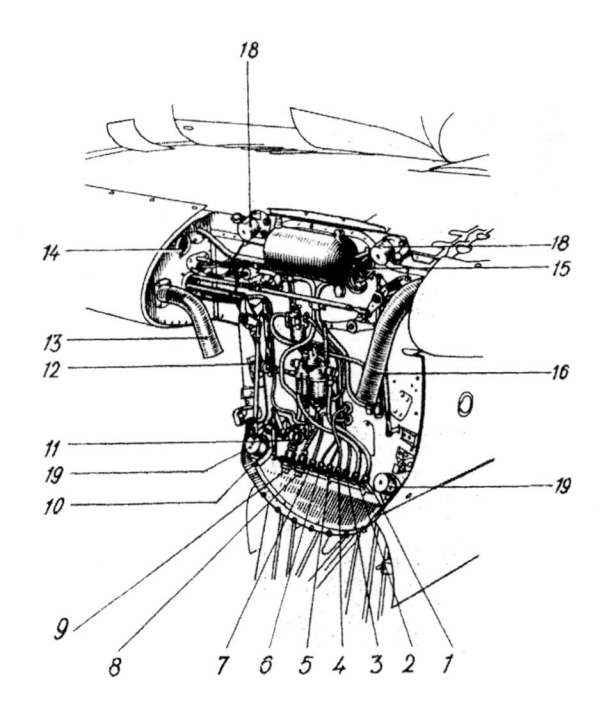

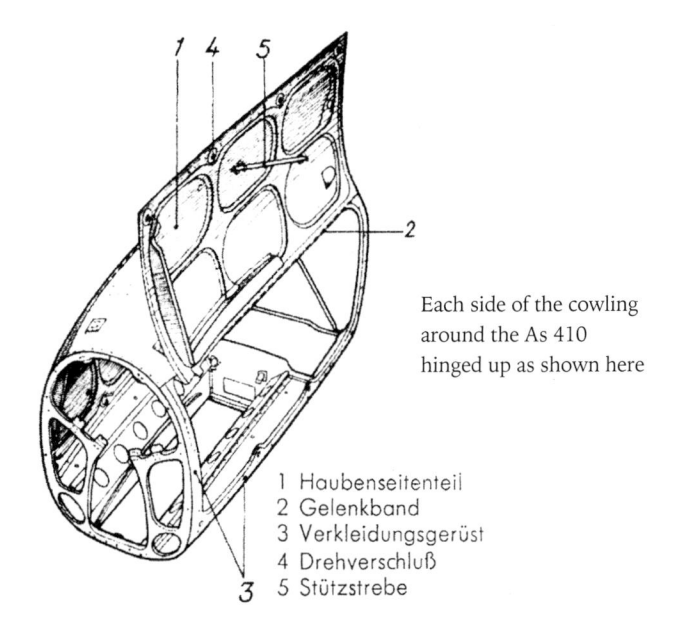

Each side of the cowling around the As 410 hinged up as shown here

1 Haubenseitenteil
2 Gelenkband
3 Verkleidungsgerüst
4 Drehverschluß
5 Stützstrebe

This diagram shows you all the various connectors on the engine bulkhead

Key
1 & 2. Kraftstoffleitungen (Fuel lines)
3. Kraftstoff-Druckmesserleitung (Fuel pressure gauge lines)
4. Einspritzleitung (Injection pipe)
5. Ladedruckmesserleitung (Boost meter line)
7. Feurlöschleitung (Fire extinguisher line)
8. Drucköl-Druckleitung (Oil pressure (pressure) line)
9. Drucköl-Saugleitung (Oil pressure (suction) line)
10. Gasgestänge (Throttle linkage)
11. Stoßstange zum Heißluftverteiler (Bumper for hot air distribution)
12. elektr. Steckkupplung V20 (Electrical plug-in coupling V20)
13. Warmluft-Zufuhr – Rumpf (Warm air supply – fuselage)
14. elektr. Steckkupplung Zündleitung 1B (Electrical plug-in coupling – ignition 1B)
15. elektr. Steckkupplung A2 für Generator (nur am linken Brandschott) (Electrical plug-in coupling A2 for generator (on the left firewall))
16. Warmluft-Abfuhr in den Außenflügel (Warm air discharge in the outer wing)
18. obere Triebwerksanschlüsse (Upper engine connections)
19. untere Triebwerksanschlüsse (Lower engine connections)

Engines
Exhausts & Cowlings

Group 5 – Side 5

53

The middle area under the cowl housed the oil cooler unit, which hinged down as shown here

When the engine was delivered to Focke-Wulf from Argus, it came in this transit cradle

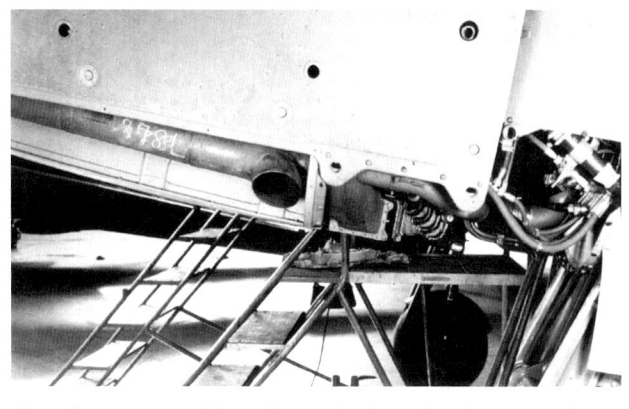

The exhaust was on either side as a single outlet pipe, as seen here on a C-0 (probably NA+WA)

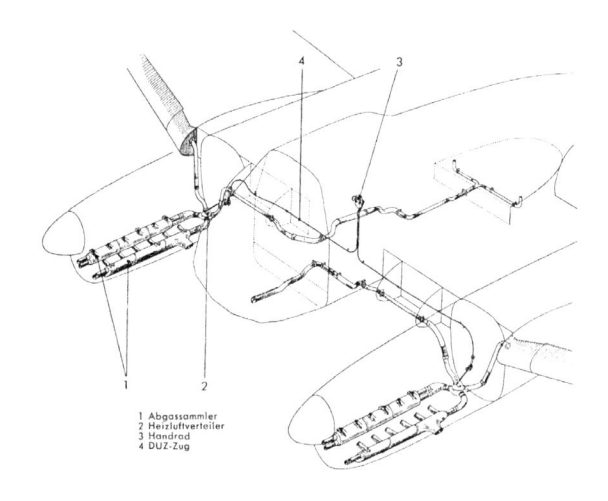

1 Abgassammler
2 Heizluftverteiler
3 Handrad
4 DUZ-Zug

The heating system took hot air off the exhaust manifold, as seen in this diagram

This period image nicely illustrates the mass of pipework etc. on the engine bulkhead before the engine is installed

The V14 with the Gnome-Rhône engines had a totally revised cowling as well as this revision to the engine/wing transition. The engine exhausts out the back, over the panels aft of the cowling, whilst the intakes at the top are on both sides

The overall revisions to the cowling for the radial Gnome-Rhône engine are apparent in this front view of the V14, as is the Ratier three-blade propeller and spinner

Group 6 – Side 1
Armament
54 Fixed Gun

This diagram shows the twin fixed MG17 machine-guns situated in each wing root of the A-series

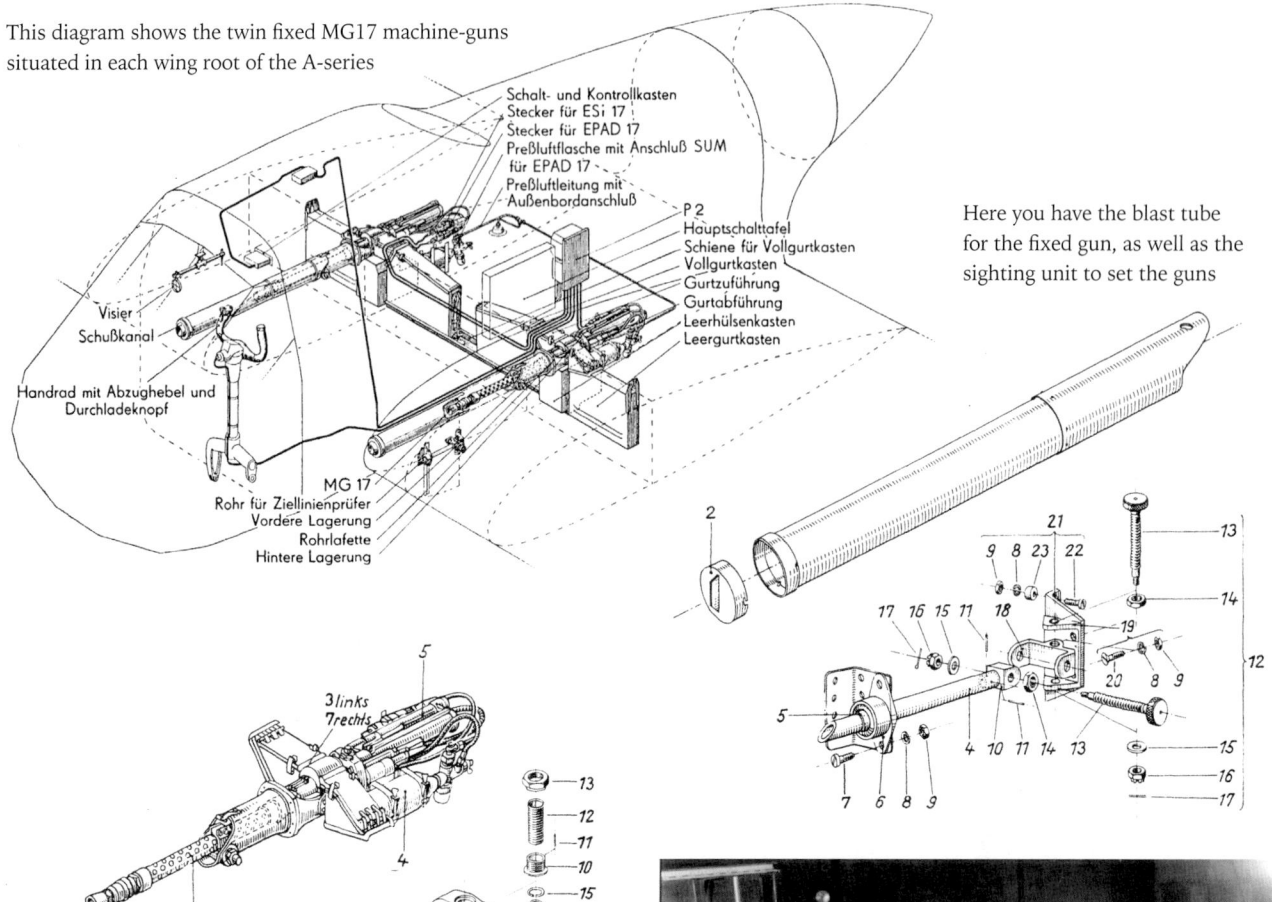

Here you have the blast tube for the fixed gun, as well as the sighting unit to set the guns

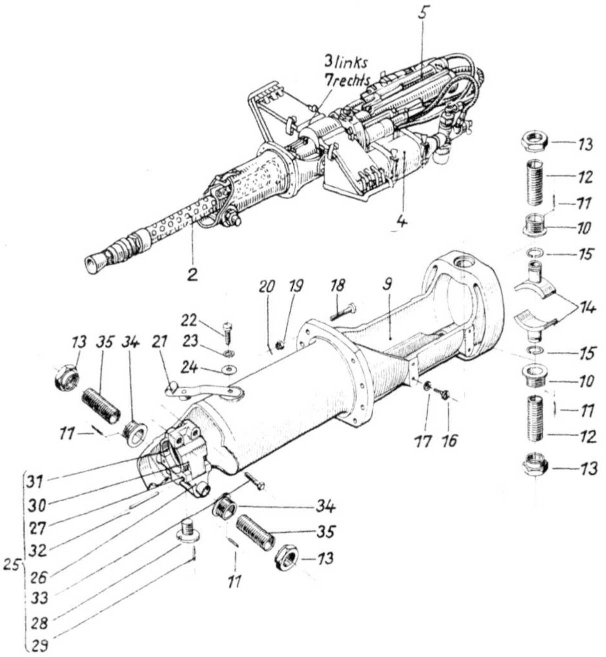

This is the fixed gun and cradle assembly for the A-series

A nice period image confirming how the gun access panel on the upper surface opened

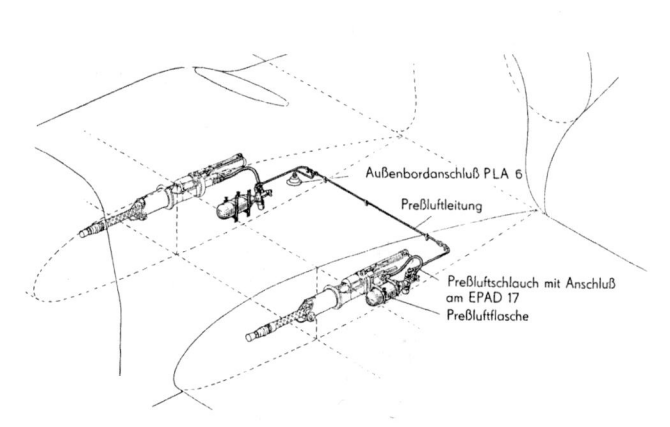

Each gun was cocked pneumatically, and this diagram shows the bottles and air lines

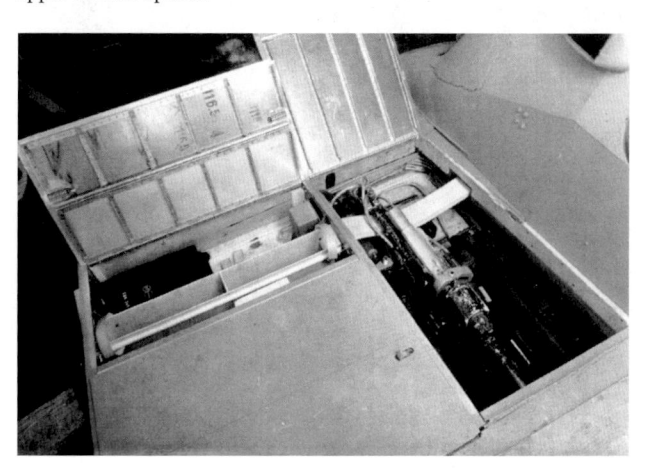

The V1b had six guns, this photo shows the revised ammo and gun bays in the port wing of the wooden mock-up

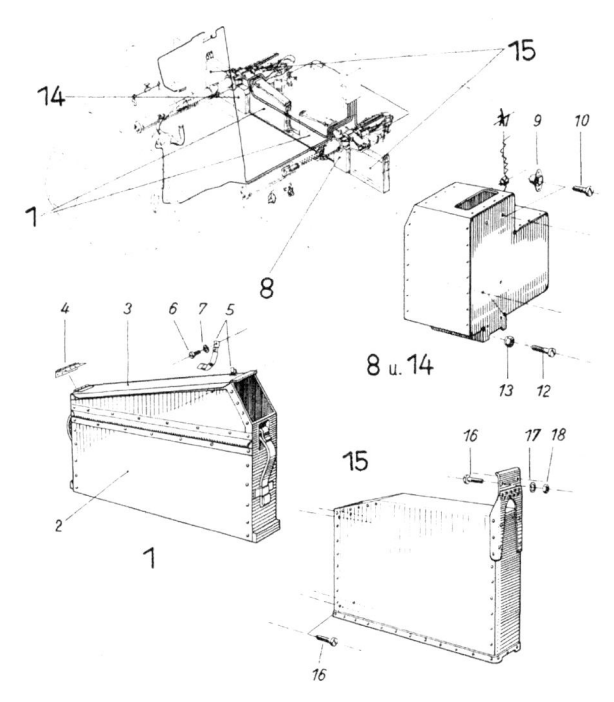

Group 6 – Side 2
Armament
Fixed Gun

The ammunition belts sat in the outer (15) boxes, and the cases collected in the inner box (1), whilst the belt clips fell out through the bottom of the wing via the box (8 & 14) below the breech of each weapon

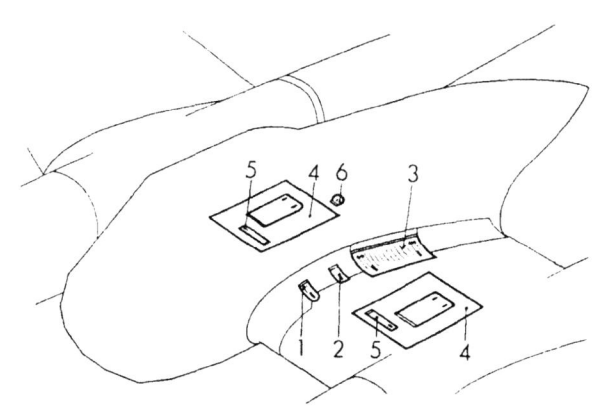

Access to the fixed guns was via a series of access panels, with those on top numbered 1 to 3 and those underneath, 4 to 6

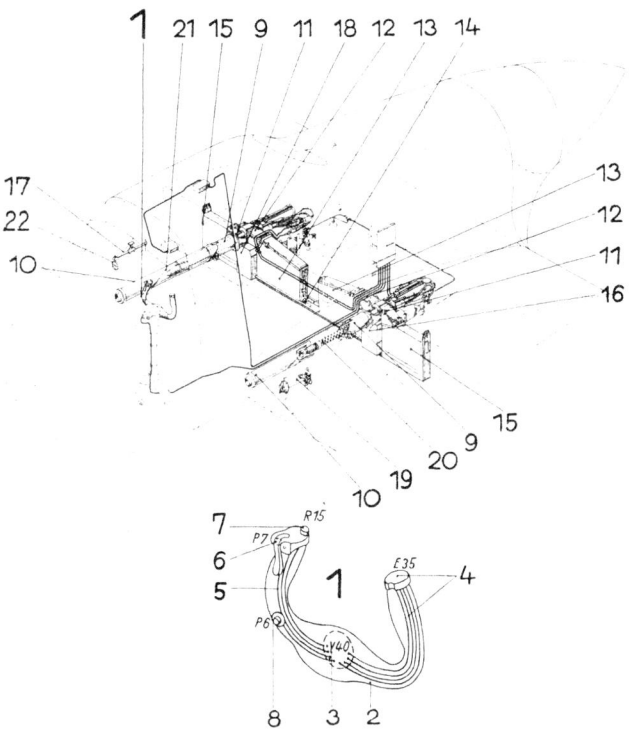

This diagram shows the firing circuit, as well as the trigger on the control column (7) and the ring and bead sight (17 & 22) in the canopy top

The armament in the C-series was similar to that in the V1b and V6, this shot therefore shows the weapons (inboard) element with the MG151/20 on the right and the two MG17s in the middle and on the left

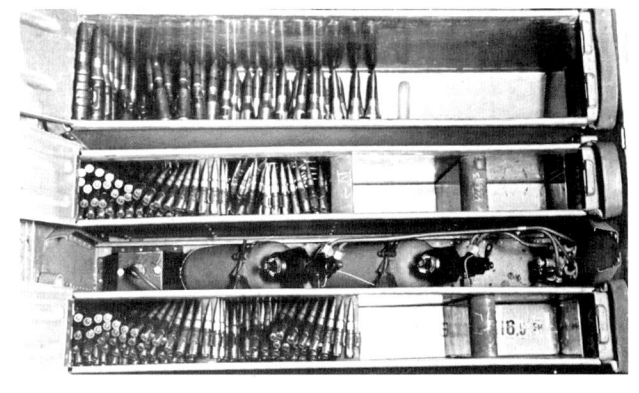

This shot shows the ammunition bays for the fixed armament of the C-series, which was outboard of the bay for the weapons themselves; this is the bay in the port wing, as the guns would be on the right

Armament
Dorsal Turret

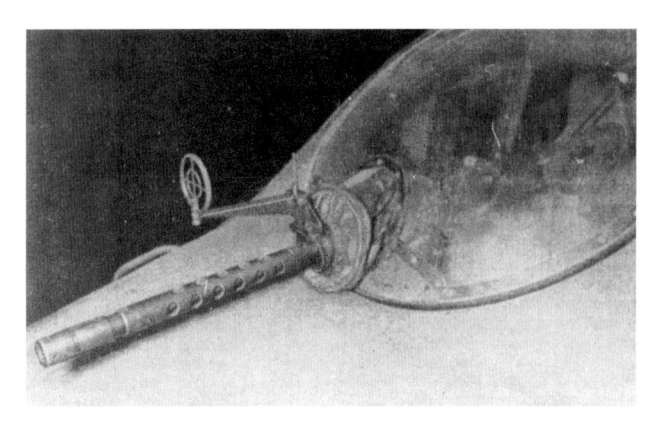

The dorsal gun position was initially fitted with the MG15, seen here with the VE22A sight

This diagram shows the mounting ring for the dorsal gun, as well as the empty ammunition drum compartment that fitted into the roof of the fuselage just aft of it

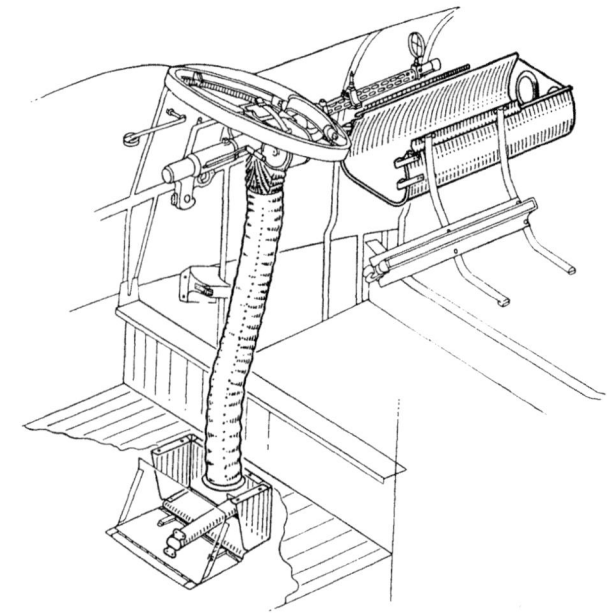

The spent cases from the dorsal gun went down this chute into a collection box built into the floor

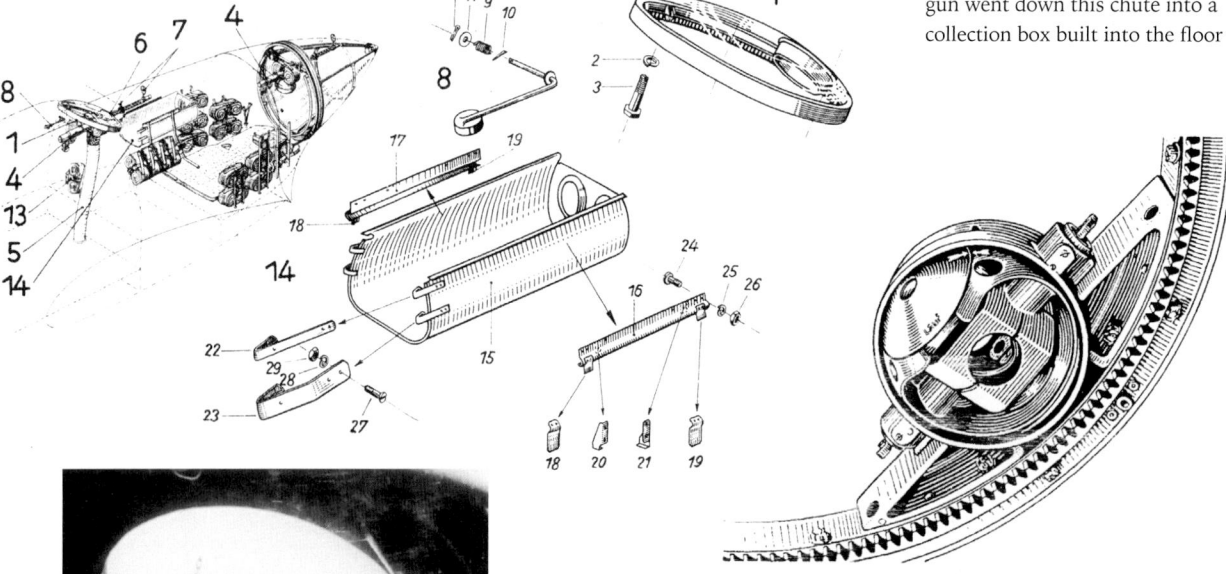

This diagram shows the LLG mounting within the gun ring on the dorsal position

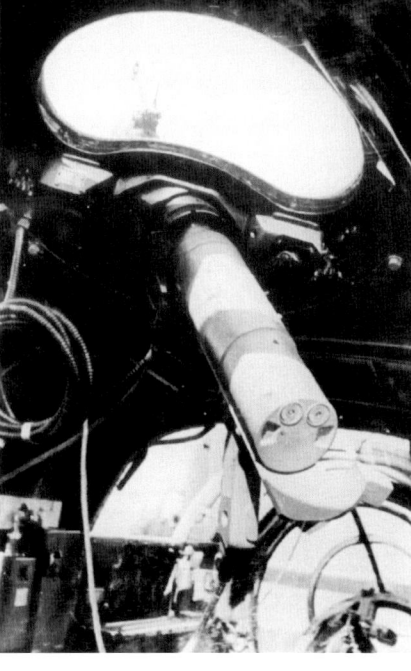

For training purposes the MG15 could be replaced with a camera gun as seen in this period image

From the A-2 series the MG15 was replaced with a twin MG81Z as seen here, or a single MG81J

Group 6 – Side 4
Armament
Rear Gun

An overall diagram of the dorsal and rear gun positions

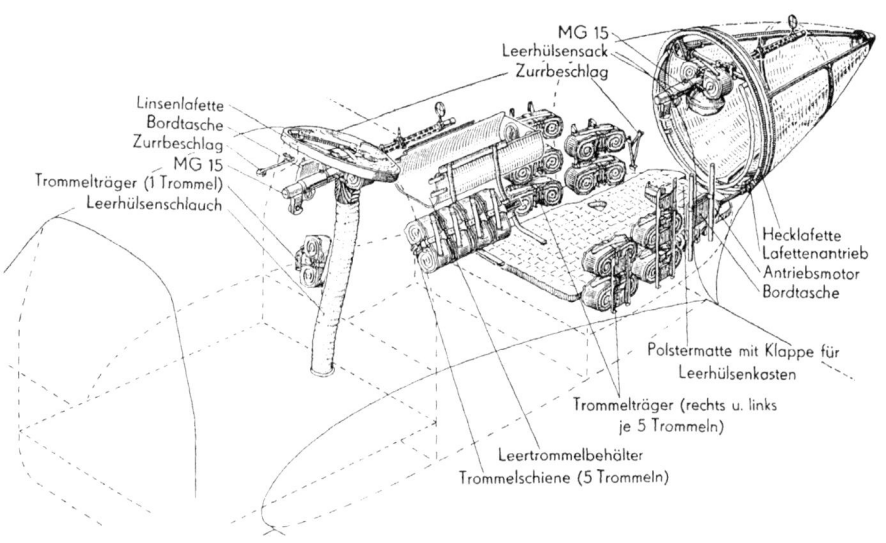

Key
- Leerhülsenschlauch (Spent cartridge tube)
- Trommelträger (1 Trommel) (Drum support (1 drum))
- MG15 (MG15 machine-gun)
- Zurrbeschlag (Gun lock – stowed position)
- Bordtasche (Board case)
- Linsenlafette (Lens (gun) mount)
- Zurrbeschlag (Gun lock – stowed position)
- Leerhülsensack (Spent cartridge sack)
- MG15 (MG15 machine-gun)
- Hecklafette (Rear (gun) mount)
- Lafettenantrieb (Carriage driving – rear gun mount)
- Antriebsmotor (Drive motor – rear gun mount)
- Bordtasche (Board case)
- Polstermatte mit Klappe für Leerhülsenkasten (Cushion mat (gunner) with flap for spent ammunition clips)
- Trommelträger (rechts u. links je 5 Trommeln) (Drum (ammunition) support (right and left, five per side))
- Leertrommelbehälter (Empty (ammunition) drum container)
- Trommelschiene (5 Trommeln) (Ammunition drum track (five drums))

This is the rearmost glazed element of the fuselage with the HL-15A-1 mount visible across the bottom

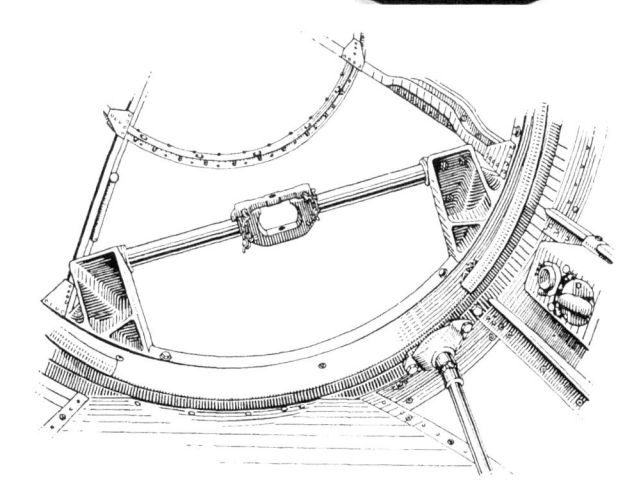

The initial rear gun mount for the A-series was the HL-15A-1 as seen here in this period drawing from the manual

A nice period view, showing the HL-15A-1 mount, MG15 with saddle ammunition drum and the spent cartridge chute

From the A-2 onwards the rear MG15 was replaced with an MG81Z as seen here, note also the revised rear cupola with the curved panel added inside (an attempt to reduce the draught caused by the original completely open area)

Group 6 – Side 5
Armament 1
Rear Gun/Ordnance

The MG81Z used a similar cross-brace unit, but it was larger and had a bigger pick-up in the middle for the bigger twin-barrelled gun

The final rear gun cupola was like this, with the gun completely enclosed via a flat glass panel; the MG81Z was now belt fed

A view inside the cupola on the final configuration, which allows you to see the ammunition feed belts for the gun

A nice clear detailed shot from the front of SC50 bombs being loaded onto the racks; note the nearest one has the sway braces still in the up position at the front of the rack, whilst the attached bomb has these down and clamped onto the nose/sides of the bombs

A nice period image showing the twin ETC 50/VIIId racks under the port wing (note the landing light in the background)

Armament

Ordnance

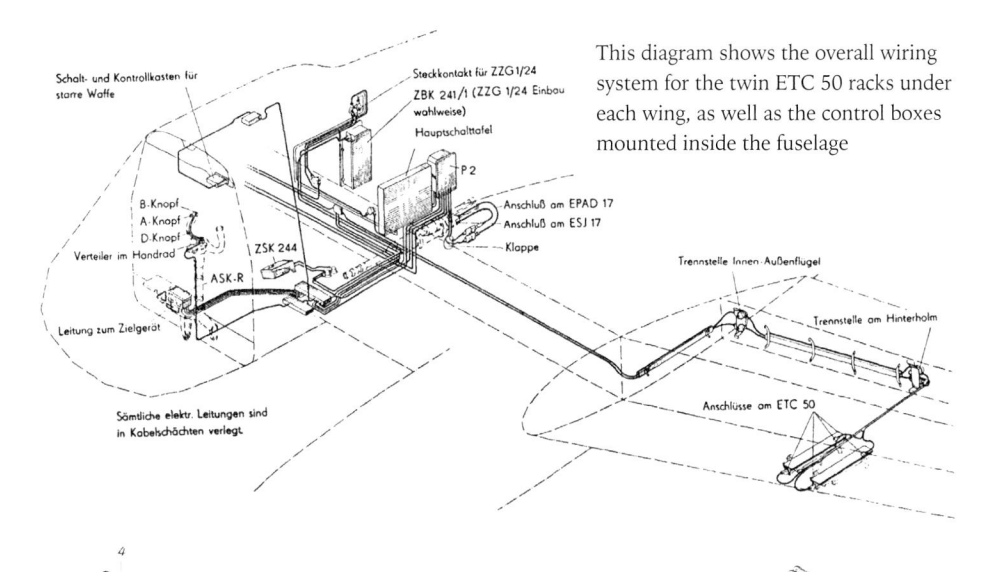

This diagram shows the overall wiring system for the twin ETC 50 racks under each wing, as well as the control boxes mounted inside the fuselage

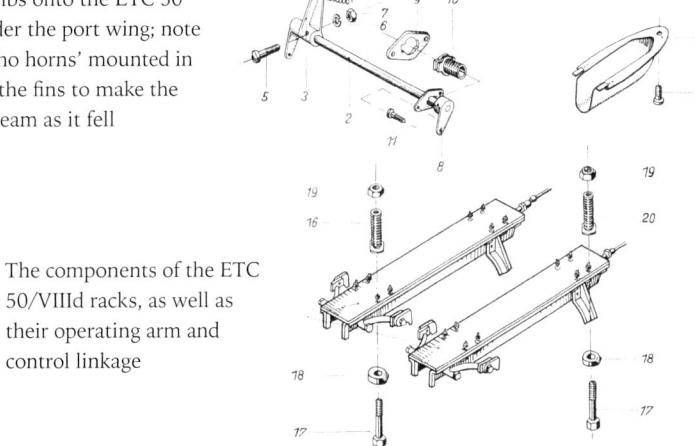

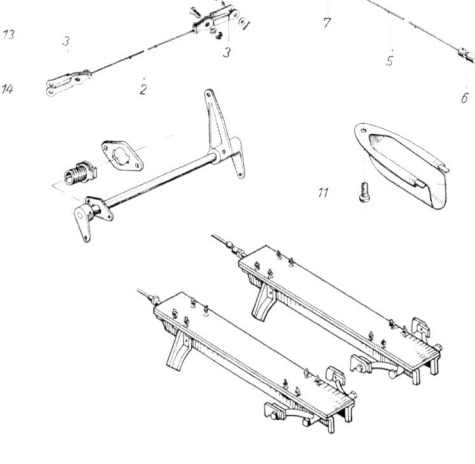

A good period image showing groundcrew man-handling 50kg bombs onto the ETC 50 racks under the port wing; note the 'Jericho horns' mounted in between the fins to make the bomb scream as it fell

The components of the ETC 50/VIIId racks, as well as their operating arm and control linkage

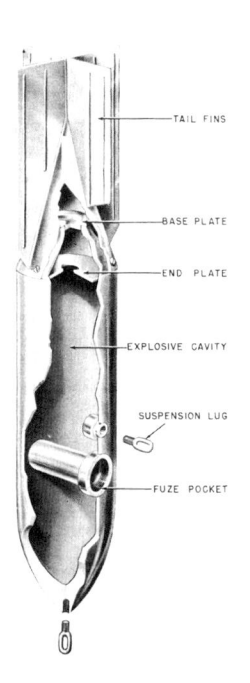

The Fw 189 could only carry 50kg SC50 bombs, which came in three different sorts. This is the Bi, which had a one-piece cast body with all the fittings welded in place; overall length was 46.1in

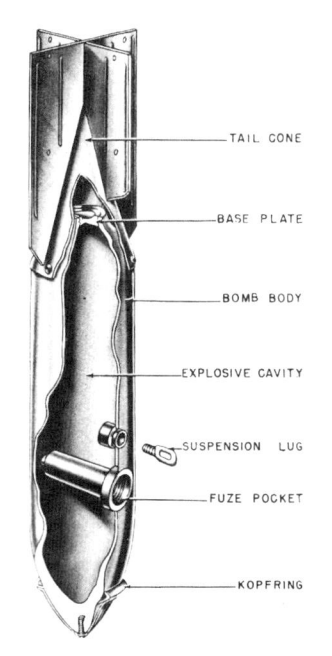

This is the SC50 Grade I, Ja, L or Stabo, which had a one-piece drawn steel (seamless) body; overall length was 43.3in (Ja and L) or 61.8in (Stabo)

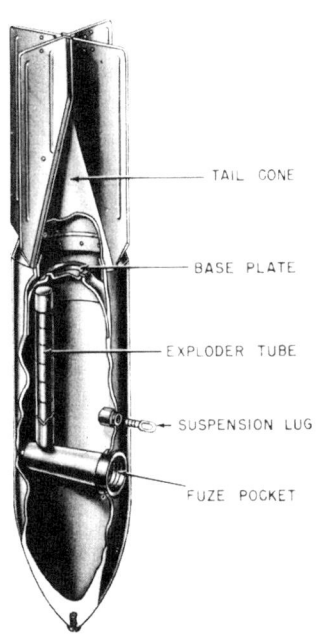

The final option is the SC50 Grade II, which came as JB, JC, J or J/2 versions. This featured a pressed-steel nose and drawn-steel body, which were welded together; overall length was 43.3in

Group 6 – Side 7
Armament
Ordnance

Here you can see SC50 bombs with the metal style of Dinort tubes fitted

The bombs on the Fw 189 often featured a Dinort Rod, attached to the front of the bomb to achieve a 'daisy cutter' effect on impact. This is the metal style unit used on the SC50

SD 50-70

This is the wooden style Dinort Rod used on the SC50

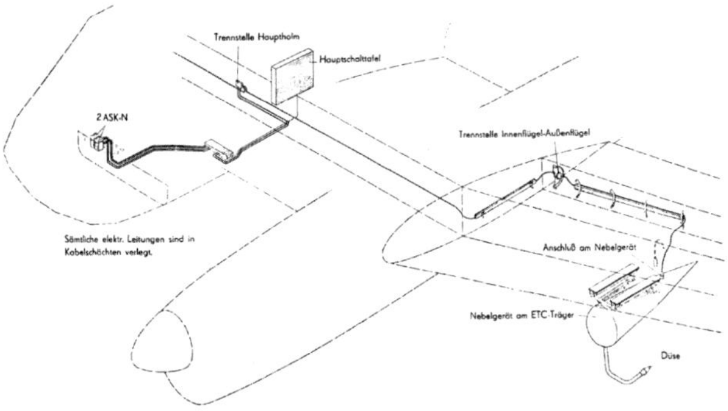

Here is the system diagram for the carriage of S 125

Being used for liaison with the ground troops, the ETC racks could also carry other items, as seen here as message tubes are loaded

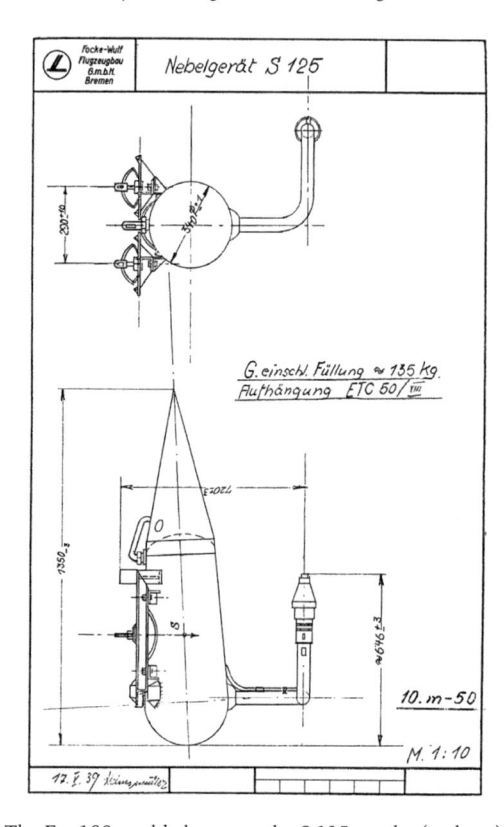

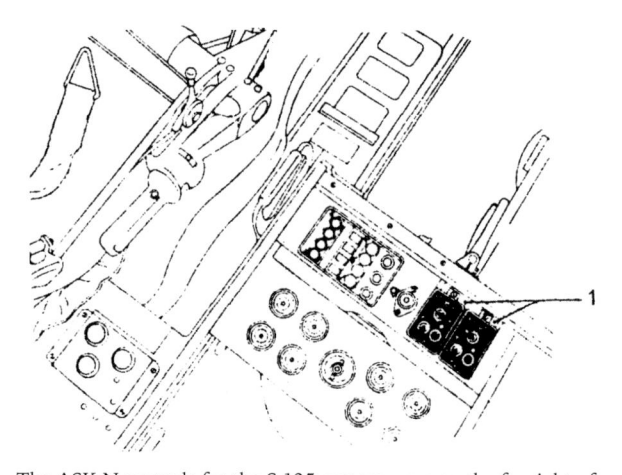

The ASK-N controls for the S 125 system were on the far right of the control cluster for the observer in the cockpit floor, as seen here

The Fw 189 could also carry the S 125 smoke (and gas) generator, one to each set of racks

Group 6 – Side 8
Armament
Sighting & Release

This period image shows all the various controls relating to ordnance in the floor of the cockpit, ahead of the observer, and they include the ASK-R (bomb release), ASK-N (S 125 smoke generators) and the bombsight (GV 219d)

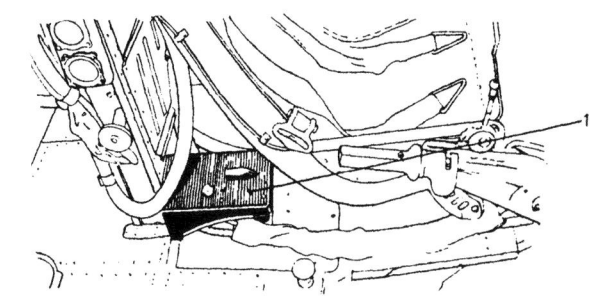

The ignite box (ZSK 244A) to arm the bombs was situated under the pilot's seat, so could only be reached by the observer

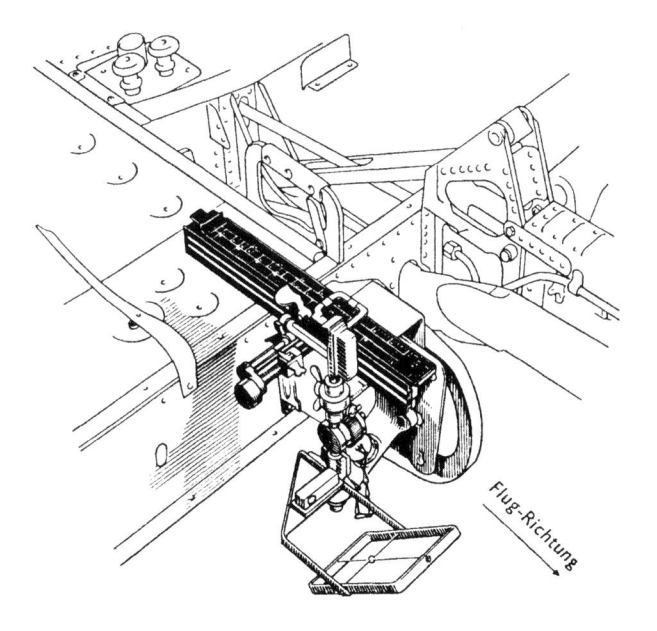

The bombsight on the Fw 189 was the simple GV 219d, termed as 'Sighting (target device) GV 219d'

In late 1943 some Fw 189s were converted to anti-partisan work, and to undertake this low-level bombing this optically flat round panel was built into the canopy, we presume to ease the use of the bombsight in a more level manner, instead of the 'top down' manner in which it was usually used for dropping bombs from a height

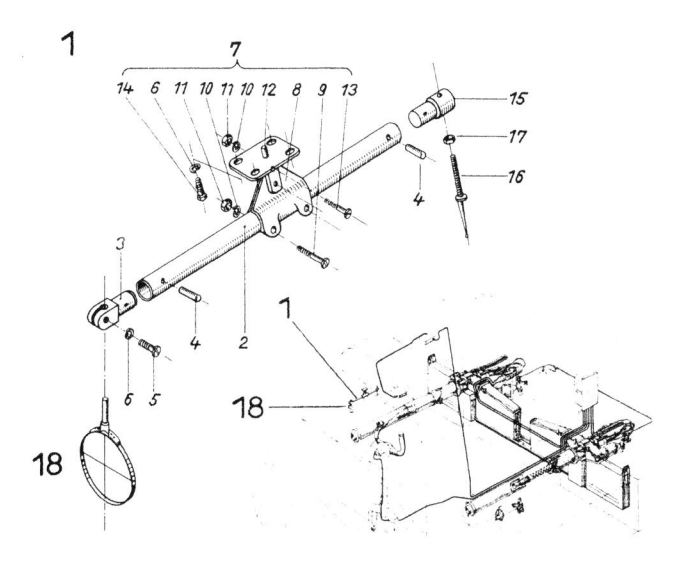

To sight the fixed guns the pilot had this ring and bead sight in the top of the canopy, just ahead of him

The C-series utilised an external Revi gunsight, as there was no space inside the tiny cockpit; this shot shows such a sight on one of the prototypes and the 'telegraph pole' with all the cross wires mounted ahead of it was to determine angles of attack during trials; the big windscreen panels denote this is most likely a C-0

Group 6 – Side 9
Armament 1

62 | Camera

This diagram shows the overall camera installation, in this case an Rb 50/30

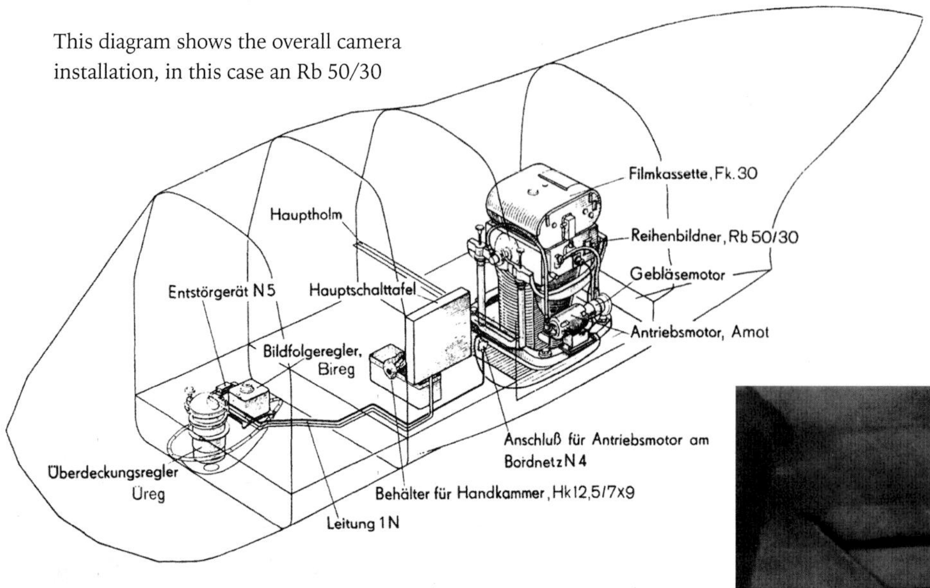

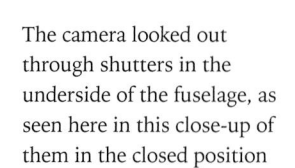

- Filmkassette, Fk.30
- Hauptholm
- Reihenbildner, Rb 50/30
- Gebläsemotor
- Entstörgerät N5
- Hauptschalttafel
- Antriebsmotor, Amot
- Bildfolgeregler, Bireg
- Anschluß für Antriebsmotor am Bordnetz N 4
- Überdeckungsregler Üreg
- Behälter für Handkammer, Hk 12,5/7x9
- Leitung 1 N

The camera looked out through shutters in the underside of the fuselage, as seen here in this close-up of them in the closed position

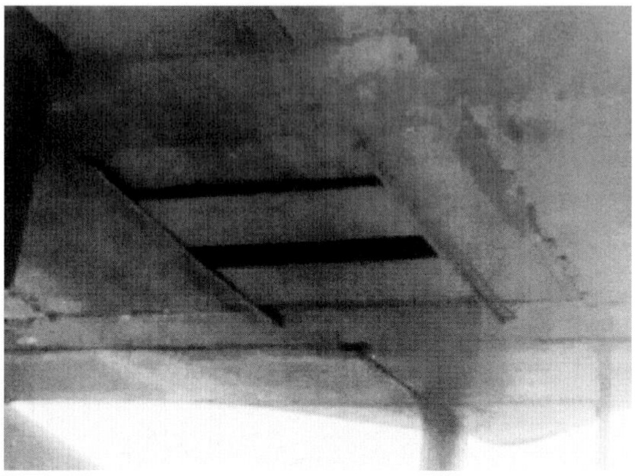

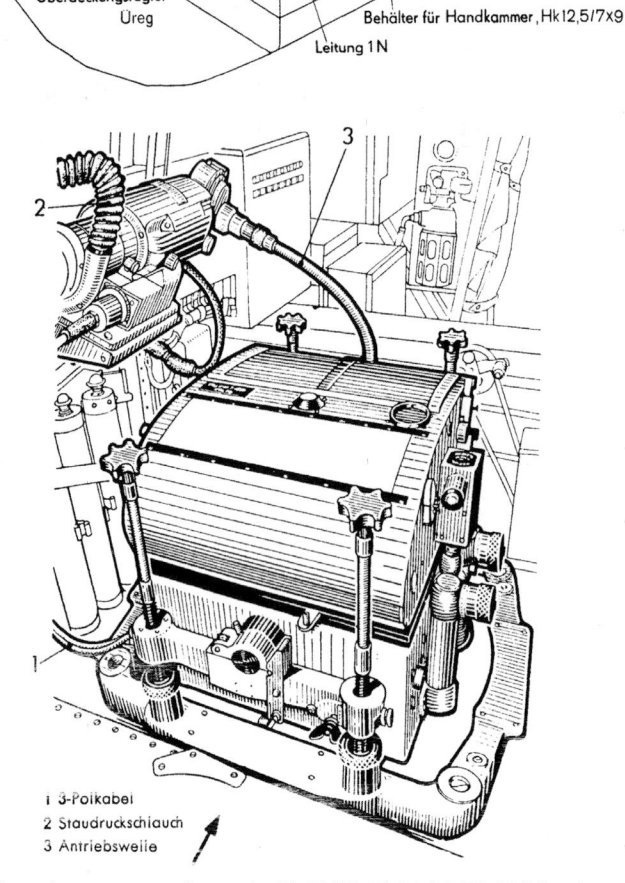

1 3-Polkabel
2 Staudruckschlauch
3 Antriebswelle

The main cameras used were the Rb 21/18, Rb 20/30, Rb 50/18 and Rb 50/30; the installation of the Rb 20/30 is shown in this diagram

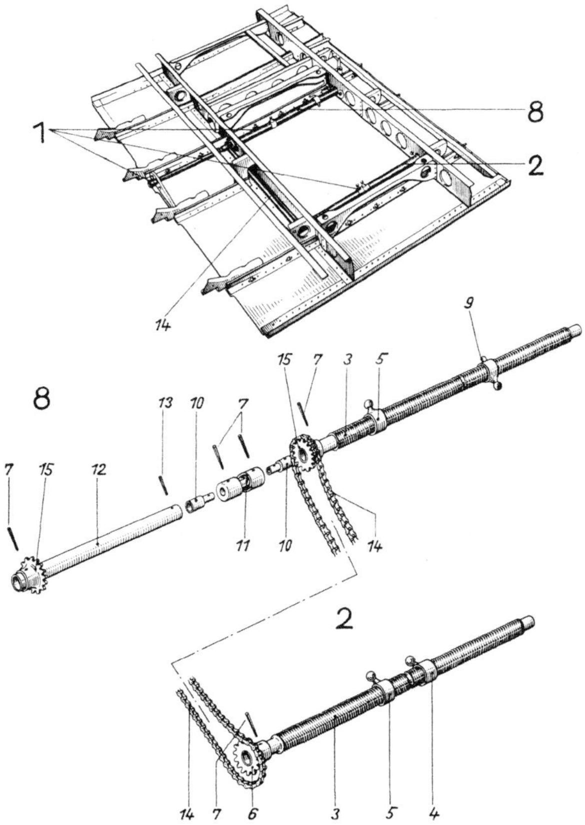

This diagram shows the opening in the floor as well as the rollers and chain drives that open and shut the covers

This is the image sequence/overlap controller (see p63 and 64 for installation)

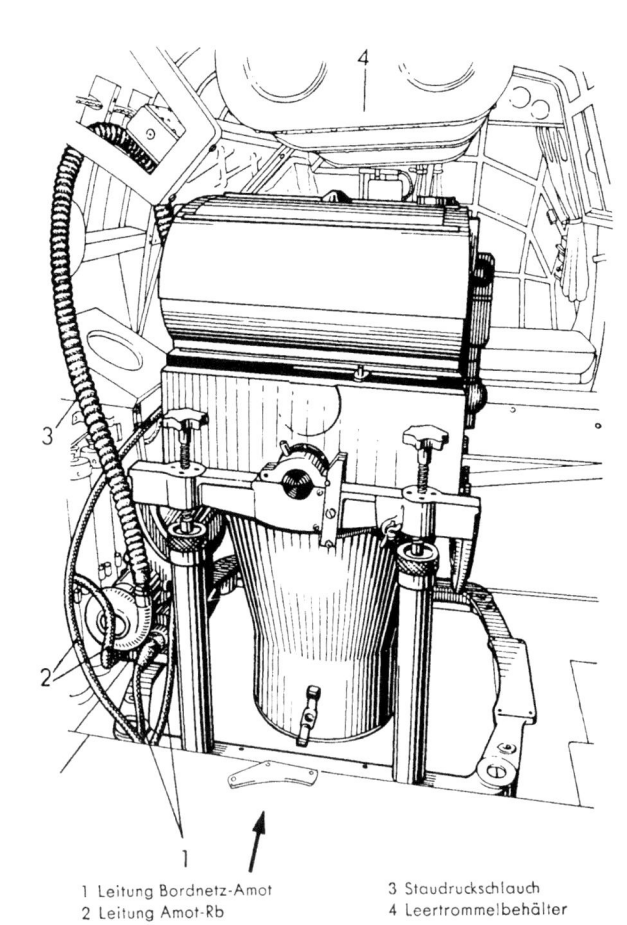

Group 6 – Side 10
Armament
Camera | 63

1 Leitung Bordnetz-Amot
2 Leitung Amot-Rb
3 Staudruckschlauch
4 Leertrommelbehälter

This is the Rb 50/30 installation

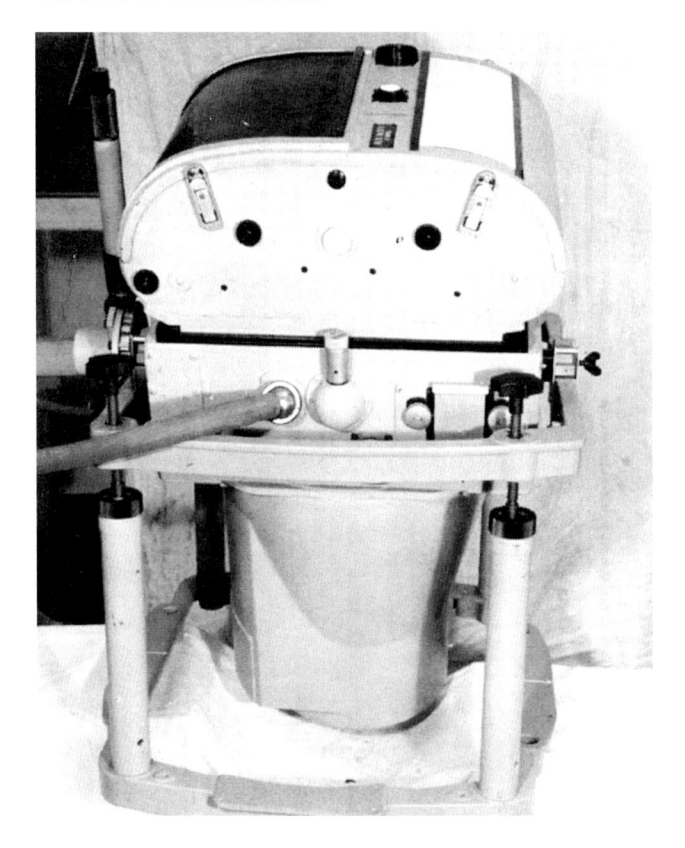

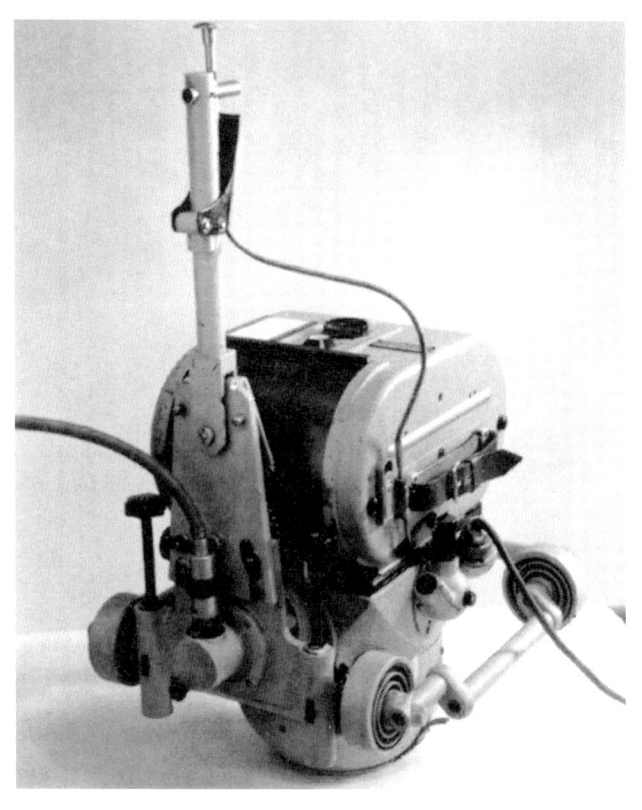

This is the Rb 21/18 in its mounting frame

This is what you can see of the sequence/overlap controller when you look up into the little bulged fairing under the starboard side of the underside of the nacelle, opposite the DF loop

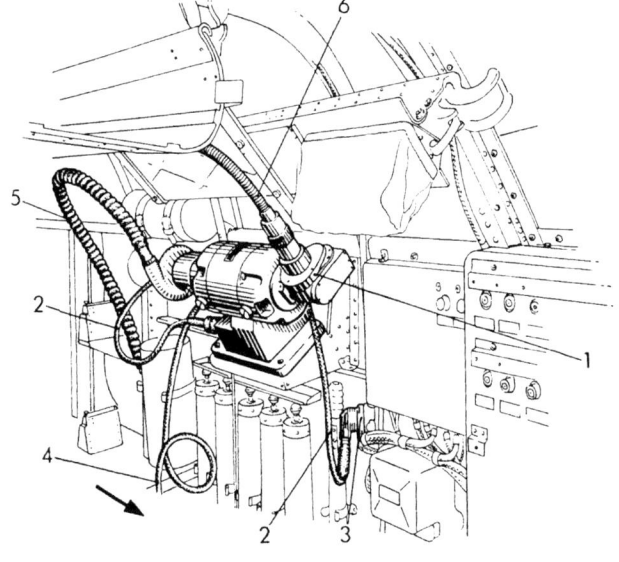

This is an Rb 50/30 in its mounting frame and complete with film cassette

1 Antriebskopf
2 Kabel Bordnetz-Amot
3 Stecker N 4 der Bordleitung
4 Kabel Amot-Rb
5 Staudruckschlauch
6 Biegsame Welle

This is the motor assembly fitted to the port side inside the mid-fuselage, which was required when the Rb 20/30, 21/18 or 50/18 cameras were installed; the Rb 50/30 did not need it

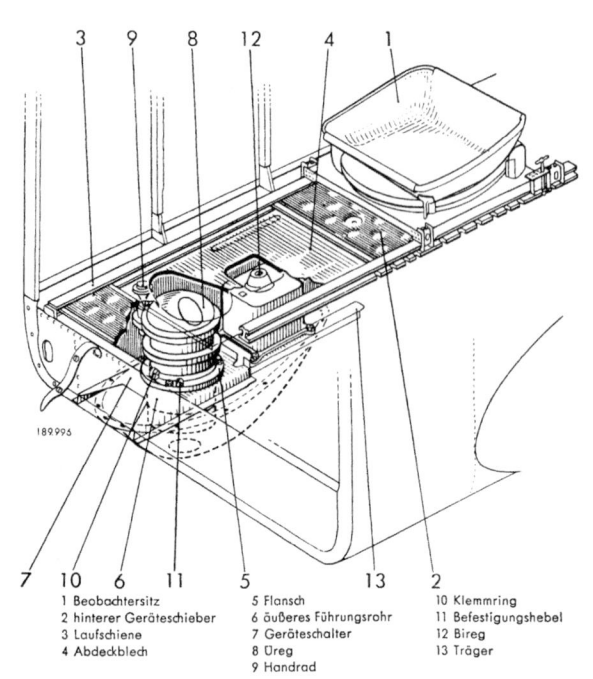

Group 6 – Side 11
Armament 1

| 64 | Camera |

1 Beobachtersitz
2 hinterer Geräteschieber
3 Laufschiene
4 Abdeckblech
5 Flansch
6 äußeres Führungsrohr
7 Geräteschalter
8 Üreg
9 Handrad
10 Klemmring
11 Befestigungshebel
12 Bireg
13 Träger

The observer controlled the camera and used an image sequence/overlap controller (8) that was mounted in the floor just ahead of his sliding seat

Manhandling the big Rb 50/30 into the fuselage of the Fw 189 was hard work, as seen in this image of one being loaded into an A-1 in Russia; the film cassette was not fitted to reduce the size/weight of the unit

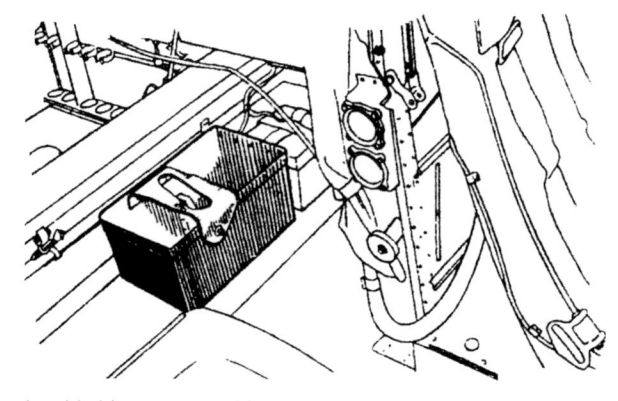

This is the Rb 21/18 camera, complete with film cassette

A hand-held camera could be used by the observer and could be stored in this box behind the pilot's seat

This is the Hk 12.5/7x9 hand-held camera

This is the Hk 19/13x18 hand-held camera

Group 7 – Side 1
Miscellaneous
Access Panels

This diagram shows the various access panels in the under surfaces

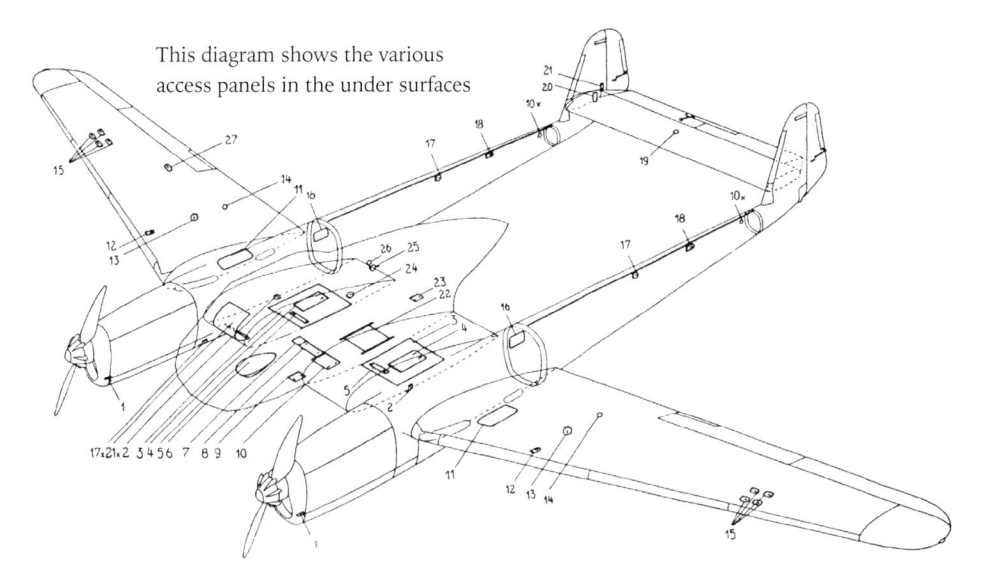

This diagram shows the various access panels in the upper surfaces

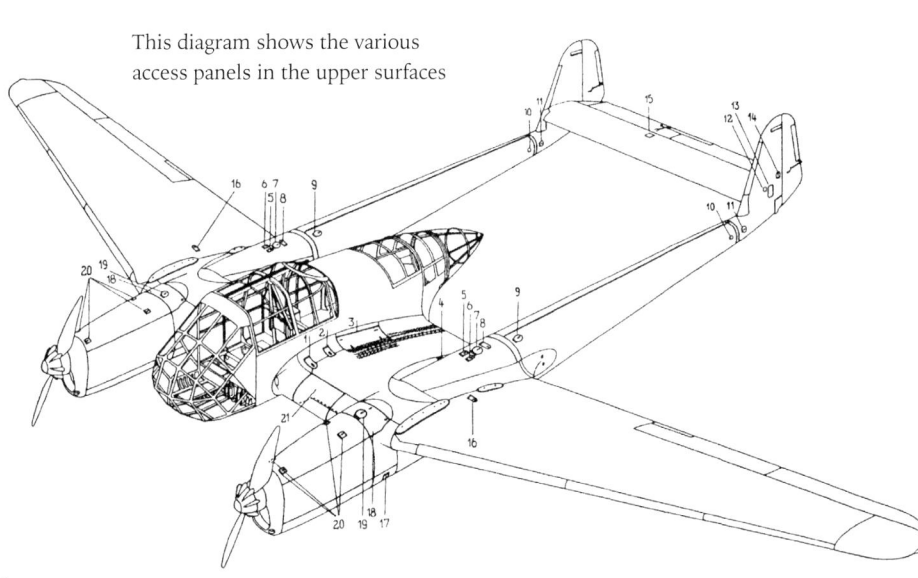

Key
1. Securing the closure of the radiator flaps
2. Injection pump
3. Overload protection relay lever for control unit, MG-bearing oxygen bottles (right only) machine-gun air tank
4. Split flap gear
5. Removal of the empty cartridges and empty ammunition belts
6. Overlap/sequence regulator
7. Lever for control unit
8. Channel for cables, bomb release
9. Lever for throttle linkage
10. Lever for control mechanism
11. Controller for the outer wing split flaps drive
12. Separation point for electrical controller, dropped weapons
13. Control shaft from dropped weapons
14. Plus for mist system (e.g. S 125 smoke generator)
15. Lever for ailerons
16. Electrical pump (defrosting) – both sides, left side only also access to Master Compass
17. Control cable roller (guide) at frame 18
18. Control cables
19. Resistant transmitter and bumper trim level
20. Intermediate lever for rudder
21. Bumper for (Flettner) servo tab
22. Flap for imaging device (e.g. camera)
23. Empty cartridge case removal
24. Compressed air bottle (for machine-guns) filling connection
25. Connection for oxygen replenishment
26. Outboard connection for electrical charging
27. Separation point for electrical line (characteristic light-end flap) [for ETC racks]

Key
1. Blast tubes for the fixed guns
2. Forward MG-bearing, channel lock, side adjustment
3. Rear MG-bearer, height adjustment and air tank
4. Rear spar root fitting
5 & 6. Fuel line separation points
7. Fuel filler connection
8. Electrical fuel sender gauge and residual (fuel) level warning
9. Control unit connected to forward fuel control unit
10. Lifting/jacking point
11. Separation points for electrical system, controller and pneumatics
12. Cable (guide pulley)
13. Bumper for left rudder, bumper for elevator, truncation point for electrical equipment-tail
14. Electrical connector for side trim with resistance transmitter
15. Electrical transmitter, trim height
16. Filters for airscrew de-icing
17. Cold start operating (e.g. starting handle)
18. Upper engine connections
19. Filler for lubricant
20. Hoisting eyes for engine
21. Hinged panel for engine and undercarriage control rods, heating pipes and fire extinguisher pipes

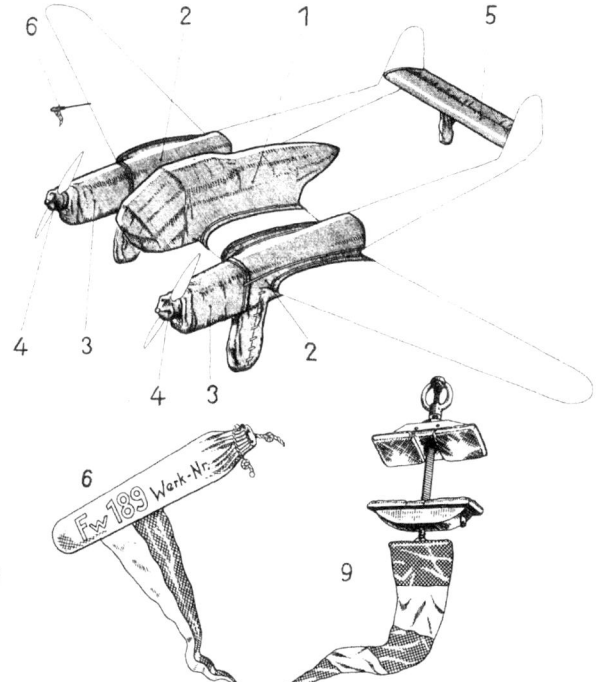

This diagram shows all the various covers in place, including those for the propeller and pitot head and a control lock (9)

Group 7 – Side 2
Miscellaneous 1
66 | Various

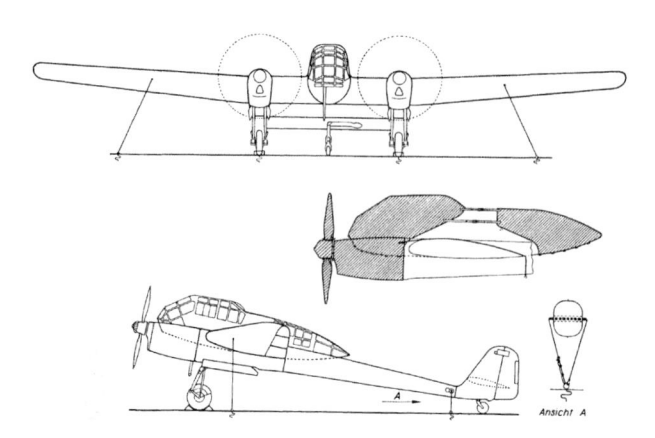

As well as the main covers, this diagram shows the tie-down locations under the wings and at the tail

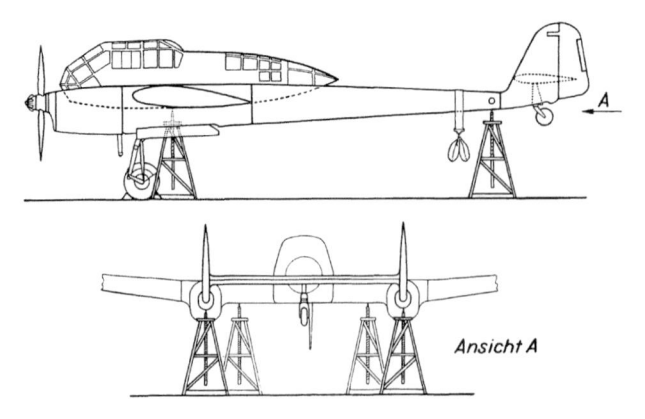

This shows how the airframe is jacked into an in-flight position for repairs or setting the fixed guns

This shot shows that probably only the covers for the fuselage were ever actually put on whilst in service

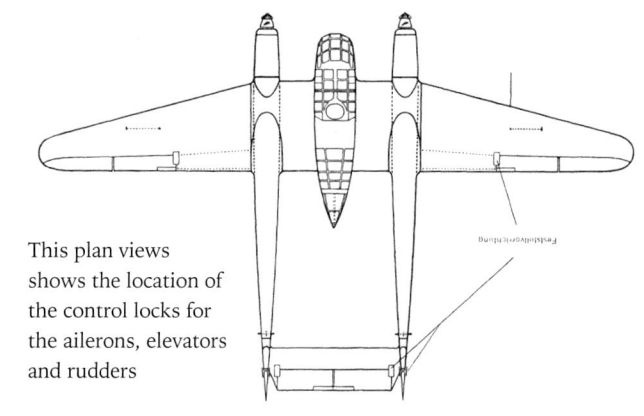

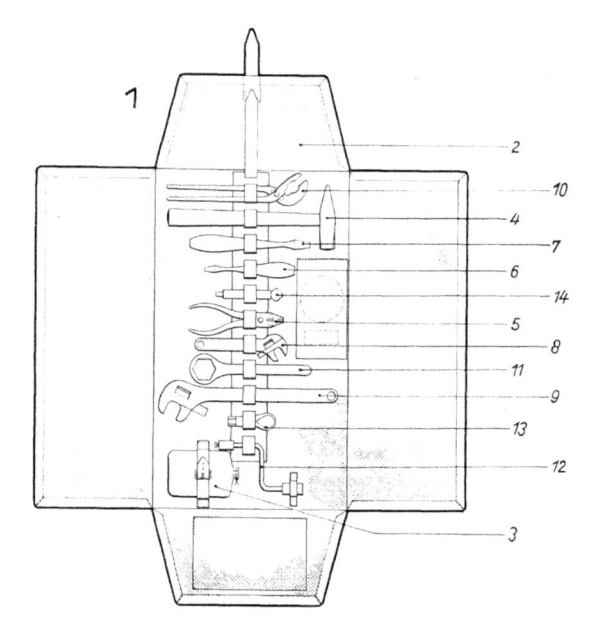

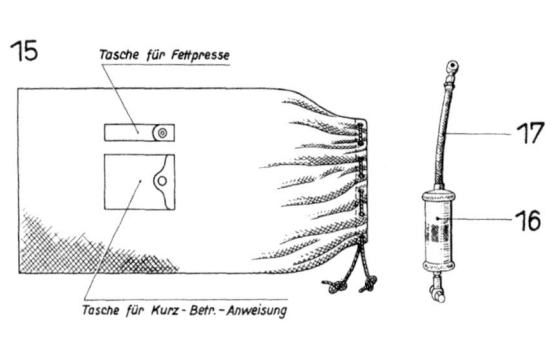

This plan views shows the location of the control locks for the ailerons, elevators and rudders

Each aircraft came with its own tool roll, as shown here

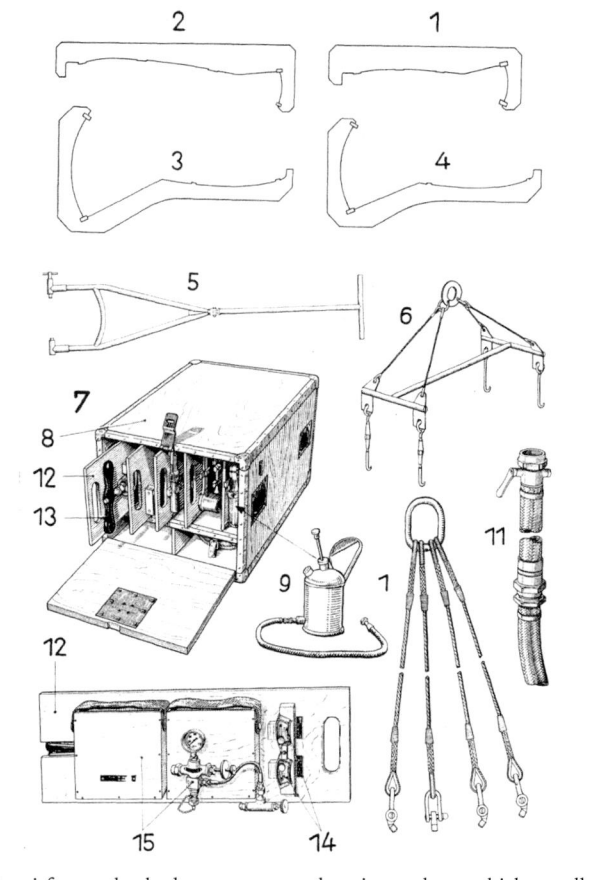

The airframe also had a more comprehensive tool set, which usually remained on the ground with the squadron

Evolution
Prototype, Production and Projected Variants

The evolution of the Focke-Wulf Fw 189 series involved a couple of prototype machines as well as production and projected armament installations. What follows therefore is a list of all the former airframes that were actually built, along with details of any armament trials, both tested and those which never got further than the design or mock-up stage.

As you would expect with a subject now 70+ years old, there is much contradiction in both period and subsequent documentation, so we have based all our drawings, where possible, on existing photos and when not, on the most likely layout based on other developments from other German aircraft manufacturers during the period.

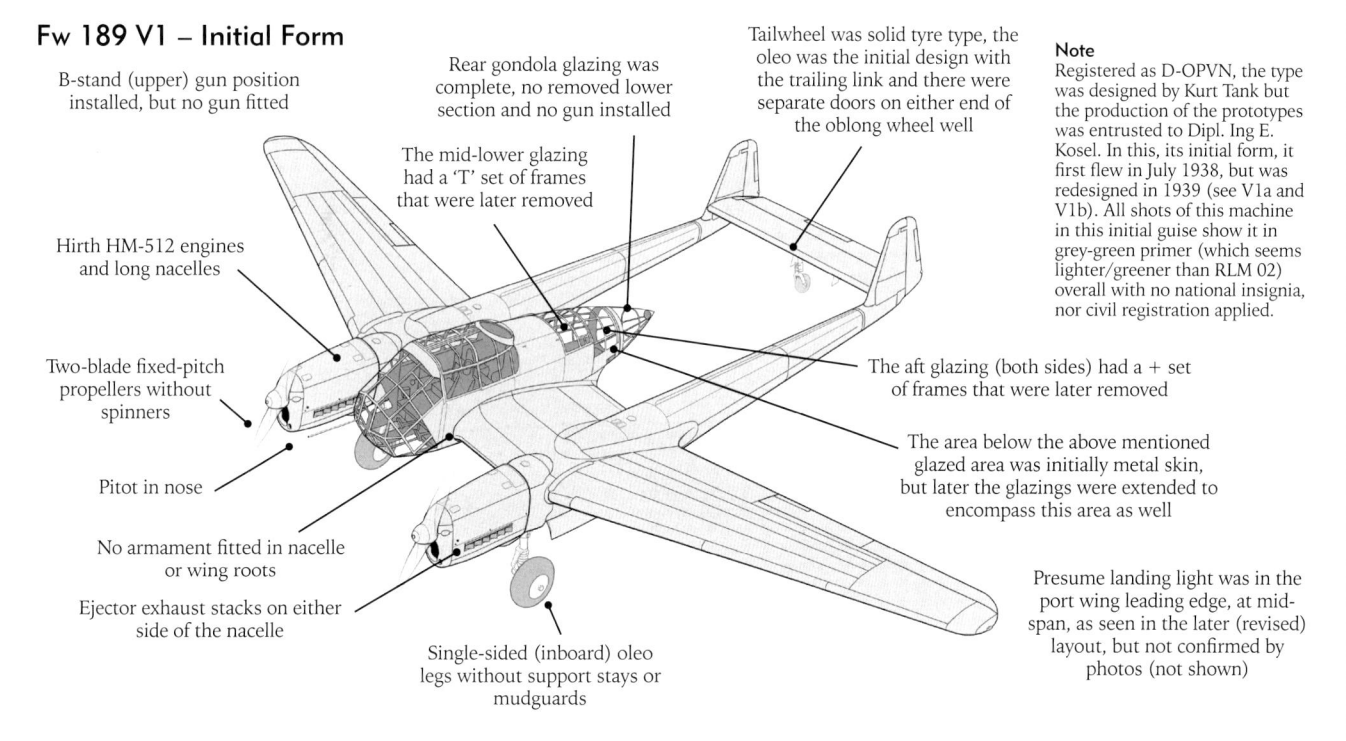

Fw 189 V1 – Initial Form

- B-stand (upper) gun position installed, but no gun fitted
- Rear gondola glazing was complete, no removed lower section and no gun installed
- Tailwheel was solid tyre type, the oleo was the initial design with the trailing link and there were separate doors on either end of the oblong wheel well
- The mid-lower glazing had a 'T' set of frames that were later removed
- Hirth HM-512 engines and long nacelles
- Two-blade fixed-pitch propellers without spinners
- Pitot in nose
- The aft glazing (both sides) had a + set of frames that were later removed
- The area below the above mentioned glazed area was initially metal skin, but later the glazings were extended to encompass this area as well
- No armament fitted in nacelle or wing roots
- Ejector exhaust stacks on either side of the nacelle
- Single-sided (inboard) oleo legs without support stays or mudguards
- Presume landing light was in the port wing leading edge, at mid-span, as seen in the later (revised) layout, but not confirmed by photos (not shown)

Note
Registered as D-OPVN, the type was designed by Kurt Tank but the production of the prototypes was entrusted to Dipl. Ing E. Kosel. In this, its initial form, it first flew in July 1938, but was redesigned in 1939 (see V1a and V1b). All shots of this machine in this initial guise show it in grey-green primer (which seems lighter/greener than RLM 02) overall with no national insignia, nor civil registration applied.

Fw 189 V1 – Revised Form
Same as V1 – Initial Form except:

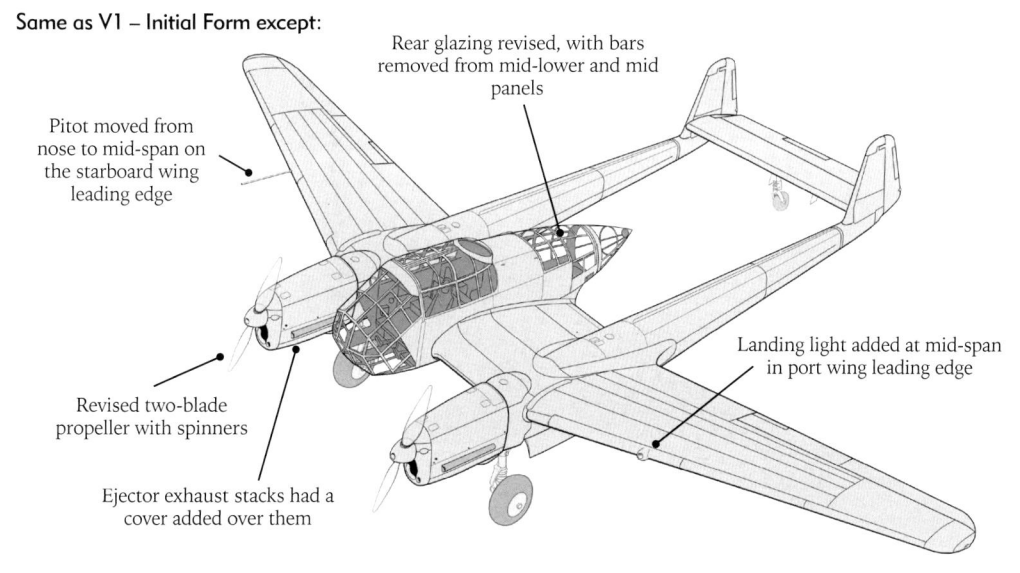

- Rear glazing revised, with bars removed from mid-lower and mid panels
- Pitot moved from nose to mid-span on the starboard wing leading edge
- Landing light added at mid-span in port wing leading edge
- Revised two-blade propeller with spinners
- Ejector exhaust stacks had a cover added over them

Note
With these modifications all images of this machine show it in full two-tone splinter-pattern camouflage on the upper surfaces and RLM 65 Lichtblau undersides. The demarcation is straight and low down on both the engine nacelles and tail booms. The registration D-OPVN is applied in the usual manner above and below the wings, in black, and repeated on the outer faces of each tail boom. No national crosses are applied but a wide red band, with a swastika surmounted on a white disc is applied across each vertical fin/rudder unit (only on the outer faces).

Focke-Wulf Fw 189
Evolution 2

Prototypes

Fw 189 V1a – Initial Form
Same as V1 – Revised Form except:

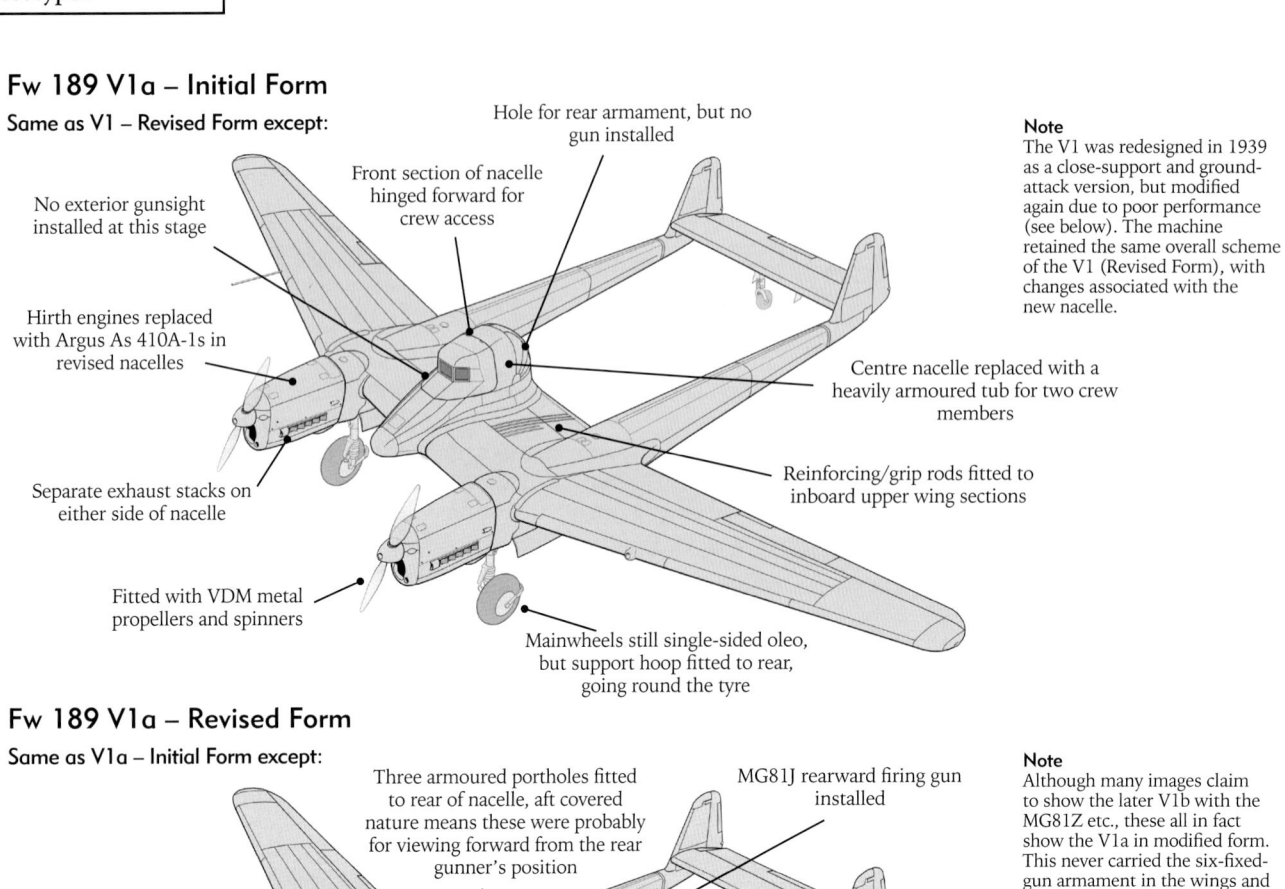

- No exterior gunsight installed at this stage
- Hirth engines replaced with Argus As 410A-1s in revised nacelles
- Separate exhaust stacks on either side of nacelle
- Fitted with VDM metal propellers and spinners
- Hole for rear armament, but no gun installed
- Front section of nacelle hinged forward for crew access
- Centre nacelle replaced with a heavily armoured tub for two crew members
- Reinforcing/grip rods fitted to inboard upper wing sections
- Mainwheels still single-sided oleo, but support hoop fitted to rear, going round the tyre

Note
The V1 was redesigned in 1939 as a close-support and ground-attack version, but modified again due to poor performance (see below). The machine retained the same overall scheme of the V1 (Revised Form), with changes associated with the new nacelle.

Fw 189 V1a – Revised Form
Same as V1a – Initial Form except:

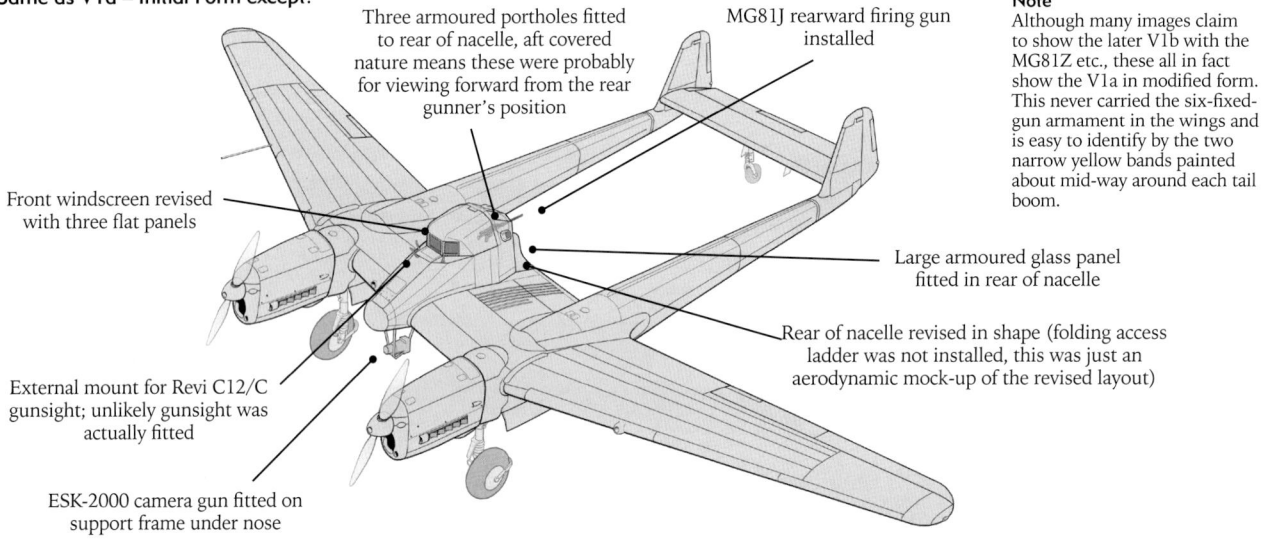

- Front windscreen revised with three flat panels
- External mount for Revi C12/C gunsight; unlikely gunsight was actually fitted
- ESK-2000 camera gun fitted on support frame under nose
- Three armoured portholes fitted to rear of nacelle, aft covered nature means these were probably for viewing forward from the rear gunner's position
- MG81J rearward firing gun installed
- Large armoured glass panel fitted in rear of nacelle
- Rear of nacelle revised in shape (folding access ladder was not installed, this was just an aerodynamic mock-up of the revised layout)

Note
Although many images claim to show the later V1b with the MG81Z etc., these all in fact show the V1a in modified form. This never carried the six-fixed-gun armament in the wings and is easy to identify by the two narrow yellow bands painted about mid-way around each tail boom.

Fw 189 V1b
Same as V1a – Revised Form except:

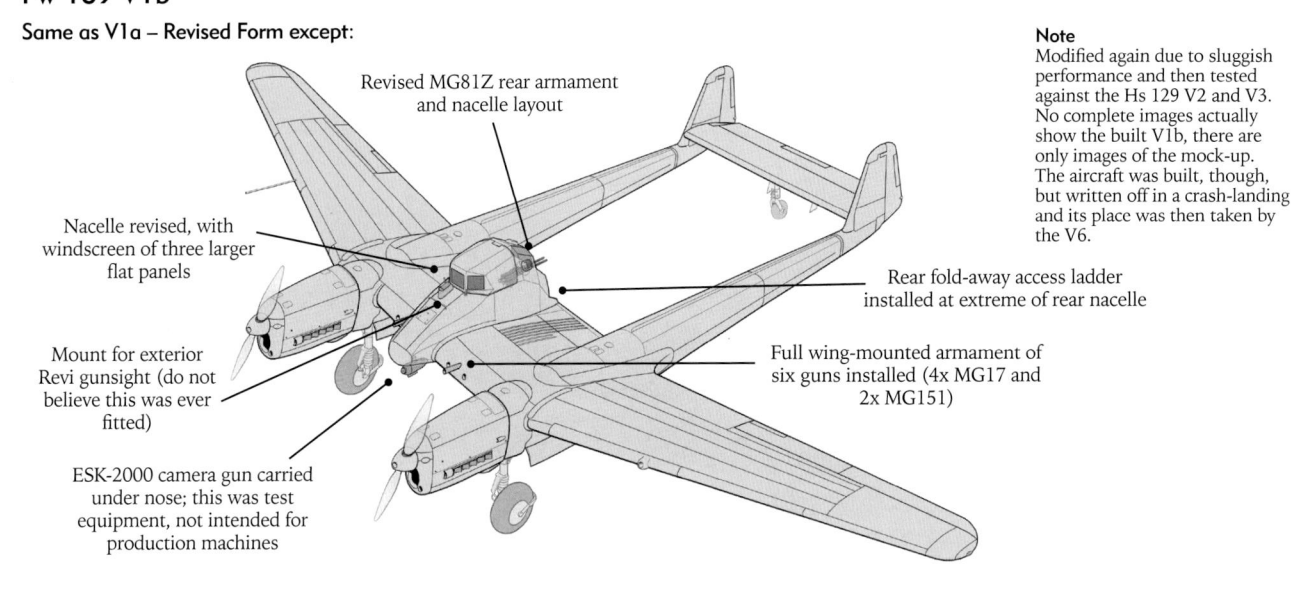

- Nacelle revised, with windscreen of three larger flat panels
- Mount for exterior Revi gunsight (do not believe this was ever fitted)
- ESK-2000 camera gun carried under nose; this was test equipment, not intended for production machines
- Revised MG81Z rear armament and nacelle layout
- Rear fold-away access ladder installed at extreme of rear nacelle
- Full wing-mounted armament of six guns installed (4x MG17 and 2x MG151)

Note
Modified again due to sluggish performance and then tested against the Hs 129 V2 and V3. No complete images actually show the built V1b, there are only images of the mock-up. The aircraft was built, though, but written off in a crash-landing and its place was then taken by the V6.

Fw 189 V1c
Same as V1b except:

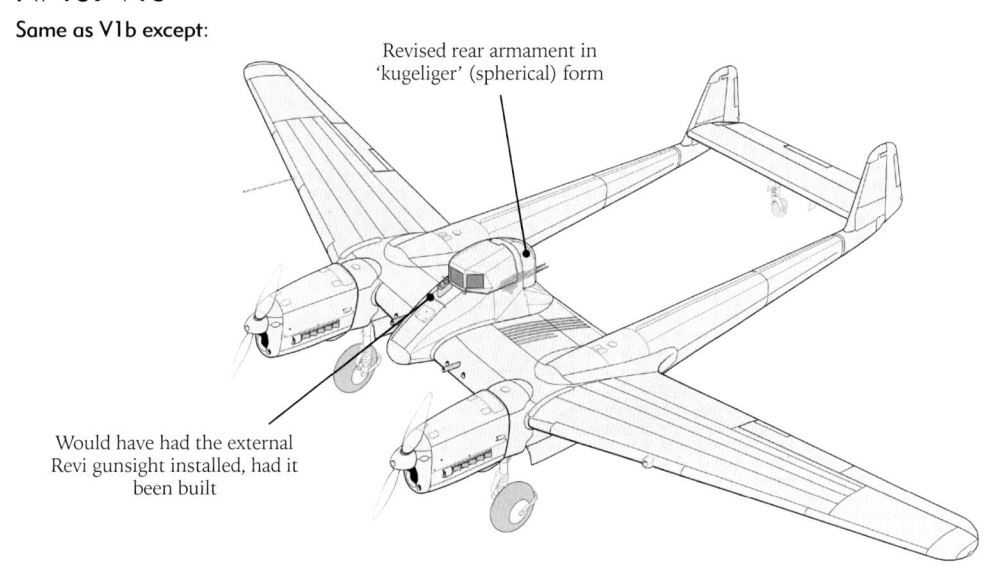

- Revised rear armament in 'kugeliger' (spherical) form
- Would have had the external Revi gunsight installed, had it been built

Note
An initial armament arrangement under consideration, this version was never actually built because the 'kugeliger' layout was not considered stable enough, so the whole project was dropped early in the development programme.

Fw 189 V2
Same as V1 – Final Form except:

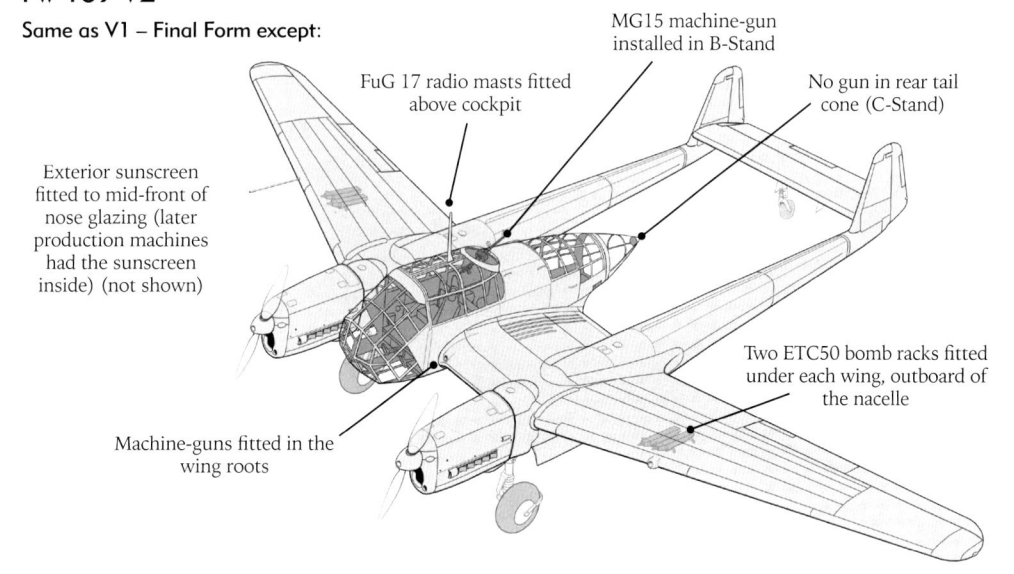

- MG15 machine-gun installed in B-Stand
- FuG 17 radio masts fitted above cockpit
- No gun in rear tail cone (C-Stand)
- Exterior sunscreen fitted to mid-front of nose glazing (later production machines had the sunscreen inside) (not shown)
- Two ETC50 bomb racks fitted under each wing, outboard of the nacelle
- Machine-guns fitted in the wing roots

Note
Registered as D-OVHD, the V2 first flew in August 1938 and was the first to have armament in the B-stand and ETC racks under the wings. Colour and markings were the same as the V1 – Final Form, except for the revised registration.

Bulge, off-set to starboard under the nose, probably a mock-up for the camera overlap control installation (not shown)

Hole in the front of the nose, probably relating to bomb sighting trials (later seen on a production A-series in the 'level bombing' modification tested for anti-partisan trials) (not shown)

Fw 189 V3 – Initial Form
Same as V2 except:

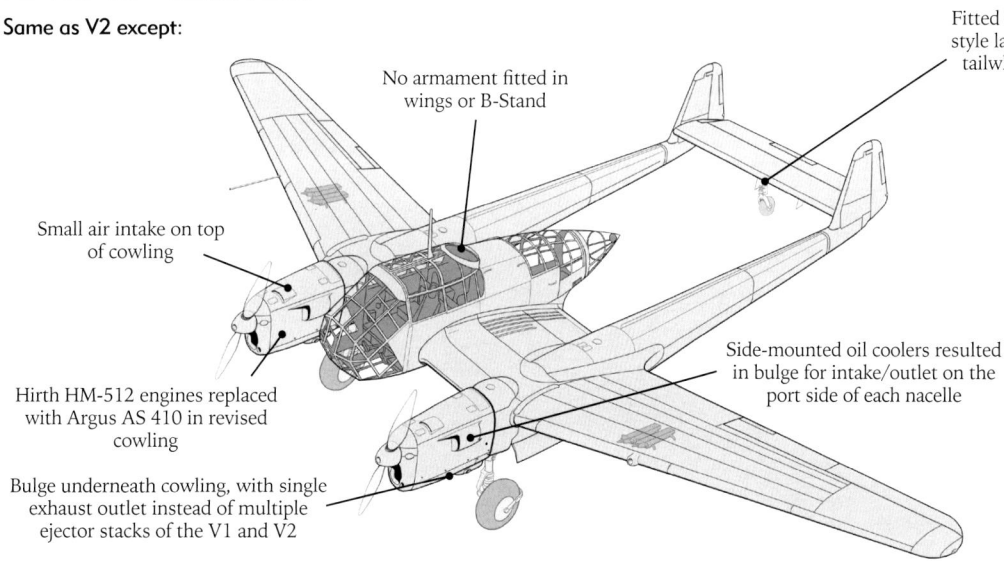

- No armament fitted in wings or B-Stand
- Fitted with the later (production) style larger pneumatic tyre on the tailwheel, with revised oleo leg assembly
- Small air intake on top of cowling
- Hirth HM-512 engines replaced with Argus AS 410 in revised cowling
- Bulge underneath cowling, with single exhaust outlet instead of multiple ejector stacks of the V1 and V2
- Side-mounted oil coolers resulted in bulge for intake/outlet on the port side of each nacelle

Note
Registered as D-ORMH, the V3 first flew in September 1938. The overall scheme was identical to the V1 and V2 in their initial form, with just the civil registration codes being different above and below the wings and on the outer face of each tail boom.

Focke-Wulf Fw 189
Evolution 2
Prototypes

Fw 189 V3 – Revised Form
Same as V3 – Initial Form except:

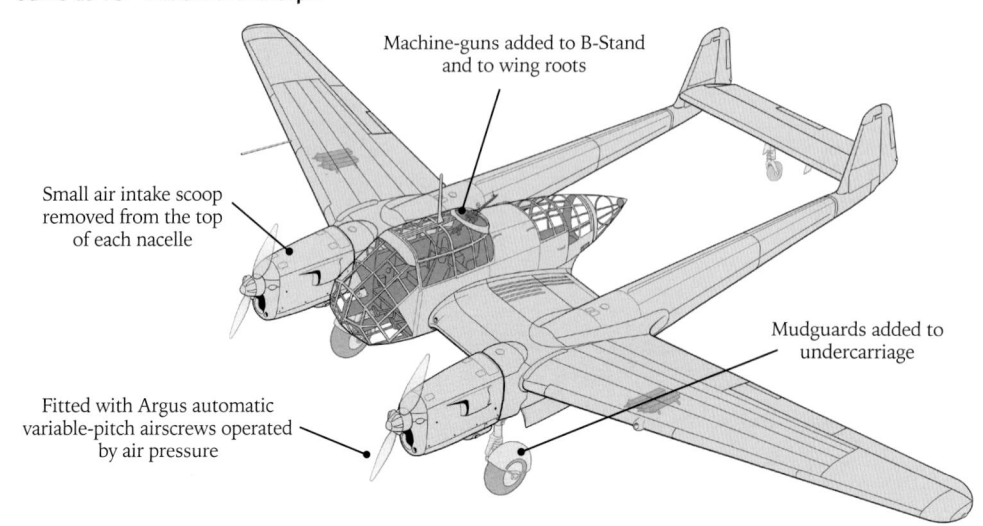

- Machine-guns added to B-Stand and to wing roots
- Small air intake scoop removed from the top of each nacelle
- Mudguards added to undercarriage
- Fitted with Argus automatic variable-pitch airscrews operated by air pressure

Note
In this revised form this airframe was the first to undertake service trials, when it became TP+AW with 9(H)LG2 at Paderborn in December 1939. The overall scheme remained unchanged, the civil registration being removed from the wings and booms, whilst crosses were applied above the wings (period images do not show any under the wings) and on each outer face of the boom, with the codes applied around them in the usual manner. We suspect the red band and white disc of the swastika on the tail/rudder was removed, resulting in a plain Type H2 swastika. Note that there are many retouched images of this machine claiming to be an operational A-series 'GJ+RT' in April 1941, the side intakes on the nacelles being the give-away feature.

Fw 189 V4
Same as V3 – Revised Form except:

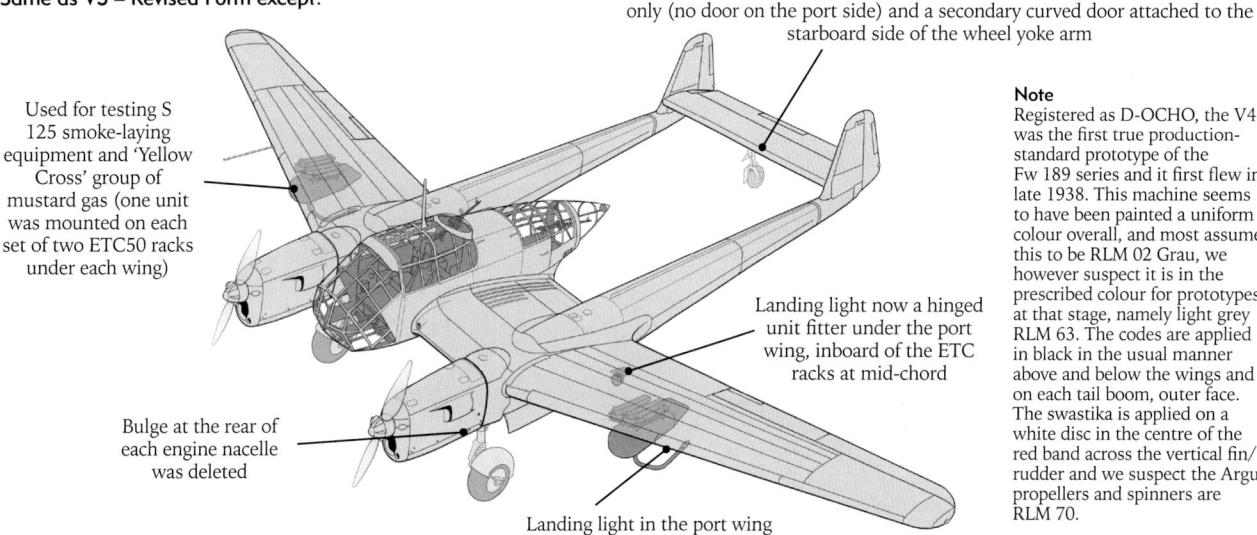

- The tailwheel was revised, with a pneumatic tyre and a rigid yoke with a trailing link that connected to a hydraulic damper unit at the back. The doors were revised to a hinged, twin-section unit on the starboard outer face of the oleo only (no door on the port side) and a secondary curved door attached to the starboard side of the wheel yoke arm
- Used for testing S 125 smoke-laying equipment and 'Yellow Cross' group of mustard gas (one unit was mounted on each set of two ETC50 racks under each wing)
- Landing light now a hinged unit fitter under the port wing, inboard of the ETC racks at mid-chord
- Bulge at the rear of each engine nacelle was deleted
- Landing light in the port wing leading edge deleted

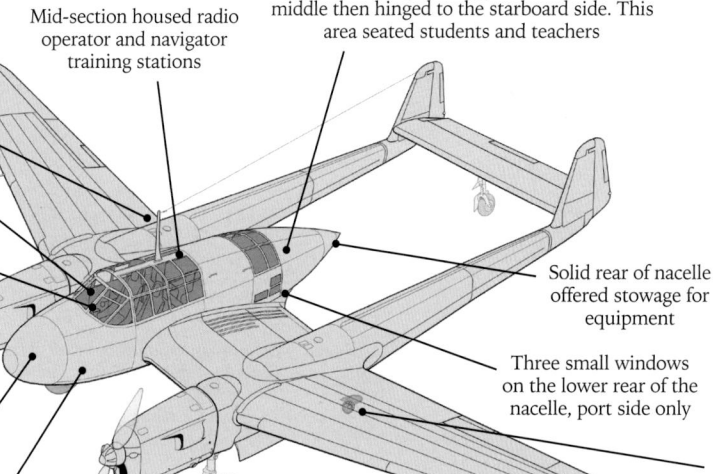

Note
Registered as D-OCHO, the V4 was the first true production-standard prototype of the Fw 189 series and it first flew in late 1938. This machine seems to have been painted a uniform colour overall, and most assume this to be RLM 02 Grau, we however suspect it is in the prescribed colour for prototypes at that stage, namely light grey RLM 63. The codes are applied in black in the usual manner above and below the wings and on each tail boom, outer face. The swastika is applied on a white disc in the centre of the red band across the vertical fin/rudder and we suspect the Argus propellers and spinners are RLM 70.

Fw 189 V5
Same as V4 except:

- Aft section has glazed upper cover, hinged in middle then hinged to the starboard side. This area seated students and teachers
- Mid-section housed radio operator and navigator training stations
- Aerial lead from top of radio mast to tip of starboard vertical fin
- New windscreen
- Front glazings hinged in two, then at the middle like the A-series (no matching glazed area to starboard though, it only extends aft on the port side)
- Solid rear of nacelle offered stowage for equipment
- Three small windows on the lower rear of the nacelle, port side only
- Front nose shape totally revised and radio equipment and DF loop now housed inside the solid nose cone
- Entire fuselage nacelle was redesigned to offer dual-control training
- Landing light moved from leading edge of wing, to a hinged unit fitted under the port wing, at mid-chord

Note
The V5 was intended as the prototype for the proposed B-series trainer and it first flew in early 1939. The aircraft was finished in an overall grey (RLM 63) scheme with Luftwaffe codes BQ+AZ applied either side of the Type B2 crosses on each outer face of the tail booms and under the wings, read as B+Q under the starboard and A+Z under the port, rear from the leading edge looking aft. Photos confirm that the codes were not applied above the wings. A Type H2 swastika is applied to the outer face of each vertical fin, at the mid-point between the tip and the top of the tailplane; this does not cross onto the rudder.

Focke-Wulf Fw 189
Evolution
Prototypes

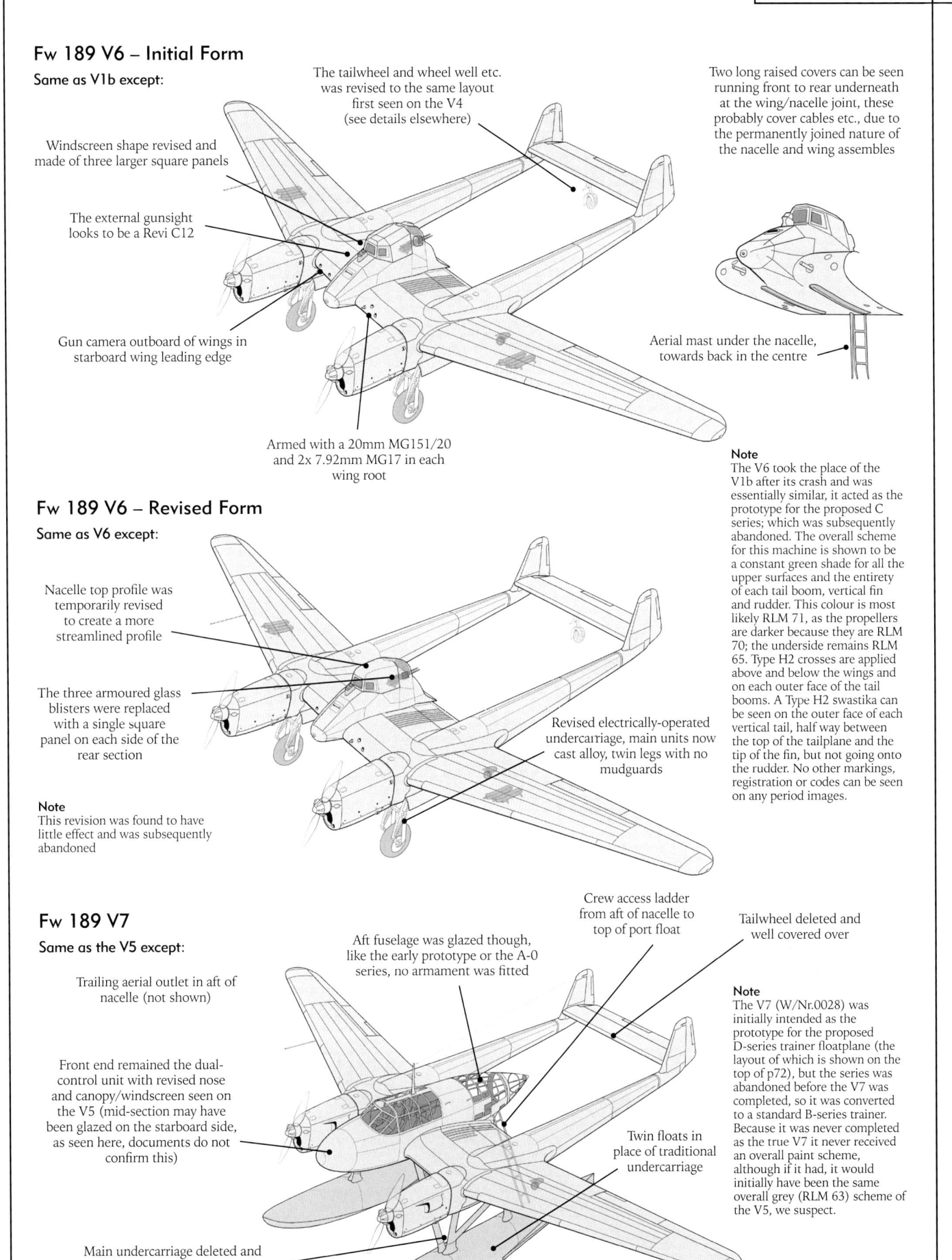

Fw 189 V6 – Initial Form
Same as V1b except:

Windscreen shape revised and made of three larger square panels

The external gunsight looks to be a Revi C12

Gun camera outboard of wings in starboard wing leading edge

The tailwheel and wheel well etc. was revised to the same layout first seen on the V4 (see details elsewhere)

Armed with a 20mm MG151/20 and 2x 7.92mm MG17 in each wing root

Two long raised covers can be seen running front to rear underneath at the wing/nacelle joint, these probably cover cables etc., due to the permanently joined nature of the nacelle and wing assembles

Aerial mast under the nacelle, towards back in the centre

Note
The V6 took the place of the V1b after its crash and was essentially similar, it acted as the prototype for the proposed C series; which was subsequently abandoned. The overall scheme for this machine is shown to be a constant green shade for all the upper surfaces and the entirety of each tail boom, vertical fin and rudder. This colour is most likely RLM 71, as the propellers are darker because they are RLM 70; the underside remains RLM 65. Type H2 crosses are applied above and below the wings and on each outer face of the tail booms. A Type H2 swastika can be seen on the outer face of each vertical tail, half way between the top of the tailplane and the tip of the fin, but not going onto the rudder. No other markings, registration or codes can be seen on any period images.

Fw 189 V6 – Revised Form
Same as V6 except:

Nacelle top profile was temporarily revised to create a more streamlined profile

The three armoured glass blisters were replaced with a single square panel on each side of the rear section

Revised electrically-operated undercarriage, main units now cast alloy, twin legs with no mudguards

Note
This revision was found to have little effect and was subsequently abandoned

Fw 189 V7
Same as the V5 except:

Trailing aerial outlet in aft of nacelle (not shown)

Front end remained the dual-control unit with revised nose and canopy/windscreen seen on the V5 (mid-section may have been glazed on the starboard side, as seen here, documents do not confirm this)

Main undercarriage deleted and well covered over, new struts to support floats installed

Aft fuselage was glazed though, like the early prototype or the A-0 series, no armament was fitted

Crew access ladder from aft of nacelle to top of port float

Tailwheel deleted and well covered over

Twin floats in place of traditional undercarriage

Note
The V7 (W/Nr.0028) was initially intended as the prototype for the proposed D-series trainer floatplane (the layout of which is shown on the top of p72), but the series was abandoned before the V7 was completed, so it was converted to a standard B-series trainer. Because it was never completed as the true V7 it never received an overall paint scheme, although if it had, it would initially have been the same overall grey (RLM 63) scheme of the V5, we suspect.

See Fw 189 V7 Schematic next page

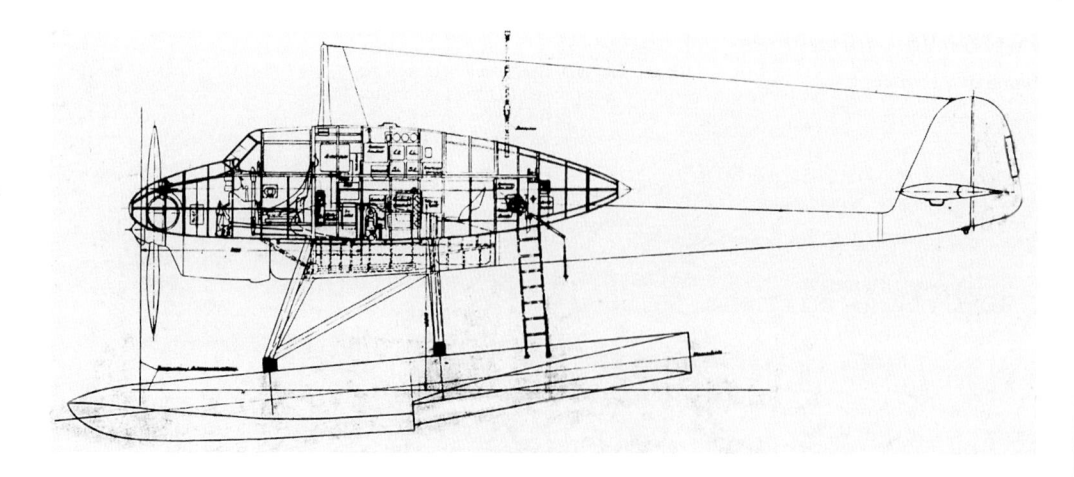

Focke-Wulf Fw 189
Evolution 2
Prototypes

Fw 189 V7 Schematic

Fw 189 V8

Note
This prototype (W/Nr.0029) was never completed, it was intended as a floatplane prototype like the V7

Fw 189 V9

Like the A-0 except:

No photos exist of the V9, so we have based our isometric on the most likely layout

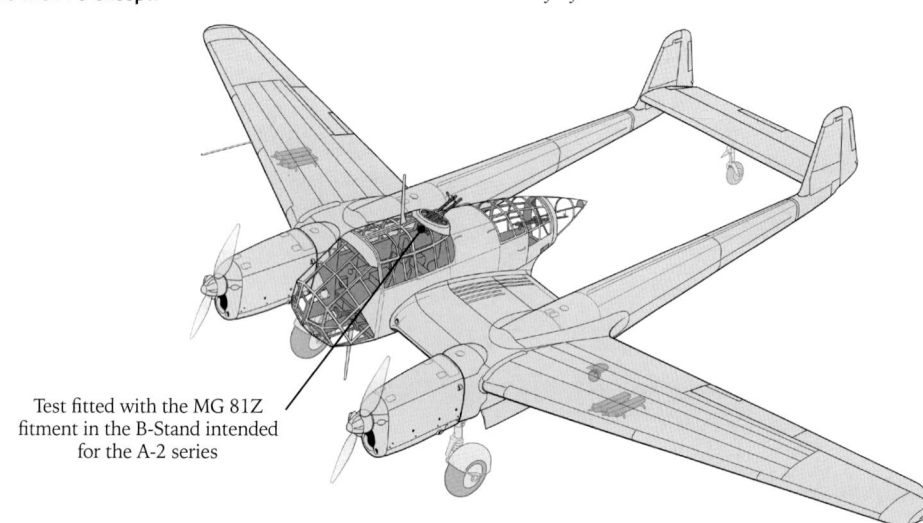

Test fitted with the MG 81Z fitment in the B-Stand intended for the A-2 series

Note
There is a bit of confusion as far as the V9 goes because surviving records show that the test facilities had no less than four airframes designated the 'V9', these being W/Nrs.0030, 0031, 0032 and 0050. Records indicate that 0031 and 0032 were in fact production A-1s and were used as duplicate V9s to test various items relating to the A-1 and A-2 series in tandem with the 'real' V9 (W/Nr.0030); we have confined our comments here to W/Nr.0030 because the 0031 and 0032 will be the same as the production A-1 series. W/Nr.0050 was another A-1, but had the armament of the A-2 and was used to test survey equipment for the proposed Fw 189Aa-2/U2 version (see below).

Fw 189 V9 – Survey Aircraft

Built as an A-1 (W/Nr.0050), this machine had the armament of the A-2, so was like the V9 except:

Note
This airframe apparently tested the feasibility of installing the survey equipment into the Fw 189 for the proposed Aa-2/U2 version

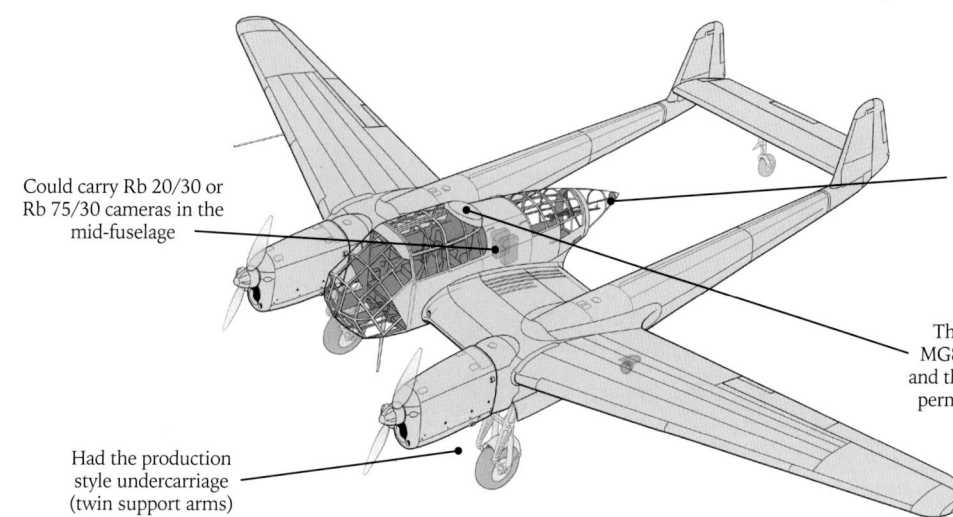

Could carry Rb 20/30 or Rb 75/30 cameras in the mid-fuselage

Instead of having the MG81Z mount (HL 81Z/A) in the rear (C-Stand) it was replaced with the HL-15A-1 unit without the pivoting motor drive installed; thus the whole unit would be moved manually

The top (B-Stand) mount for the MG81Z (LL-G 81 VE) was removed and the canvas cover in the mount was permanently sealed with new canvas (no gun installed)

Had the production style undercarriage (twin support arms)

Focke-Wulf Fw 189
Evolution
Prototypes

Fw 189 V10
Like the A-0 except:

No photos exist of the V10, so we have based our isometric on the most likely layout

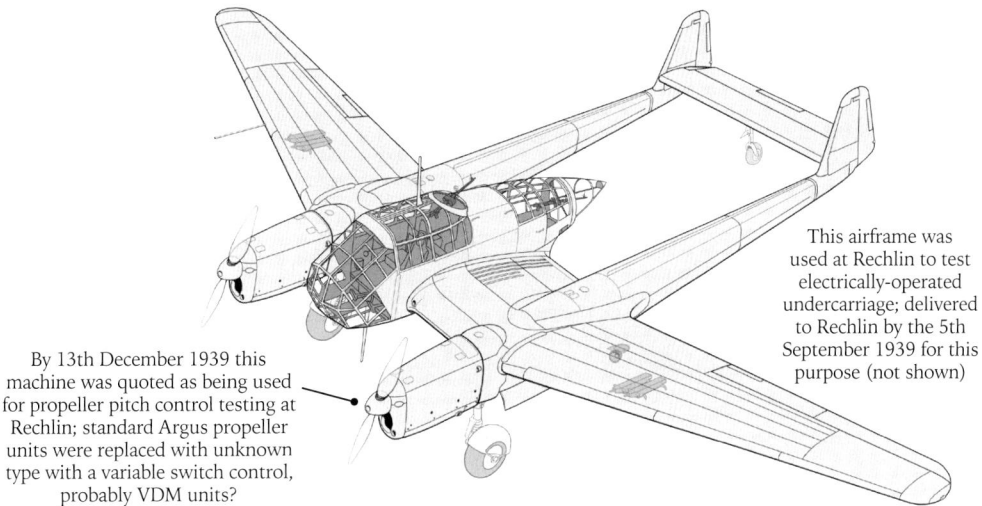

This airframe was used at Rechlin to test electrically-operated undercarriage; delivered to Rechlin by the 5th September 1939 for this purpose (not shown)

By 13th December 1939 this machine was quoted as being used for propeller pitch control testing at Rechlin; standard Argus propeller units were replaced with unknown type with a variable switch control, probably VDM units?

Note
Most previously published accounts list this as W/Nr.0047, however that was just a production A-1. The V10 was W/Nr.0006, initially registered as D-OHVC then taken on to Luftwaffe charge for trials as BQ+AW. The aircraft continued trials at Rechlin, mainly engines and propellers related, until at least 21st September 1941. We have found no photographs of this machine, so cannot make any comments on its likely scheme, but suspect in Luftwaffe service is was in the standard RLM 70/71 over 65 scheme with Type B2 crosses on the wings and tail booms and a Type H2 swastika on the vertical tail. The codes would be applied on the outer side of each boom, read left to right (BQ+AW) on either side and this would be repeated under the wings as B+Q under the starboard and A+W under the port, read from the leading edge looking aft.

Fw 189 V11
Like the A-0 except:

No photos exist of the V11, so we have based our isometric on the most likely layout

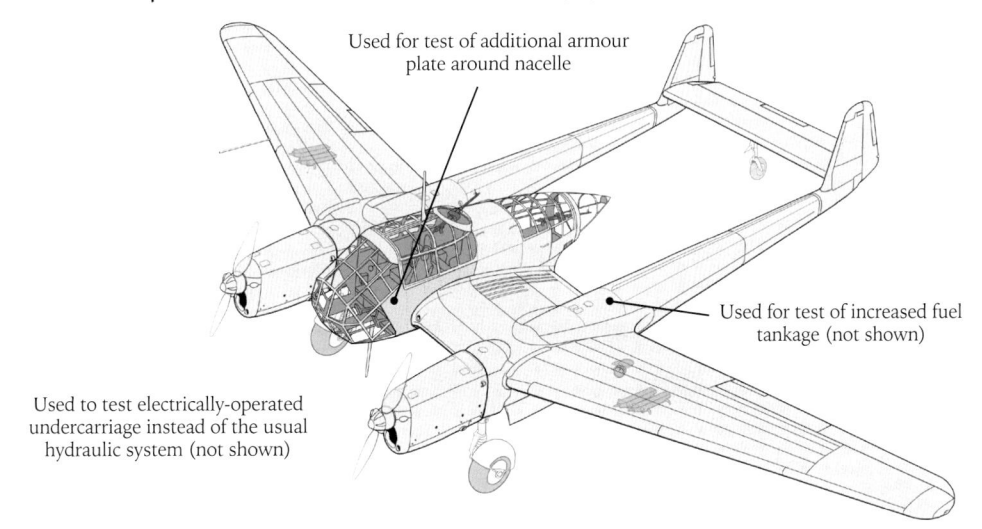

Used for test of additional armour plate around nacelle

Used for test of increased fuel tankage (not shown)

Used to test electrically-operated undercarriage instead of the usual hydraulic system (not shown)

Note
Many published sources state that this machine was in relation to the proposed E-series, however more recent German research of remaining data show this machine, like the V10 and V-13, to have been A-0 series machines used for development work on the proposed F-series. This machine was W/Nr.0007 and it carried the codes BQ+AX. As no photos survive, we assume it to be in the standard RLM 70/71 over 65 scheme, with Type B2 crosses in the usual positions and the codes carried on the booms and under the wings.

Fw 189 V11 (C-1)
Same as the V6

Note
Most published works list this as W/Nr.0048 (built as an A-1, modified to A-2) and a test airframe for the proposed E-series, however more recent German research states this was the first and only C-1 and was W/Nr.0310302, however its actual construction is still considered 'questionable'

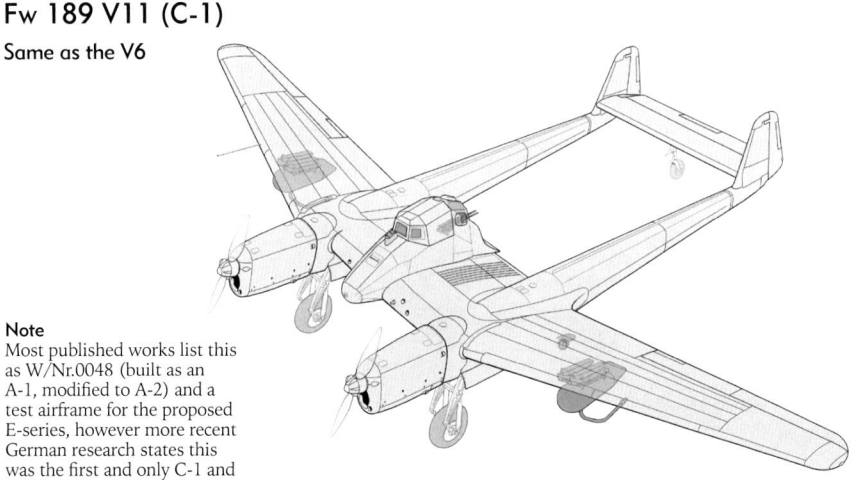

Fw 189 V12

Note
Many published works state that this machine was used for development work on the proposed F-2 series, however recent German research does not show any machine designated the V12 in surviving records, although oddly the F-related prototypes were the V10, V11 and V13* (*which is also not accounted for, see below), so the V12 is suspiciously absent?

Fw 189 V13

Note
Just like the V12, many previously pubished works state that this machine was used for development work on the proposed F-series and in particular the F-1, however recent German research does not show any machine designated the V13 in surviving records, although oddly the F-related prototypes were the V10 and V11 (plus the V12, which is also not accounted for, see above), so the V13 is suspiciously absent?

Evolution

Prototypes

Fw 189 V14
Similar to the A-1 except:

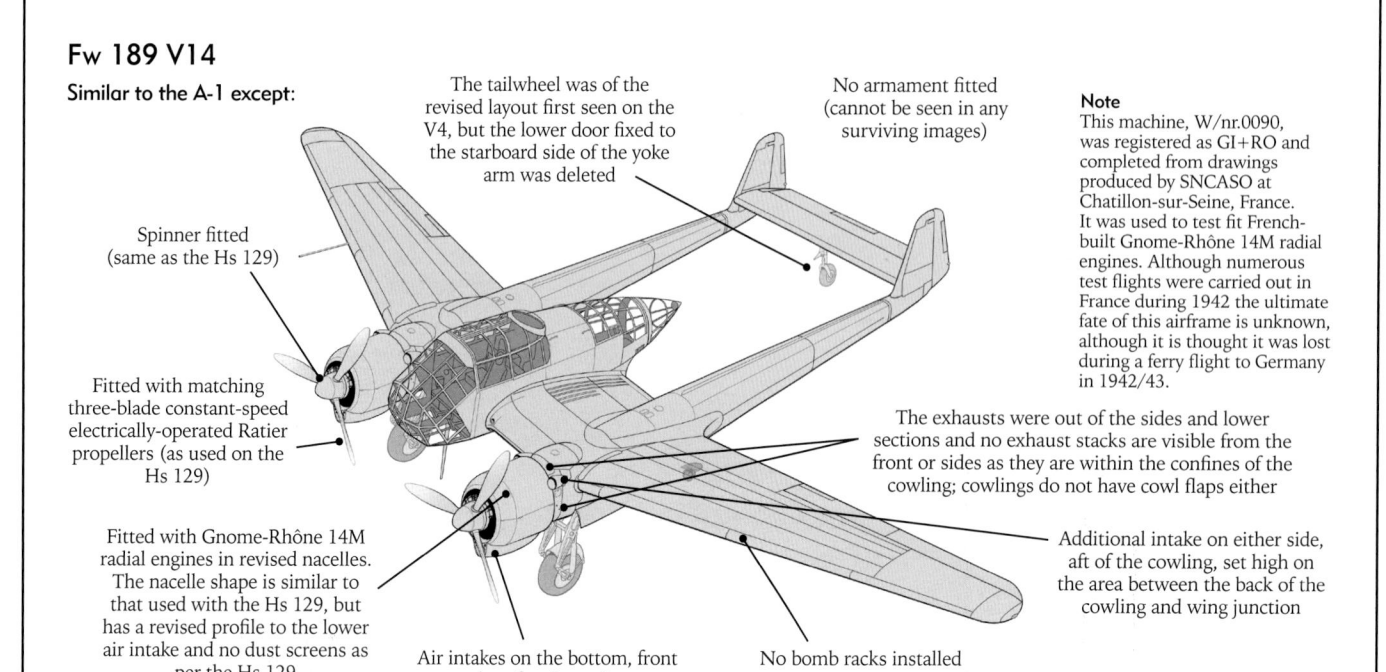

- Spinner fitted (same as the Hs 129)
- Fitted with matching three-blade constant-speed electrically-operated Ratier propellers (as used on the Hs 129)
- Fitted with Gnome-Rhône 14M radial engines in revised nacelles. The nacelle shape is similar to that used with the Hs 129, but has a revised profile to the lower air intake and no dust screens as per the Hs 129
- The tailwheel was of the revised layout first seen on the V4, but the lower door fixed to the starboard side of the yoke arm was deleted
- No armament fitted (cannot be seen in any surviving images)
- Air intakes on the bottom, front edge of each cowling
- The exhausts were out of the sides and lower sections and no exhaust stacks are visible from the front or sides as they are within the confines of the cowling; cowlings do not have cowl flaps either
- No bomb racks installed
- Additional intake on either side, aft of the cowling, set high on the area between the back of the cowling and wing junction

Note
This machine, W/nr.0090, was registered as GI+RO and completed from drawings produced by SNCASO at Chatillon-sur-Seine, France. It was used to test fit French-built Gnome-Rhône 14M radial engines. Although numerous test flights were carried out in France during 1942 the ultimate fate of this airframe is unknown, although it is thought it was lost during a ferry flight to Germany in 1942/43.

Fw 189 V15
Same as the A-2 except:

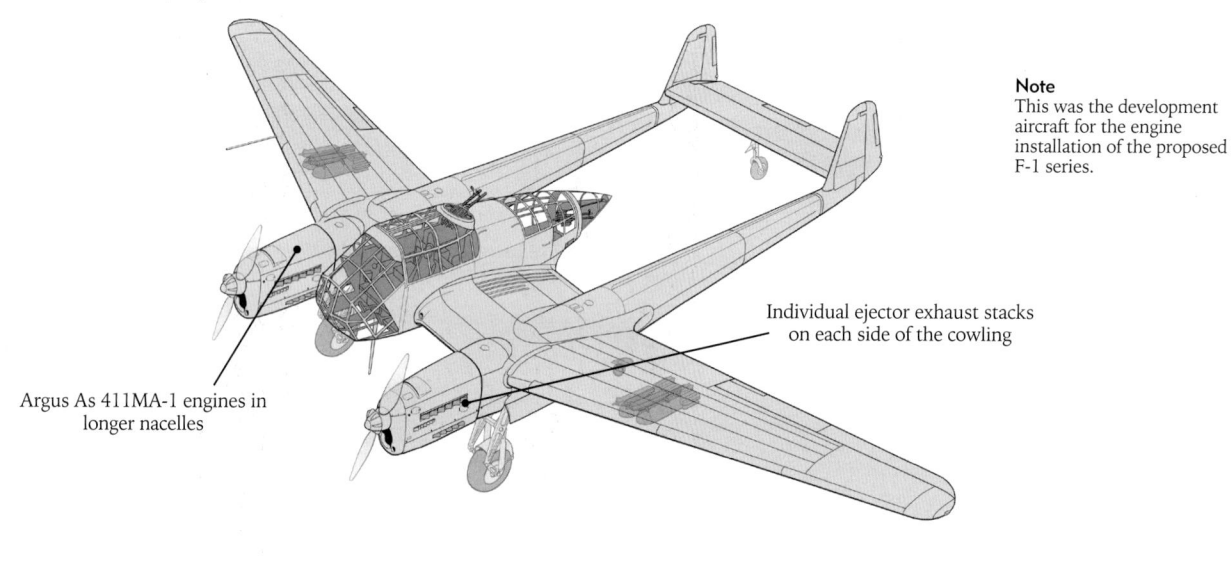

- Argus As 411MA-1 engines in longer nacelles
- Individual ejector exhaust stacks on each side of the cowling

Note
This was the development aircraft for the engine installation of the proposed F-1 series.

An Fw 189A-0 being ground-run, it lacks the upper MG15 and has no FuG17 aerial mast fitted

Focke-Wulf Fw 189
Evolution
Pre-production

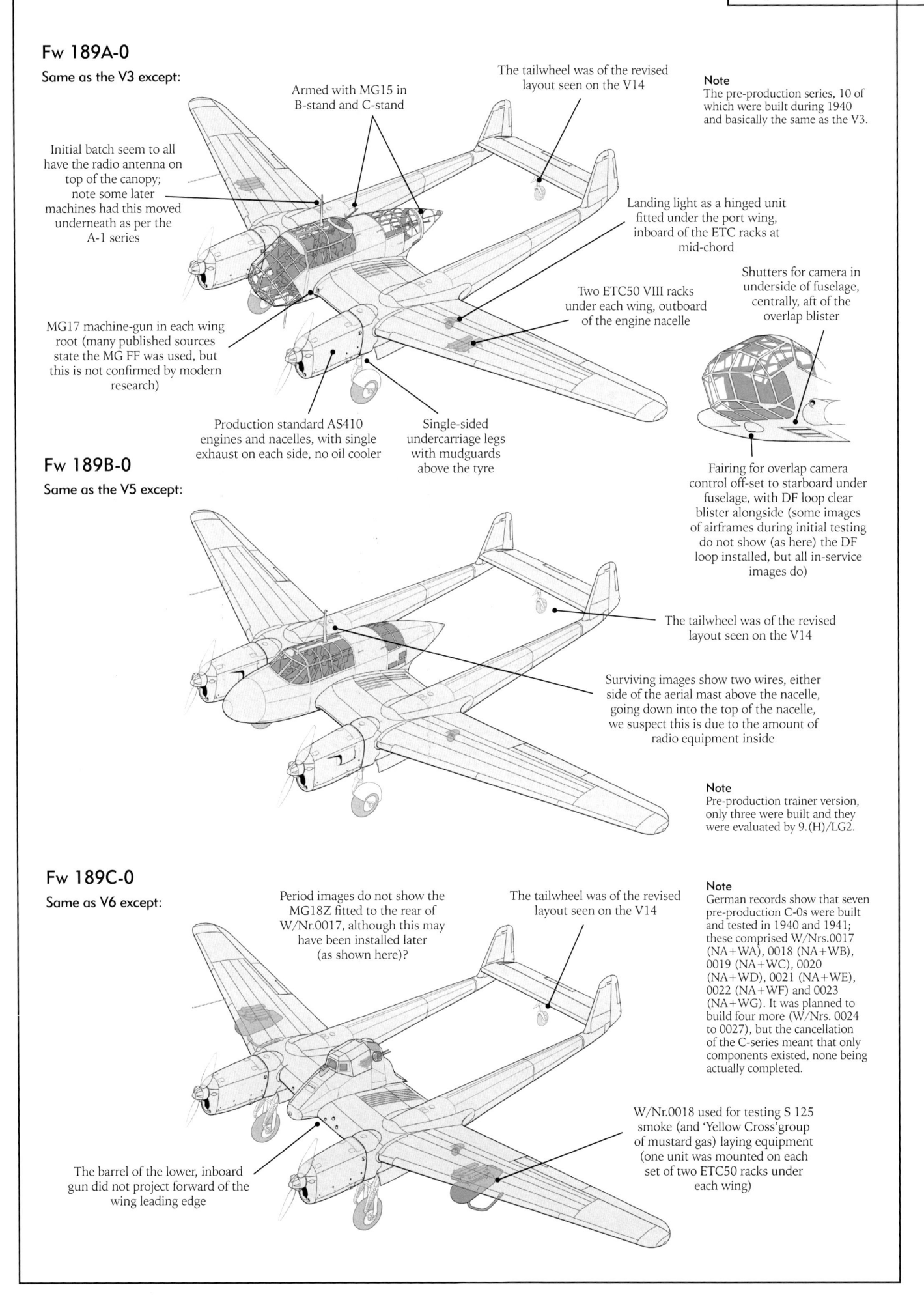

Fw 189A-0
Same as the V3 except:

Initial batch seem to all have the radio antenna on top of the canopy; note some later machines had this moved underneath as per the A-1 series

Armed with MG15 in B-stand and C-stand

The tailwheel was of the revised layout seen on the V14

Note
The pre-production series, 10 of which were built during 1940 and basically the same as the V3.

Landing light as a hinged unit fitted under the port wing, inboard of the ETC racks at mid-chord

MG17 machine-gun in each wing root (many published sources state the MG FF was used, but this is not confirmed by modern research)

Two ETC50 VIII racks under each wing, outboard of the engine nacelle

Shutters for camera in underside of fuselage, centrally, aft of the overlap blister

Production standard AS410 engines and nacelles, with single exhaust on each side, no oil cooler

Single-sided undercarriage legs with mudguards above the tyre

Fairing for overlap camera control off-set to starboard under fuselage, with DF loop clear blister alongside (some images of airframes during initial testing do not show (as here) the DF loop installed, but all in-service images do)

Fw 189B-0
Same as the V5 except:

The tailwheel was of the revised layout seen on the V14

Surviving images show two wires, either side of the aerial mast above the nacelle, going down into the top of the nacelle, we suspect this is due to the amount of radio equipment inside

Note
Pre-production trainer version, only three were built and they were evaluated by 9.(H)/LG2.

Fw 189C-0
Same as V6 except:

Period images do not show the MG18Z fitted to the rear of W/Nr.0017, although this may have been installed later (as shown here)?

The tailwheel was of the revised layout seen on the V14

Note
German records show that seven pre-production C-0s were built and tested in 1940 and 1941; these comprised W/Nrs.0017 (NA+WA), 0018 (NA+WB), 0019 (NA+WC), 0020 (NA+WD), 0021 (NA+WE), 0022 (NA+WF) and 0023 (NA+WG). It was planned to build four more (W/Nrs. 0024 to 0027), but the cancellation of the C-series meant that only components existed, none being actually completed.

The barrel of the lower, inboard gun did not project forward of the wing leading edge

W/Nr.0018 used for testing S 125 smoke (and 'Yellow Cross' group of mustard gas) laying equipment (one unit was mounted on each set of two ETC50 racks under each wing)

Focke-Wulf Fw 189
Evolution
Production Versions

Fw 189A-1
The first production series, 20 were built during 1940. Same as the A-0 except:

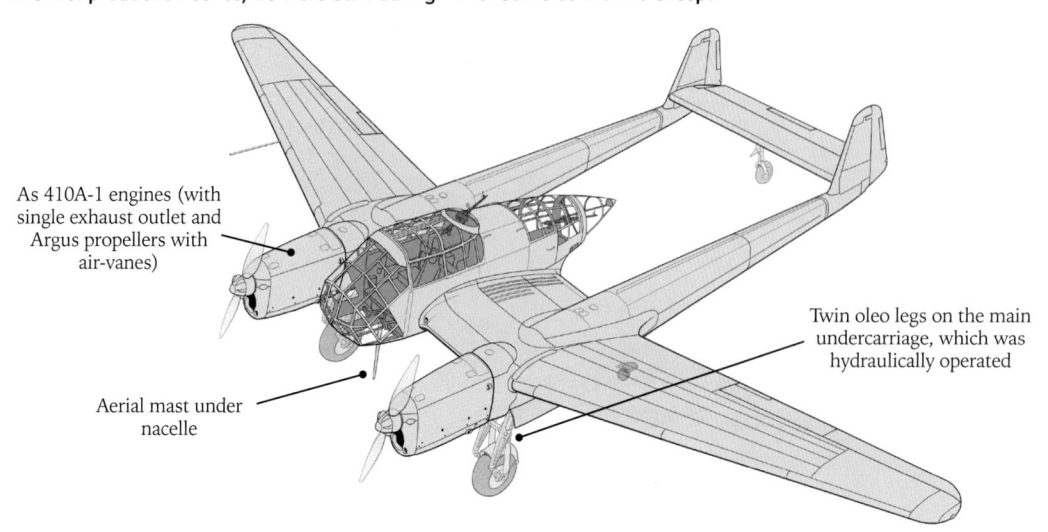

- As 410A-1 engines (with single exhaust outlet and Argus propellers with air-vanes)
- Aerial mast under nacelle
- Twin oleo legs on the main undercarriage, which was hydraulically operated

Fw 189A-1/U2
Same as the Fw 189A-1 except:

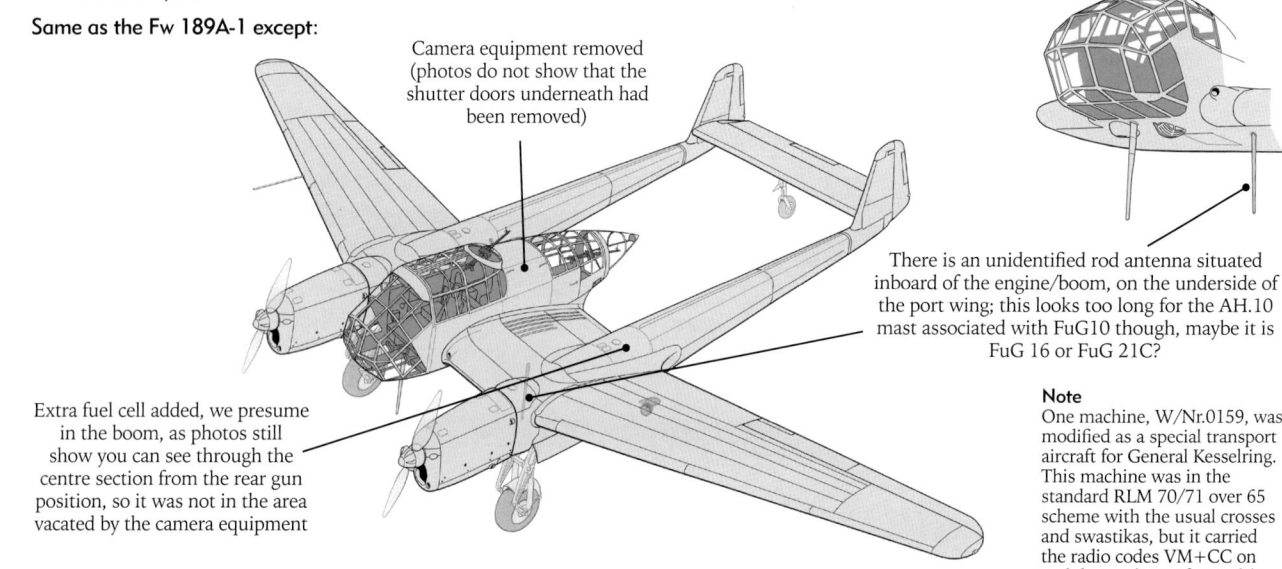

- Camera equipment removed (photos do not show that the shutter doors underneath had been removed)
- Extra fuel cell added, we presume in the boom, as photos still show you can see through the centre section from the rear gun position, so it was not in the area vacated by the camera equipment
- There is an unidentified rod antenna situated inboard of the engine/boom, on the underside of the port wing; this looks too long for the AH.10 mast associated with FuG10 though, maybe it is FuG 16 or FuG 21C?

Note
One machine, W/Nr.0159, was modified as a special transport aircraft for General Kesselring. This machine was in the standard RLM 70/71 over 65 scheme with the usual crosses and swastikas, but it carried the radio codes VM+CC on each boom (outer face only) and, most likely) under the wings, read as 'V+M' under the starboard and 'C+C' under the port, read from the trailing edge looking forward. The aircraft had yellow bands around the rear of each tail boom and the underside tips of each wing were also painted yellow. This machine had the emblem of Luftflotte 2 applied to either side of the nose, forward and below the glazed panels that open for crew access.

Fw 189A-1/U3
Same as the Fw 189A-1/U2

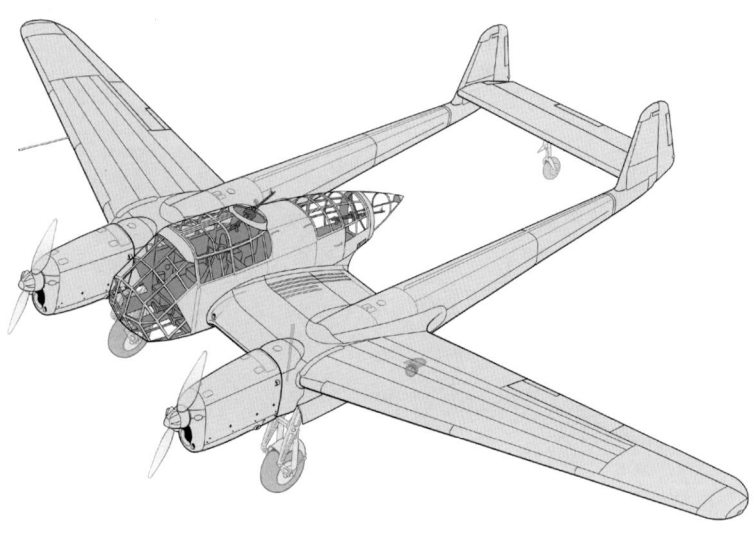

Note
One machine was modified as a special transport aircraft for Generaloberst Hans Jeschonnek. Chief of the Luftwaffe General Staff. Although this machine was most likely in the standard RLM 70/71 over 65 scheme with the usual crosses and swastikas, its radio codes and any other markings remain unknown.

Fw 189A-1 with skis
Same as the Fw 189A-1 except:

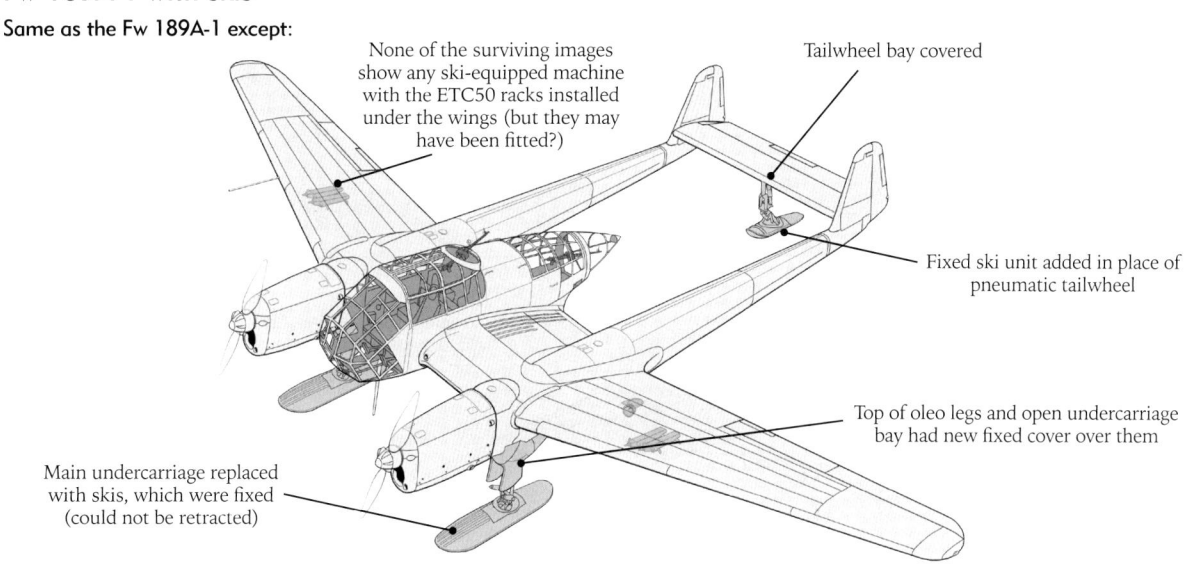

- None of the surviving images show any ski-equipped machine with the ETC50 racks installed under the wings (but they may have been fitted?)
- Tailwheel bay covered
- Fixed ski unit added in place of pneumatic tailwheel
- Top of oleo legs and open undercarriage bay had new fixed cover over them
- Main undercarriage replaced with skis, which were fixed (could not be retracted)

Fw 189A-2 – Initial Form
Appeared in the summer of 1941, same as the A-1 except:

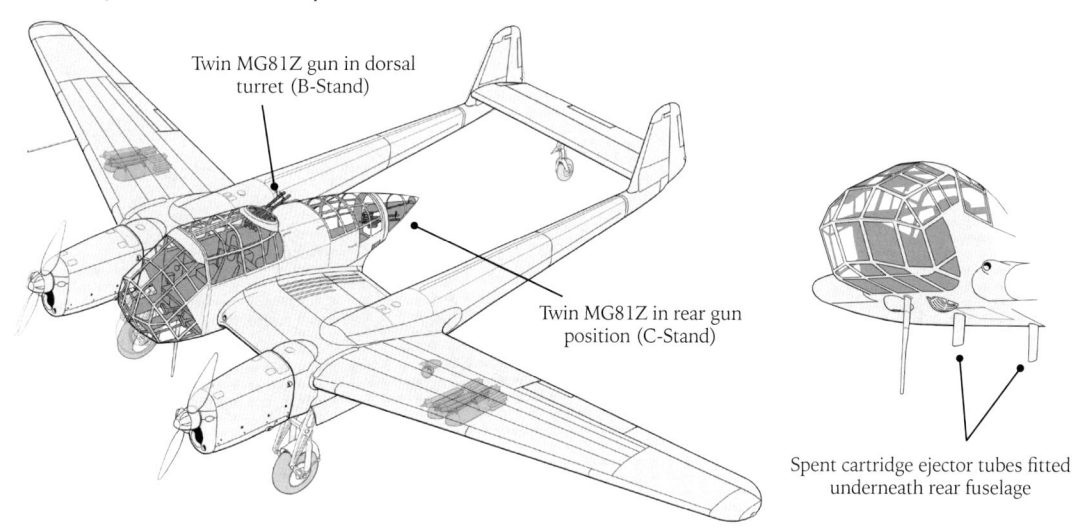

- Twin MG81Z gun in dorsal turret (B-Stand)
- Twin MG81Z in rear gun position (C-Stand)
- Spent cartridge ejector tubes fitted underneath rear fuselage

Fw 189A-2 – Later Form
Same as the A-2 – Initial Form except:

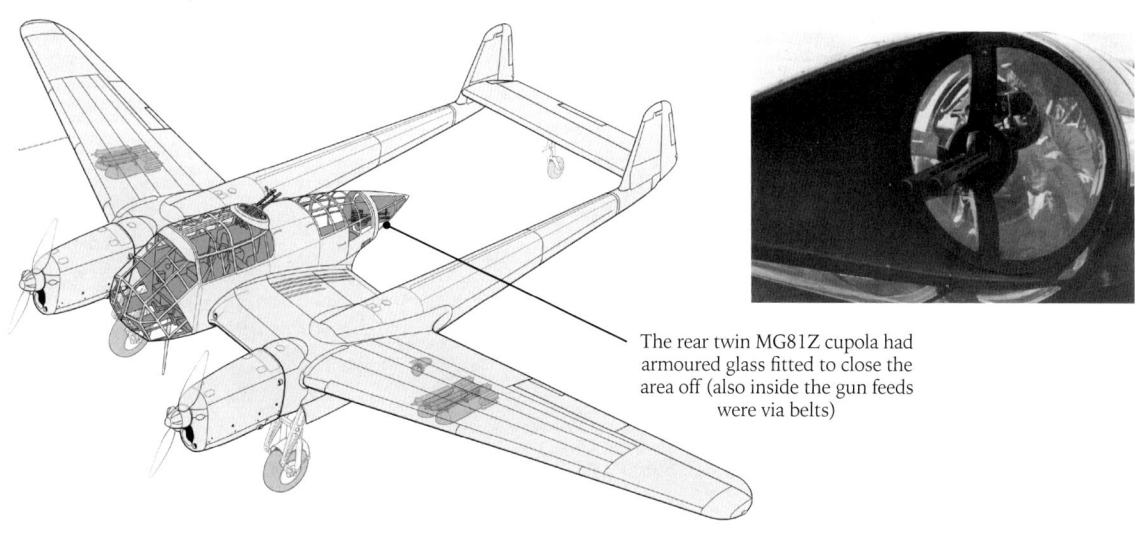

- The rear twin MG81Z cupola had armoured glass fitted to close the area off (also inside the gun feeds were via belts)

Fw 189A-2 Nightfighter
Same as the A-2 – Initial Form except:

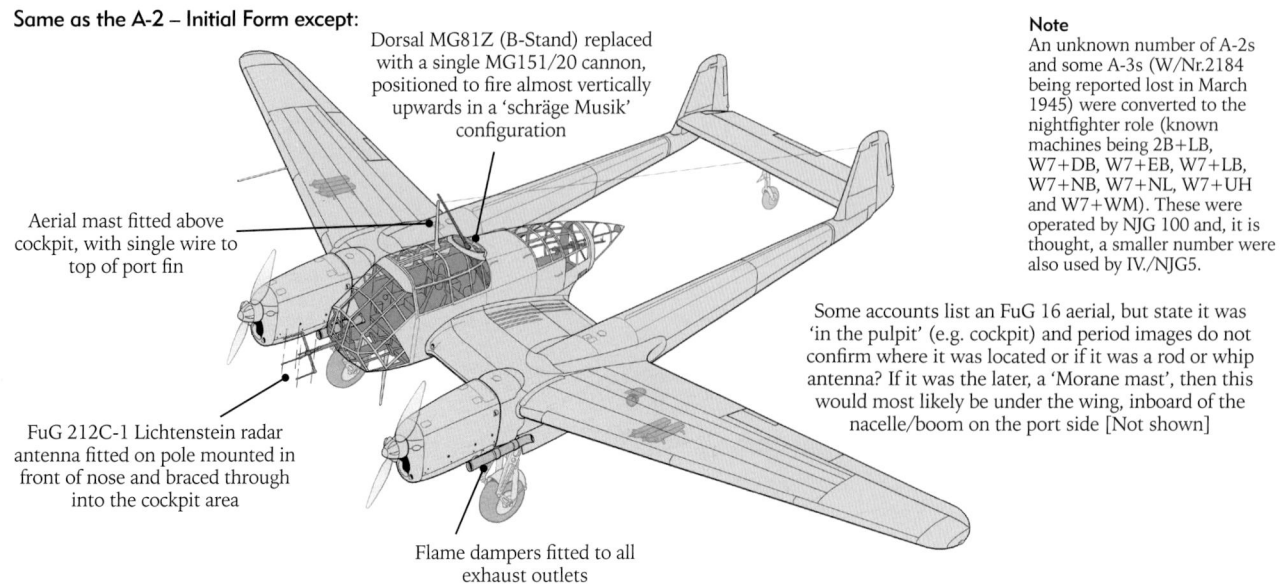

Dorsal MG81Z (B-Stand) replaced with a single MG151/20 cannon, positioned to fire almost vertically upwards in a 'schräge Musik' configuration

Aerial mast fitted above cockpit, with single wire to top of port fin

FuG 212C-1 Lichtenstein radar antenna fitted on pole mounted in front of nose and braced through into the cockpit area

Flame dampers fitted to all exhaust outlets

Note
An unknown number of A-2s and some A-3s (W/Nr.2184 being reported lost in March 1945) were converted to the nightfighter role (known machines being 2B+LB, W7+DB, W7+EB, W7+LB, W7+NB, W7+NL, W7+UH and W7+WM). These were operated by NJG 100 and, it is thought, a smaller number were also used by IV./NJG5.

Some accounts list an FuG 16 aerial, but state it was 'in the pulpit' (e.g. cockpit) and period images do not confirm where it was located or if it was a rod or whip antenna? If it was the later, a 'Morane mast', then this would most likely be under the wing, inboard of the nacelle/boom on the port side [Not shown]

Fw 189Aa-2/U2
All standard A-2s except:

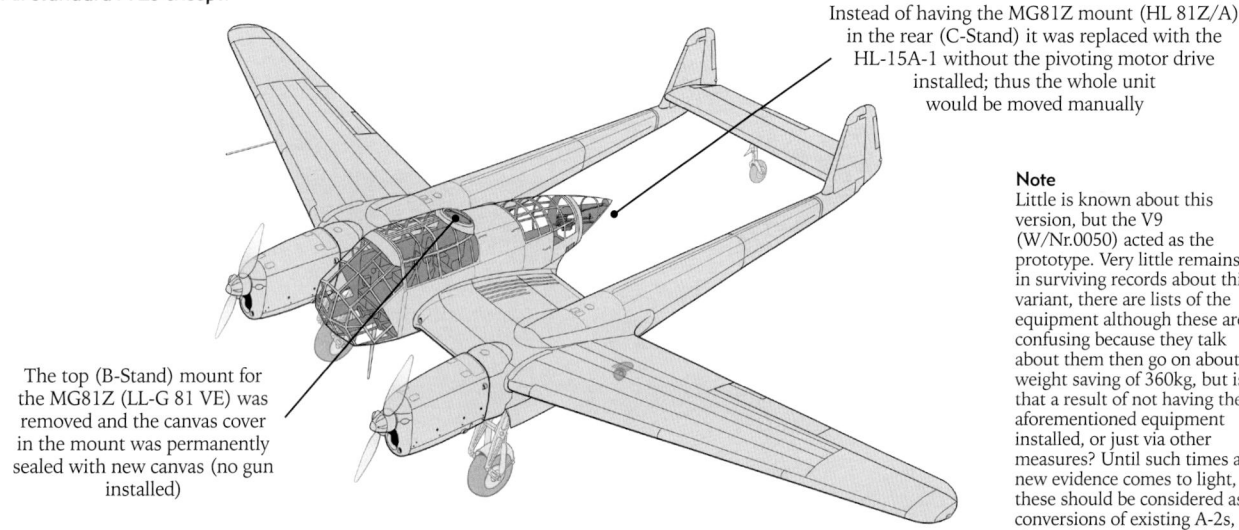

Instead of having the MG81Z mount (HL 81Z/A) in the rear (C-Stand) it was replaced with the HL-15A-1 without the pivoting motor drive installed; thus the whole unit would be moved manually

The top (B-Stand) mount for the MG81Z (LL-G 81 VE) was removed and the canvas cover in the mount was permanently sealed with new canvas (no gun installed)

Note
Little is known about this version, but the V9 (W/Nr.0050) acted as the prototype. Very little remains in surviving records about this variant, there are lists of the equipment although these are confusing because they talk about them then go on about weight saving of 360kg, but is that a result of not having the aforementioned equipment installed, or just via other measures? Until such times as new evidence comes to light, these should be considered as conversions of existing A-2s, although the actual number involved is unknown.

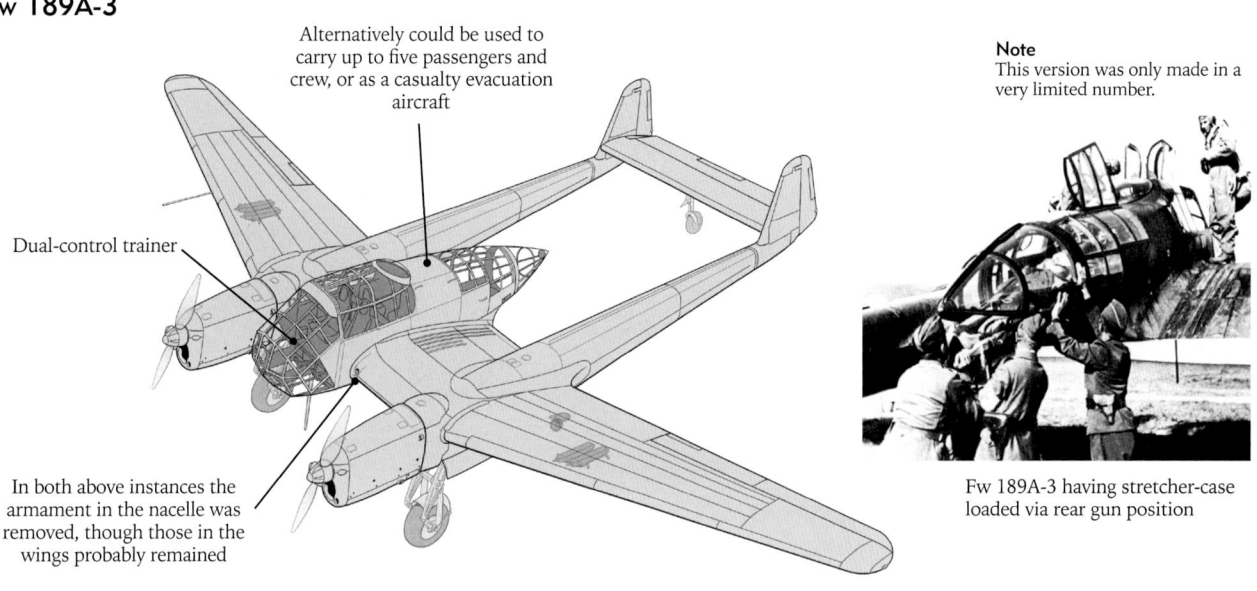

Fw 189A-3

Alternatively could be used to carry up to five passengers and crew, or as a casualty evacuation aircraft

Dual-control trainer

In both above instances the armament in the nacelle was removed, though those in the wings probably remained

Note
This version was only made in a very limited number.

Fw 189A-3 having stretcher-case loaded via rear gun position

Fw 189A-3 Nightfighter
This is the same as the A-2 Nightfighter except:

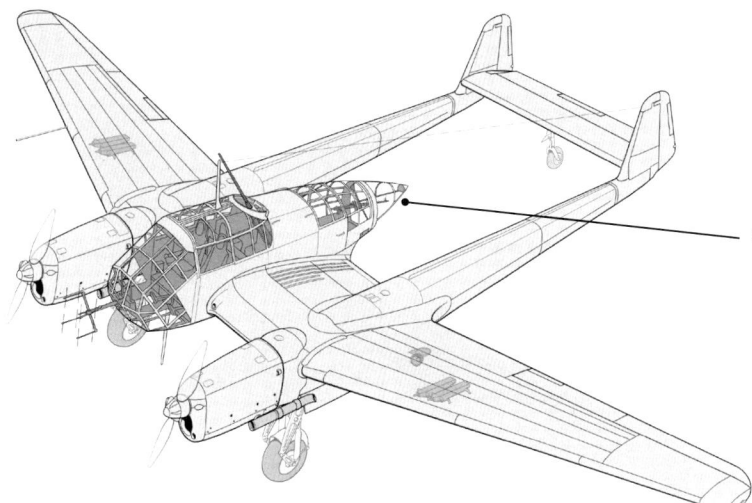

This version was based on the A-3, so we suspect it did not have the gun in the rear tail cone, though there are no surviving images to confirm either way

Fw 189B-1

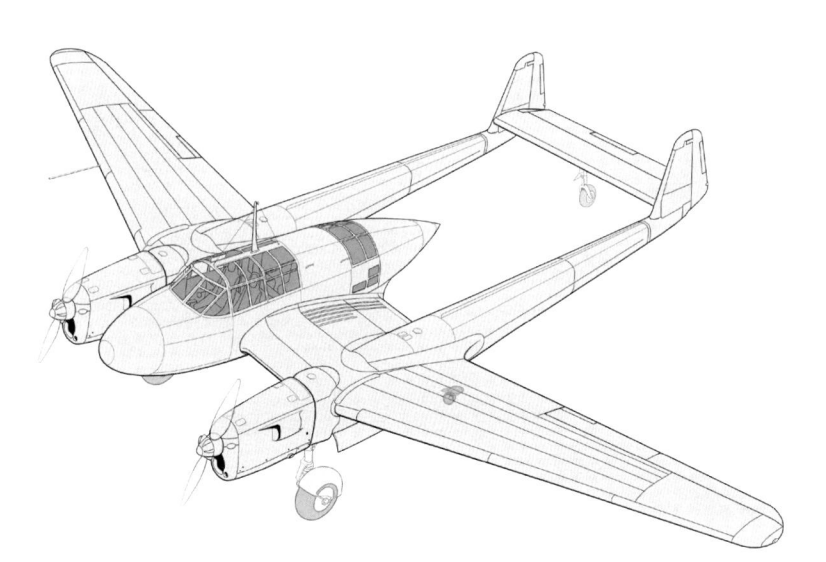

Note
This was the production trainer version and 10 were built. It was basically the same as the V5, although it would have been fully equipped internally for its intended role.

Note that all the B-series airframes were built before any A-series ordered were even placed.

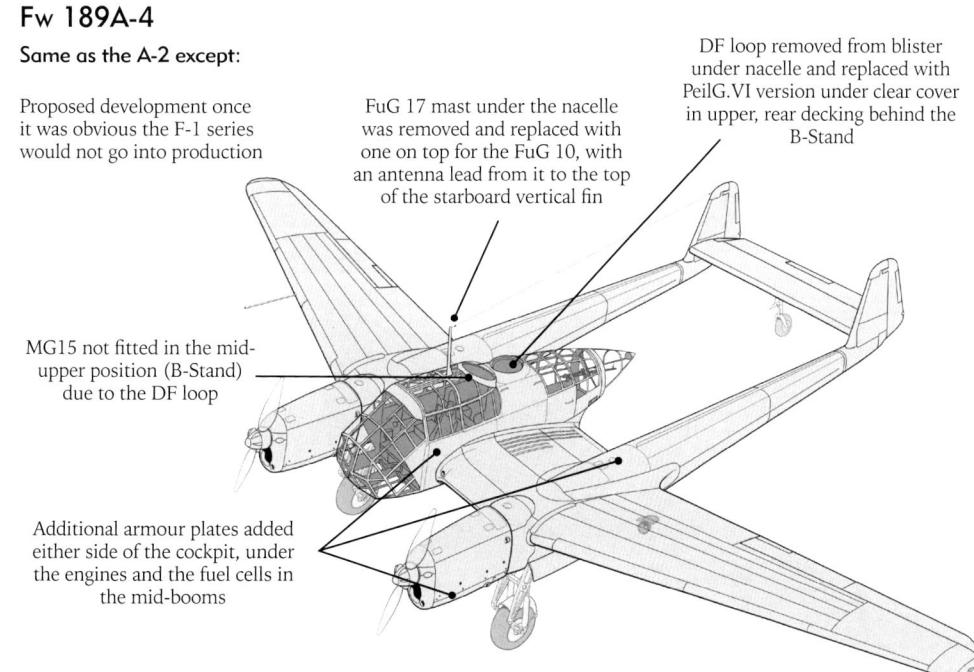

Fw 189A-4
Same as the A-2 except:

Proposed development once it was obvious the F-1 series would not go into production

FuG 17 mast under the nacelle was removed and replaced with one on top for the FuG 10, with an antenna lead from it to the top of the starboard vertical fin

DF loop removed from blister under nacelle and replaced with PeilG.VI version under clear cover in upper, rear decking behind the B-Stand

MG15 not fitted in the mid-upper position (B-Stand) due to the DF loop

Additional armour plates added either side of the cockpit, under the engines and the fuel cells in the mid-booms

Note
Although some published sources over the years have stated that this version went into production in 1942, more recent research in Germany shows that no production of the A-4 (or A-5) was ever actually undertaken. The situation was such that by July 1942 the RLM had not even decided on series production of the A-4, they felt modifying the A-2 in this manner would be a simpler option, thus removing the need for any separate A-4 production. Many previously published sources also stated that the fixed MG17s were to be replaced with the MG FF, however no surviving documents in Germany support this and it is thus felt to be very unlikely.

Focke-Wulf Fw 189
Evolution
Projected & One-offs

Fw 189A-5
Proposed development from the A-4 except:

The FuG 17 radio was replaced with the FuG 21C, again with an aerial mast on top of the nacelle and lead to the top of the starboard fin

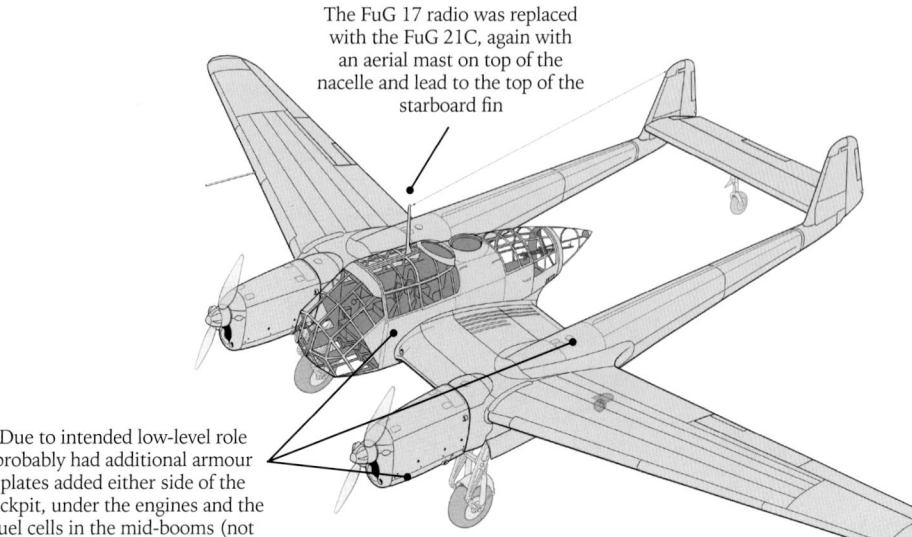

Due to intended low-level role probably had additional armour plates added either side of the cockpit, under the engines and the fuel cells in the mid-booms (not confirmed

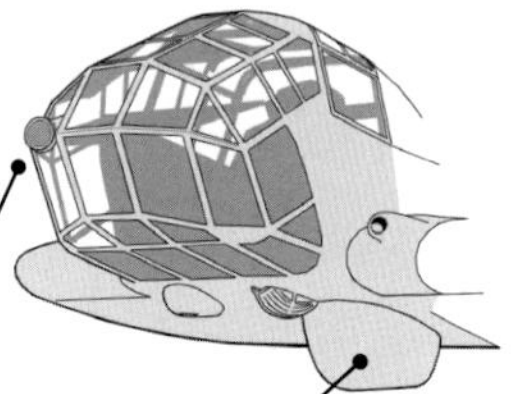

The low-level nature of its intended role meant that the round optically-flat panel off-set to starboard in the nose would have been installed

Note
Little is known of this type, although a set of three-view drawings does exist, it would seem that the type may have been envisaged to meet the RLM's requirement for a type used in anti-partisan work and thus would have been for low-level bombing and may also have had the flat (round) disc in the nose glazing for a low-level bombsight.

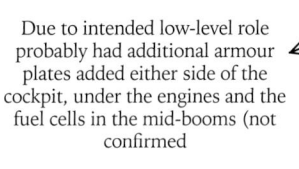

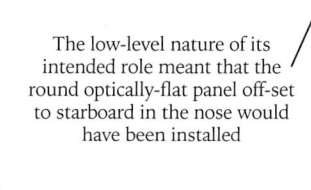

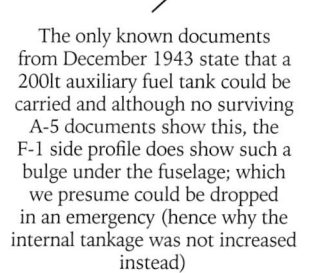

The only known documents from December 1943 state that a 200lt auxiliary fuel tank could be carried and although no surviving A-5 documents show this, the F-1 side profile does show such a bulge under the fuselage; which we presume could be dropped in an emergency (hence why the internal tankage was not increased instead)

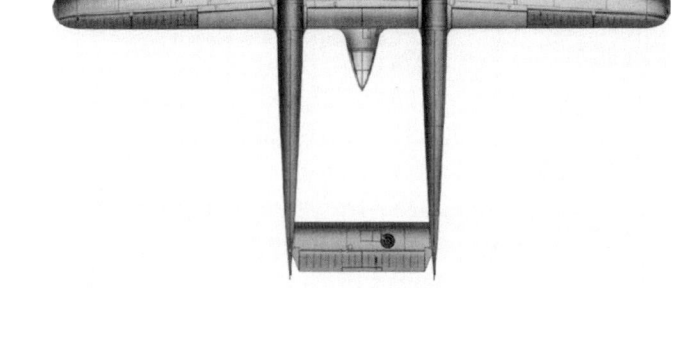

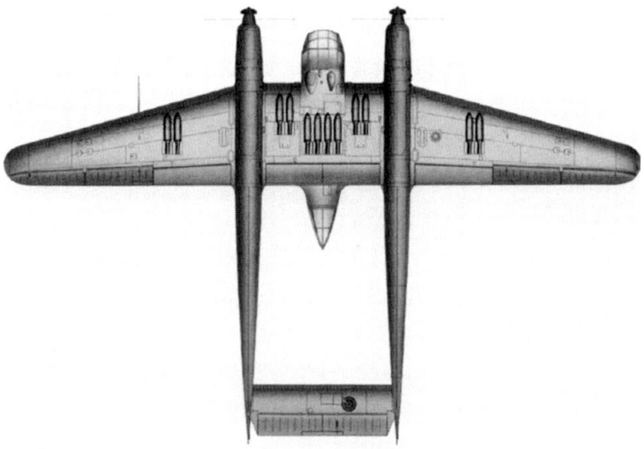

It is possible that this version was intended to be the one shown in the 18th December 1943 diagram with 12x SC50 bombs on separate ETC racks; two under each outer wing panel as normal, plus two on each inner wing panel and four more under the aft nacelle

Fw 189C-1
Proposed ground-attack version, similar to the V6:

Note
Not proceeded with

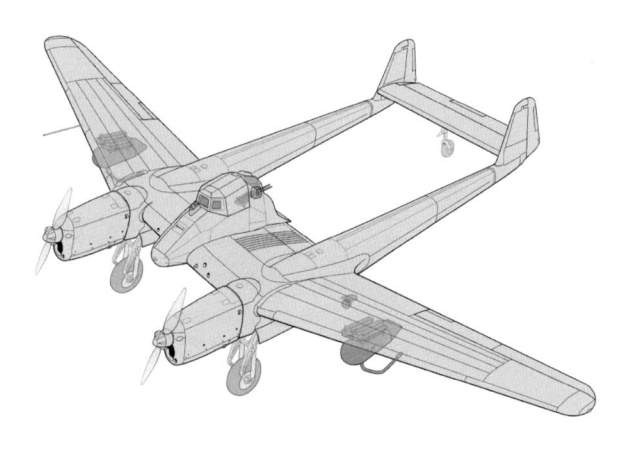

Fw 189D
Proposed floatplane trainer version, similar to the V7:

Note
Not proceeded with

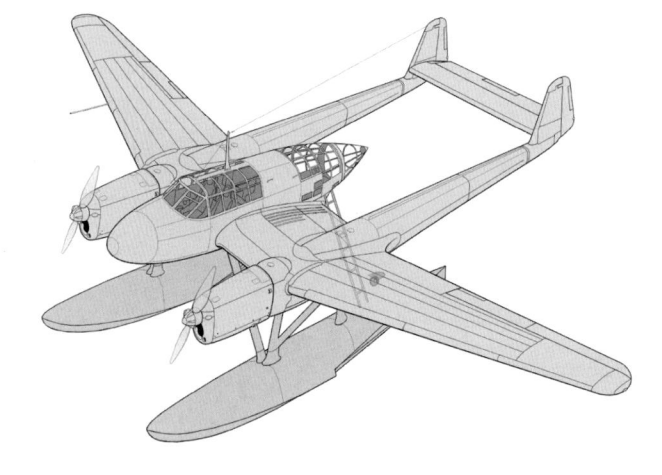

Focke-Wulf Fw 189
Evolution
Projected & One-offs

Fw 189E

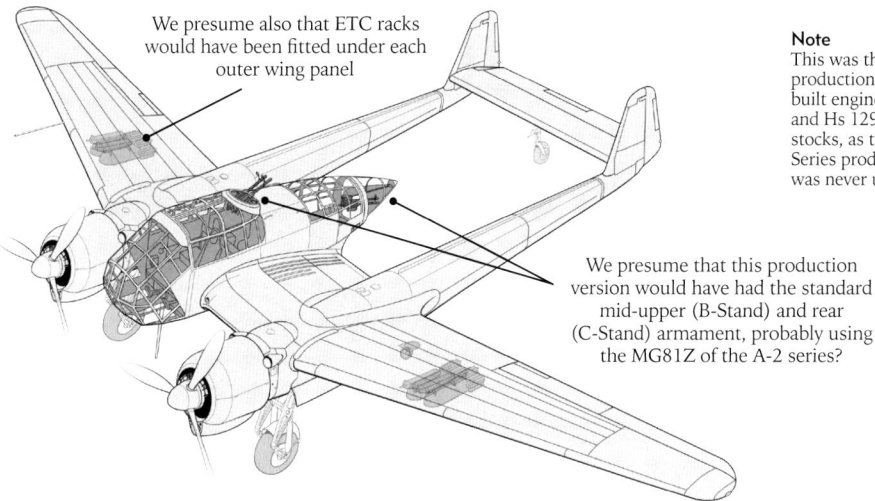

We presume also that ETC racks would have been fitted under each outer wing panel

Note
This was the proposed production version using French-built engines (as per the Go 244 and Hs 129) to use up captured stocks, as tested in the V14. Series production of this version was never undertaken.

We presume that this production version would have had the standard mid-upper (B-Stand) and rear (C-Stand) armament, probably using the MG81Z of the A-2 series?

Fw 189F-1

Same as A-2 except:

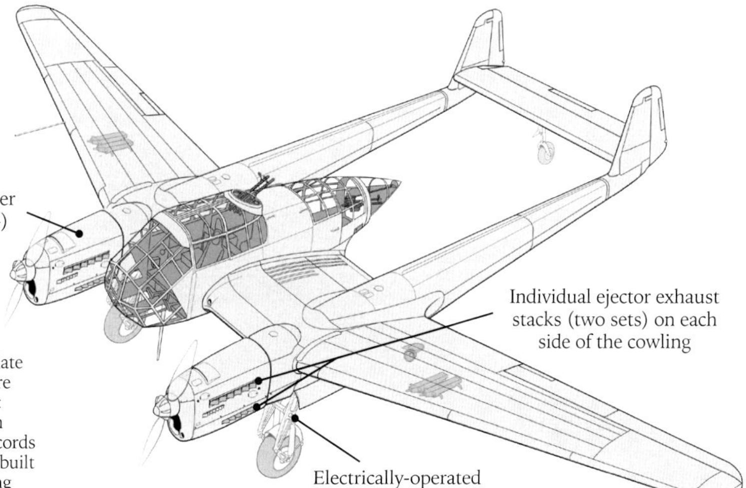

Fitted with Argus As 411MA-1 engines in longer cowlings (like the Si 204)

Diagrams of the era show a large bulged fairing under the nacelle, what this was for is unknown because no documents exist that clarify it role. The details for the A-4 (from which the F-1 would be derived) in late 1943 stated that a 200lt auxiliary fuel tank could be carried, so we suspect that is what this 'bulge' is; we presume it is external so it can be dropped in an emergency

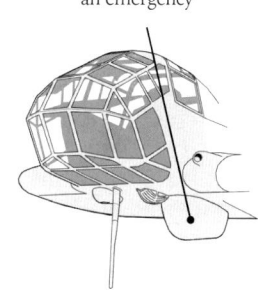

Individual ejector exhaust stacks (two sets) on each side of the cowling

Electrically-operated undercarriage

Note
All published accounts to date list that seventeen F-1s were built at Bordeaux-Merignac before production ceased in 1944. However German records state that the type was not built due to difficulty in procuring the engines in sufficient numbers (they were needed for the Si 204) and that no serial production ever took place. There are also accounts of F-1s being used by NAGr.16 (such as 5H+RK), but this was not the case, the most likely version for this machine being an A-2 or A-3

Fw 189F-2

No F-2s were ever built, even though some claim the V12 acted as a prototype, as modern German research has not found any mention of the V12 in surviving records. So until such times as its (and the V12s) existence is proven, this variant remains a 'project only'.

Fw 189G

This versions was abandoned when its intended powerplant failed to even get as far as the prototype stage

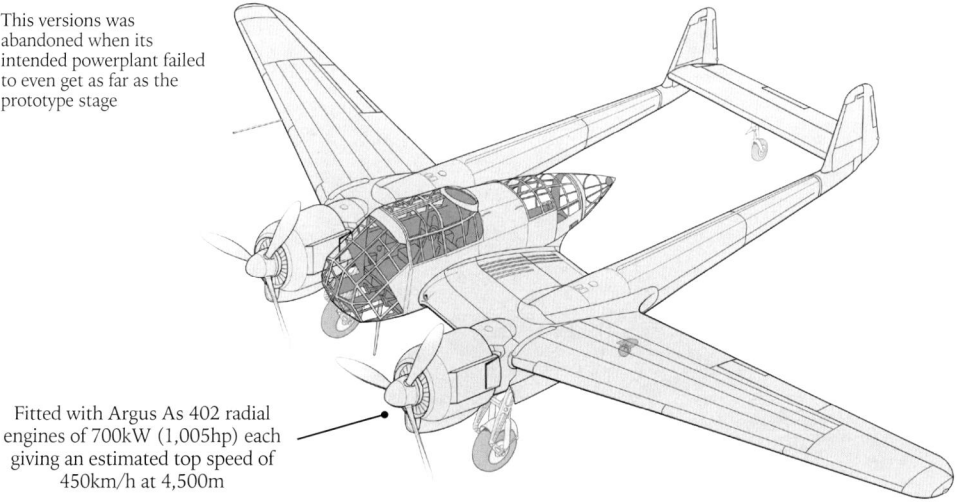

Fitted with Argus As 402 radial engines of 700kW (1,005hp) each giving an estimated top speed of 450km/h at 4,500m

Note
Little is known about the As 402 engine, as no accounts detail it in any way. The As 403 however is known, in two variants, and as this is a 2,500+ or 3,000+ hp engine, it would be pretty big. Argus have no history of building true radial engines, but they did previously built the mighty As 5, which was a 24-cylinder engine made by joining six 4-cylinder banks on a common crank. We therefore think it is most likely that the As 402 was along similar lines, thus being more of an 'X' (or 'star') configuration than a true radial engine. The most likely configuration is therefore four banks of three cylinders, although it might be six banks of 2-cylinders? Our isometric is based on the initial configuration but still has to be accepted as pure speculation, because no documentation survives on any likely configuration for either engine or airframe.

Camouflage & Markings

This is the Fw 189 V1 prior application of any camouflage and markings, so it is probably a pale green overall, which is slightly darker than the RLM 02 we all know

As always, I will start by saying that nothing is certain when trying to determine colours from old black and white photographs. The best you can make is an educated, and with luck, intelligent guess using both photographic and documentary evidence. The regulations with regard to the camouflage and markings of Luftwaffe aircraft during the war period are well known and most survive, the problem is that at the front line when the regulations changed it was highly unlikely that the ground crew rushed out to paint every aircraft in their charge, it was simply not practical. Also, in Nazi Germany, as the war situation worsened during 1944 and 1945 the haste with which machines were needed at the front

Fw 189 V1, D-OPVN, in flight, showing the standard RLM 70/71/65 scheme, but with German civil registration applied to the wings and booms

A good comparison, first here (top) you have the Fw 189 V1a, carrying civil registration letters and swastikas on the tails. The hard-edged demarcation between upper and lower colours is very evident. The second shot (below) of the Fw 189 V1a shows it after being modified (although not as the V1b), with the lower nacelle unit (which now can't be seen over the wing tip), but the most noticeable additions are the two thin yellow bands around the tail boom that look to be very roughly applied: see p95 for a colour profile of this machine in a reported RLM 61/62/63 scheme and compare it with this photo to see if you feel that scheme is likely

Camouflage & Markings
Prototypes

Nice in-flight shot of the Fw 189 V2, D-OVHD, showing the registration under the wings and the hard-edged nature of the camouflage pattern and demarcation between upper and lower colours

Nice clear starboard side view of the Fw 189 V3, still marked as D-ORMH but with Argus propellers fitted. Note the aerial mast on the top of the nacelle, the early single-leg undercarriage units and the early engine nacelles

Old photos can be deceptive, as this top view of the Fw 189 V5 (BQ+AZ) proves because it looks as it the upper surfaces are camouflaged, but other shots of this machine clearly show it is a uniform colour overall; often quoted as RLM 02, but it is grey, so more likely RLM 63

A very useful shot showing what looks to be a mottled scheme of greens, but what is identified as 'Dark Green and Olive Brown'. This machine is V7+IJ of 1/1.(H)32 operating in Russia so the colours are almost certainly field-mixed shades and not official ones (many list the brown shade as RLM 79, but the contrasts in this image are just not enough for the lighter areas to be anything other than a brown, not yellow, shade?). We think the base colour is in fact the original RLM 70/71, with the brown mix just applied to break up its overall dark effect

Camouflage & Markings 3
Production

When the Fw 189 was built it was initially in a mix of primer and bare metal, as seen here in this lovely period colour photo

An Fw 189A-1, H1+NH of Aufkl Gr (H) 12 parked on an aerodrome. Note the outlined 'N', probably done in white, and the yellow band around the boom, which is quite wide, but not placed far aft, nor under the cross or code letters

An Fw 189A-1 claimed to be in Russia, which oddly sports no yellow under the wing tips nor any around the tail booms. A Heinkel He 46 can be seen in the background along with what looks like a captured North American Yale? The lack of theatre colours combined with the presence of the other aircraft makes us think this is not Russia but a training base somewhere in Northern Germany

A nice period colour image showing the demarcation of the upper and lower colours on this brand-new Fw 189A-1. Note that although the demarcation is quite tight, it is still sprayed on and thus soft-edged. It is also interesting to note the curved line to the leading and trailing edges, with the former actually done well inboard of the leading edge

| Camouflage & Markings | 3 |
| Production | 85 |

This shot of Fw 189A, H1+HN, from Auskl. Gr. (H)12 clearly shows the yellow bands around the tail booms, in this instance applied underneath the crosses

This shot of an Fw 189 in Russia shows the yellow wing tip theatre markings, plus the application of the individual aircraft letter 'F' under each outer wing panel and on each tail boom; the latter is applied over the four-letter codes previously used and is apparently done in RLM 76, which we doubt considering the possible era

and the lack of paints when they got there meant that inevitably the regulations were adhered to less and less. This whole subject is massive, you can write volumes on the subject, but we will try and keep it concise. Just remember, nothing is an absolute when it comes to camouflage and markings, and nothing illustrates that more graphically than late-war Luftwaffe C&M!

Although we all use the term 'RLM' to prefix Luftwaffe colours it should be noted that in period documents the only colour designated in this manner was RLM 02, the rest were simply prefixed 'Farbton' (shade/tone/hue of a colour). The confusion lies in the fact that the main paint manufacturer (Warnecke und Böhm) issued paint charts that prefixed all colours with 'RLM', followed by Farbton 74, 75, 76 etc. However for consistency throughout this book we will prefix all colours with 'RLM'

Fw 189 Prototypes (V-series)

See the individual entries for each prototype in Section 2 for their camouflage and marking details.

Production Fw 189 Series

The standard scheme for production A-series machines was RLM 70 Schwarzgrün and RLM 71 Dunkelgrün in straight-edged disruptive camouflage pattern on the upper surfaces and down the tail booms and engine cowls, with RLM 65 Hellblau underneath. Demarcation between these tended to be straight-edged, but their low level resulted in sweeping curves up to the wing trailing and leading edges. Usually the entire vertical fin and rudder was in the upper colours, as the demarcation along the booms followed a straight line; the entire

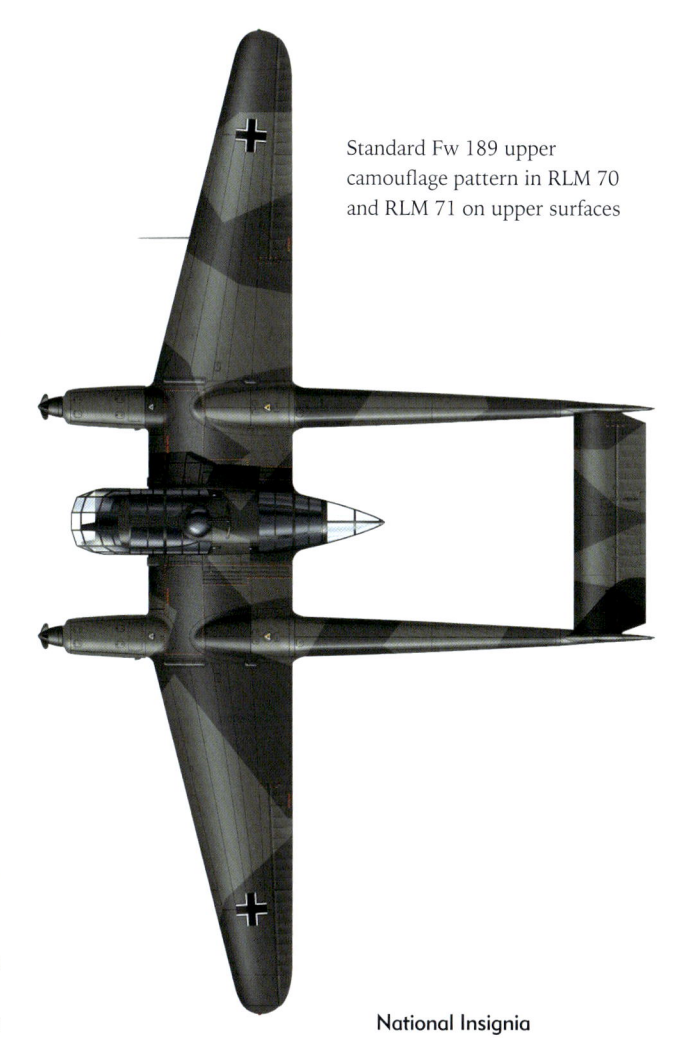

Standard Fw 189 upper camouflage pattern in RLM 70 and RLM 71 on upper surfaces

National Insignia

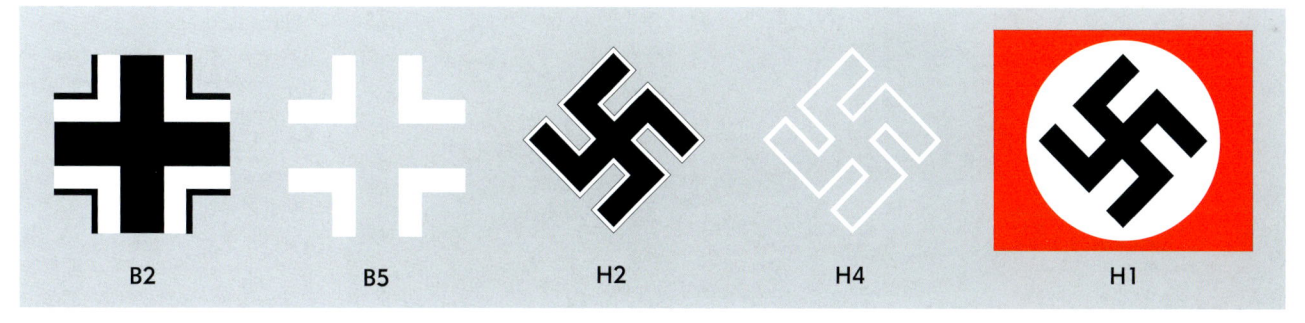

| B2 | B5 | H2 | H4 | H1 |

rudder was in the upper scheme, so only the lower edges of the boom/vertical fin saw any RLM 65. Theatre bands comprised 1,000mm bands under each wing tip and a 500mm band around the aft of each tail boom, or, underneath the cross. Unit codes and individual aircraft numbers were applied in black for the former with a combination of colours for the latter usually comprising a coloured thin edge to the black character, although you will also see coloured letters with white edges as well. These codes were applied either side of the cross on the tail boom, orientated the same way so they read left to right regardless of which side of the aircraft you are looking. A swastika, usually of H2 style was applied to the vertical fin, about half way up with no part of it crossing on to the rudder. Above this, usually following the panel line for the cap of the vertical fin, was the Werke number, usually applied as 'W.Nr.xxxx' in black, with a stencil type of character often employed for the number itself. The wing and tail boom crosses are usually of Type B2 and those under the wings are applied inboard of the yellow tips. You can find images of machines with the individual aircraft letter (the third in the four-character system) applied under the wing tip on the yellow area, with this being the case under each wing. Yellow was also often applied to the entire rudder and part or all of the engine cowlings. As the war came to a close another yellow band was applied to the remaining Fw 189s in accordance with the instruction issued on the 7th March 1945, and this was in the form of a 50cm wide band around the middle of each engine

Nice close-up of the wide yellow theatre band on the tail boom, which in this instance is situated aft of the crosses and codes, but not as far aft as you sometimes find it

Excellent top view of SI+EC again showing how irregular the mirror-wave pattern is, plus how close to the crosses it gets. The other Fw 189 in the top of the photo is in the mix of primer and bare metal, so these images of SI+EC were official ones to show the 'new' scheme

nacelle. This was almost certainly to aid recognition for ground troops, as few Luftwaffe aircraft were still flying by this stage in the war.

To break up the dark expanses of the overall upper colours, you will see many Fw 189s with a wavy, irregular application of RLM 65 on the upper surfaces; it has been said that this colour is RLM 76 Lichtblau or even RLM 75 Grauviolett, but we doubt that considering the era. Initially this was thought to have been applied by the units operating the type in the northern regions (Finland, Norway and Russia), but close study of construction numbers in relation to photos seems to show that it was done at factory level by Aero in Prague. This application was overall on the upper surfaces and is not to be confused by the application of RLM 65 (some again state RLM 76), over areas to create a soft-edged pattern. This was seen in certain areas of Northern Europe and results in a scheme that looks to be soft-edged, but is in fact just the squiggles applied in this manner over the existing RLM 70/71 hard-edged scheme and was again in an attempt to reduce the darkness of the original scheme over the terrain in which these machines operated (snow, scrubland, tundra, woodland etc., but not the dark mass of green seen further south in Europe where the type initially saw service). The other scheme seen in Russia is quoted as being 'Dark Green and Olive Brown' applied with the green as the overall base colour and then the olive

Port side of SI+EC, showing how the mirror-wave pattern was applied to the booms and tail; the codes have been touched-up on this print, as they were most likely applied after the mirror wave

Camouflage & Markings

Production

One of a series of images showing Fw 189A-1, SI+EC, with the mirror-wave pattern applied over the upper surfaces in RLM 76. Note that the application of the waves is not consistent when you look at things like the port and starboard engine nacelles, proving it was applied freehand to no official drawings etc

V7+IG of Aufkl Gr (H)32 showing the uneven application of RLM 65 or 76 to the upper surfaces in an attempt to break up the overall dark mass of the basic RLM 70/71 scheme

An Fw 189A-2, as identified by the spent ammo chutes under the fuselage, shows the white winter distemper applied to machines in Russia etc. Note the lack of this distemper on the majority of the canopy framework or on the front sections of the propeller spinners

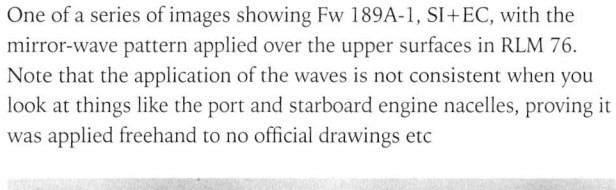

An unidentified Fw 189A in winter distemper warms up its engines. Note the wear on the outer faces of the port engine nacelle, whilst the inner face of the starboard nacelle is almost perfect. This machine differs in that it has all of the propellers and spinners done in white, many just had the back sections done, but it does exhibit the usual lack of distemper on the upper canopy framework

Winter distempers wore off very quickly resulting in very patchy aircraft, as seen here on Fw 189A-1, 5D+KH, of Auskl Gr (H)31

When you look at the port side of 5D+KH from Auskl Gr (H)31, you can see the distemper has worn off even more on this side

Camouflage & Markings 3
Production

Once the winter distemper really starts to wear off and the winter passes, you will see examples as heavily weathered as this Fw 189A

An interesting shot shows Fw 189A-2, 5D+EH after its starboard wheel went through the ice, because it seems to show that the winter whitewash was not applied to the fabric elements of the control surfaces. This makes sense otherwise the unit would have to be retrimmed due to the extra weight of the distemper

A contradictory application, here you see an Fw 189A-2, 4E+MK of 2./(H)13 on the Eastern Front in 1943 with distemper upper surfaces and then black temporarily and roughly applied to the undersides for night operations. Note the contrast of the original (faded) black of the underwing cross centre and the newly applied black elsewhere. The lighter shades on the mid-sections of the tail boom and nacelles are, we suspect, the base scheme with some of the white removed, while you can see just how high the demarcation on the inside of the tail booms seems to be

A well known shot, this Fw 189A-2, 4E+TK of 2./(H)13 is shown wrecked and used for spares in Russia during 1943. It exhibits the winter white distemper, but you can see that in this instance the canopy framework was painted as well. The '4E' of the codes are a 5th the size of the remaining letters

In this shot of an Fw 189A-2 in Russia you can see how the white distemper has been applied to create the shape of a bird on the nacelle. Also of note is the mottle edge demarcation wrapping round the wing leading edge

A front view of Fw 189A-2, 4E+MK of 2./(H)13 in which you can see the odd demarcation along the inner faces of the port and starboard booms. The photo also confirms that the underside of the tailplane was black

Camouflage & Markings

Production

A well known shot, but one of the very few showing a Fw 189A-1 nightfighter, seen here at Werneuchen. You can clearly see the radar, oblique-firing cannon and flame dampers, plus the mottling of RLM 76 on the upper surfaces. This was sprayed on and is very irregular, with the aft cowl line being used as the demarcation point, which is very different from the earlier curved demarcation seen in this area

brown is applied in an irregular fashion to produce a mix of bands and blotches from the green below. The demarcation of the two colours looks to be hard-edged, so this was not sprayed on and there is much debate as to the likely colours involved; we suspect it is in fact RLM 70/71 with a field mixed 'brown' shade applied over the top (all colours mixed make brown, so the actual colour could vary greatly and may even be a case of the Luftwaffe using up captured VVS paint stocks?) Winter operations again called for breaking up the dark upper colours, so these machines had whitewash (distemper) applied roughly to all the upper surfaces, usually going around the swastika and crosses, but not that precisely and you will also see the white encroaching the yellow bands on each tail boom. This paint wore off quickly, so these machines soon lost it over large areas and there were the inevitable touch-ups. Night operations and those machines operating far enough north to experience the long winters, had the undersides painted black (RLM 22), following the same demarcation as used for the RLM 65. Later this night scheme was revised to see the application of RLM 74 Graugrün and RLM 75 Grauviolett applied on the upper surfaces and black underneath. There are claims that the entire airframe was black, with a dense and random mottling of one of the greys on the upper surfaces, but this seems unlikely. The demarcation between the upper and lower colours is extremely soft, though, as if it is all airbrushed on. Machines used in the nightfighter role usually only had a single identifying letter applied aft of the cross on either side of the tail boom.

Only one unit operated the type in the Middle East and that was 4.(H)/12 as part of Fliegerführer Afrika. Their machines adopted the desert scheme of RLM 79 Sandgelb on the upper surfaces with irregular blotches of RLM 80 Grün, while the undersides were in RLM 78 Hellblau. Theatre markings comprised the lower tips of each wing being in white (approx. to a point 1m inboard of the tip) and bands around each tail boom, towards the rear. There are published sources showing machines in the RLM 79 upper scheme, but with the blotches now more densely applied and in RLM 71 Dunkelgrün with the undersides in RLM 65. These usually apply to those machines used on the Northern Front and probably actually relate to the application of a field-mixed brown over the standard RLM 70/71 scheme to break up the darkness of that scheme for the terrain these machines would be operating over (e.g. tundra) and this will explain the

This shot of Fw 189A, W/Nr.125715, 5H+RK of NAGr 16 in Germany in 1945 shows the 50cm yellow bands applied around the cowlings which were adopted on the 7th March 1945

Camouflage & Markings 3 — Production

Oddity 1; Fw 189A, KC+JN used as a training aircraft for a Ju 88 unit in the Baltic states, shown with a large '109' in white on the tail

Oddity 2; Fw 189A, W/Nr.0241 seen wrecked at Berlin-Gatow in the summer 1945 with a single kill marking on the rudder

Oddity 3; A crashed Fw 189A of (H)31 with some sort of slogan painted on the engine nacelle?

use of the 'later' RLM 79 with the 'older' RLM 71 and 65 and it is therefore most likely that the areas stated as RLM 71 are in fact a mix of exposed areas of RLM 70 and 71 in the original splinter pattern.

The B-series is usually depicted as being RLM 02 Grau overall, but that would be at odds with the usual procedure for training aircraft and it is much more likely that these aircraft were all finished in RLM 63 Lichtgrau overall. Codes and swastikas on the production B-1 series machines match those seen on the A-series, but some of the B-0 pre-production machines have a very small H2 swastika on the tail, about half the size seen on the B-1s. Again the four-character codes were applied around the crosses on the tail booms, but the training nature of the type meant they never carried any yellow bands on the tail booms or under each wing tip. Once again unit badges were often applied to the outward-facing cowling of each engine.

Operational Markings

See the colour profiles on pages 96 to 101 for a selection of unit markings and insignia applied to the operational Fw 189 series.

This image is often quoted as the V6, but various aspects make it more likely it is one of the Fw 189C-0s produced. The overall drab RLM 70/71/65 scheme remained on the C-series, made even darker by the lack of glazing on the new nacelle. Note that this machine does not have any Stammkennzeichen (code letters) applied

Camouflage & Markings
Production

An Fw 189A-1 of 5./(H)12 with the unit badge on the nacelle

The unit badge of 2./(H)31

The unit badge of 6./(H)15, comprised a stylised eagle over a tank

The unit badge of 3./(H)12Pz in Russia, the raven motif was chosen due to the unit's commanding office Oblt Raabe [Raven]

In service the Fw 189B adopted the same RLM 70/71 over 65 scheme of the A-series. This machine was operated by the flight instructor school at Brandenburg-Briest and this is probably the V5 airframe. Note the large unit badge on the nose along with the large '1', which is probably yellow

Foreign Service

Bulgarian Air Force

The Fw 189s operated by Bulgaria retained their overall Luftwaffe camouflage and markings but had the crosses on the wings and tail booms replaced with a similar-sized white square on which was placed the black Cross of St. Andrew. Depending on the area of operation these machines can be found with yellow tail boom bands along with half of the underside of each outer wing panel (actually thereby going underneath the white square/black cross insignia), or with these markings plus the rudder and each engine cowling also in yellow, or with the rudder yellow and the tail boom band and wing panels now in white; note that some post-war artwork shows the application of white to the upper wing tips

Fw 189A, FO+63 of the Hungarian Air Force is inspected by everyone on its arrival with the squadron. The higher contrast shows the tail band to be yellow, but it is impossible to confirm the overall scheme as being one colour, or the Luftwaffe RLM 70/71 version?

A Bulgarian Air Force Fw 189A with the Tzyklon (eye) motif on the engine cowling

as well, but we have found no period images to support this. The identification codes for these machines were numeric, consisting of a single (1 to 9) or double (10 onwards) character in white, aft of the national insignia on each tail boom; this was only on the outer face. Usually all of these machines carried the famous 'Tzyklon (eye)' marking on the outer engine cowling; as the name implies, this was an eye, mainly made up of white outlines, but with a blue iris and nine or ten white lines radiating downwards from it. When Bulgaria changed sides in September 1944 the national insignia changed from the black cross to a white roundel with a green centre and a red horizontal bar.

Hungarian Air Force

Hungarian machines tend to be a mix of two schemes, the first is the standard two-colour green over light blue Luftwaffe scheme, but later some machines seem to sport an overall green over blue scheme. As we write, we have no idea if the latter green and blue scheme

This Pegasus squadron motif was applied to the cowling, this is probably a machine from 4/1 Kozelfelderito Szazad, Hungarian AF

A lovely shot of a Slovakian Fw 189A-2, showing the style and location of the national insignia. Of note is the size of the new markings in comparison with the original Luftwaffe crosses, which were much smaller and more outboard, and traces of which you can still just make out on the wings

used Luftwaffe colours, or locally manufactured ones? National insignia comprised a black square with a white X superimposed on it and we suspect the dimensions of the black square were the same as those for the Luftwaffe cross. Usually a yellow band was applied on the aft of each tail boom, and this could range in size and location from narrower and right back on the tail transit line, or three-times as wide running forward from the same point. The tips of each wing underside were also done in yellow, following the same demarcation point as this marking on Luftwaffe examples. No swastika was carried, instead the national colours were applied in 50cm wide stripes from the top of the fin/tail downwards; red at the top, then white, then green. Usually a four-digit code was carried with known examples being F6+04 and DI+ZJ; the former is from 3/1 Kozelfelderito Szazad and the latter from 4/1 Kozelfelderito Szazad.

Rumanian Air Force

Initially all the machines used in Rumania were for training and they retained both their Luftwaffe camouflage and markings. After the coup d'état on the 23rd August 1944 the remaining machines received the later style of national markings, comprising the red/yellow/blue roundel, applied to the upper and lower wings and on each tail boom. These machines all show signs of the original Luftwaffe markings being painted out in a light green colour. The entire rudder, tail boom band and wing tips were all painted white. No other markings, nor unit identification, seem to have been applied

Slovakian Air Force

All machines operated by this nation retained their overall Luftwaffe camouflage. The national insignia was identical in size to the Luftwaffe cross, but the centre black section was applied in blue and in the very

Initially Rumanian Air Force examples flew with Luftwaffe markings, but after August 1944, as seen here, the new Rumanian AF roundels were applied

middle, only on the blue section, was superimposed a red dot. These were applied above and below the wings, whilst the crosses on the tail booms were deleted. The swastika on the vertical fin/rudder was replaced by another cross, again with the blue areas and red dot in the centre and this was of dimensions that put it across the fin and rudder unit. Usually the aircraft also carried the yellow theatre bands around the mid-section of each tail boom. No codes or other identifying marks seem to have been applied to these machines.

VVS

A number of Fw 189s were captured by Russia during WWII and one was tested by the NII VVS, so it had all its Luftwaffe markings removed and red stars applied to the upper wing, each tail boom and right across the fin and rudder. Photos do not seem to show red stars under the wings for some reason and no other markings were applied. There is another well-known captured machine being used in Russia and this again had the Luftwaffe markings removed and red stars put in their place, although this time that also included those under the wings; the type had the yellow theatre tips, which remained, so the underwing stars were well inboard,

An Fw 189A-2 of the Slovakian Air Force seen at Trenčín airfield

Nice shot of the Fw 189 captured and tested by the NII (Research Institute) of the VVS and complete with red stars on the wings, tail booms and across both vertical fin and rudder

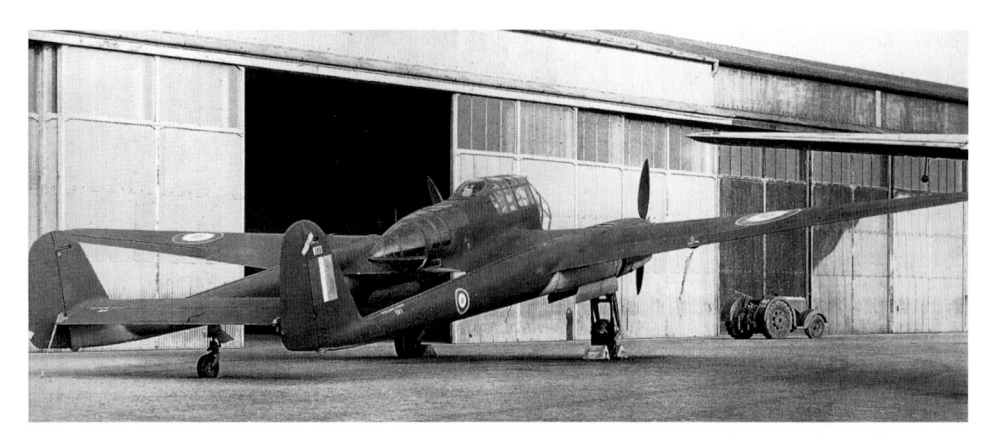

Camouflage & Markings 3
Foreign Service

One Fw 189A-2, W/Nr.0173, was captured by the RAF and returned to the UK, it is seen here in RAF markings at Farnborough in October 1945. Sadly it was later destroyed in gales whilst stored outside at RAF Brize Norton

A machine captured and flown in Russia, this machine still has the unit badge of its previous operator (Aufkl Gr (H) 16) on the engine nacelle

alongside the bomb racks. The yellow band around each tail boom was retained and the swastika on the fin was covered with another red star running across the vertical fin and rudder. No other markings can be seen but the type retained the unit badge of its previous owners on the outer face of each engine cowling, this comprising a Germanic-looking rampant lion surmounted on a black-edged white shield.

We would also recommend the following titles for those wishing to read more on the complex subject of Luftwaffe camouflage and markings.
- Luftwaffe Camouflage & Markings 1933-1945 Volume Two by K.A. Merrick & J. Kiroff
  (Classic Publications 2005 ISBN: 1-903223-39-3)
- Luftwaffe Camouflage & Markings 1933-1945 – Photo Archive 1 by K.A. Merrick, E.J. Creek & B. Green
  (Midland Publishing 2007 ISBN: 978-1-85780-275-7)
- The Official Monogram Painting Guide to German Aircraft 1935-1935 by K.A. Merrick & T.H. Hitchcock
  (Monogram Aviation Publications 1980
  ISBN: 0-914144-29-4)

Fw 189A-2 in very neatly applied distemper, with the propellers all remaining in RLM 70 and the unit badge of a Viking longship on the engine cowl

Fw 189A-2, 5H+RK as found by Allied troops at the end of the war, this machine has yellow rudders and 50cm bands on the cowls, as per the March 1945 instructions

Focke-Wulf Fw 189 V1a (modified) Uhu, D-OPVN, Erpobungstelle, Rechlin, spring 1939
RLM 61/62/63 upper surfaces with RLM 65 undersides. White spinner. Black registration letters, repeated above and below wings. RLM 23 band across vertical tail surfaces with black Swastika over a white disk (*Author's note: This scheme is quoted/shown in many published works, but surviving images do not seem to show enough contrast to allow for such a three-colour scheme?*)

Focke-Wulf Fw 189 V4 Uhu, W.Nr. 0001, D-OCHO, 1938-39
RLM 63 overall with black registration letters on tail booms, above and below wings. RLM 23 Rot (red) band across vertical tail surfaces with black Swastika over a white disk. Note chemical containers below wings

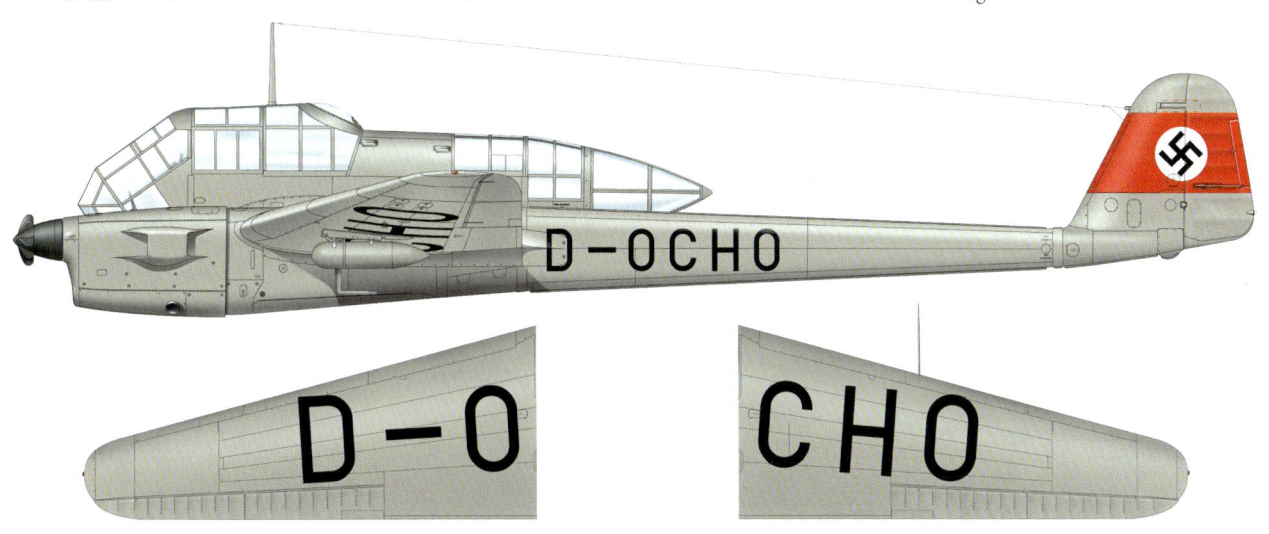

Focke Wulf Fw 189 V6 Uhu, NA+WB, 5 (Schacht)/St.LG 2 Luftwaffe, 1940
RLM 70/71 upper surfaces with RLM 65 undersides. Registration is carried in black on tail booms and below wings

Focke-Wulf Fw 189B-1 Uhu, W.Nr.0010, BQ+AZ, 9(H)/LG2 Luftwaffe, 1940
Medium green (RLM 62 or 71?; initially painted RLM 63 grey) overall with black lettering, the codes on the tail booms being repeated below the wings

Camouflage & Markings 3
Profiles, Side 2

©2015 Richard J. Caruana

Focke-Wulf Fw 189A-1 Uhu, C2+EH, 1.(H)/Aufkl. Gr.41 Luftwaffe, Eastern Front, spring 1942
RLM 70/71 upper surfaces with RLM 65 undersides. RLM 04 Gelb (yellow) below wingtips and bands around rear fuselage. Black codes, with 'E' repeated below wingtips. Scrap view shows the starboard side camouflage pattern

Focke-Wulf Fw 189A-1 Uhu, H1+BI, 3.(H)Pz./Aufkl. Gr.12 Luftwaffe, Don River area, 1942
RLM 70/71 upper surfaces with RLM 65 undersides. RLM 04 Gelb (yellow) underside of wingtips and bands around tail booms. Codes in black, with 'B' thinly outlined in red. Unit badge on engine cowling

Focke-Wulf Fw 189A-1 Uhu, S1+EG, of an unknown Luftwaffe reconnaissance unit
RLM 70/71 upper surfaces overpainted in RLM 76 'waves'; RLM 65 undersides. Black codes

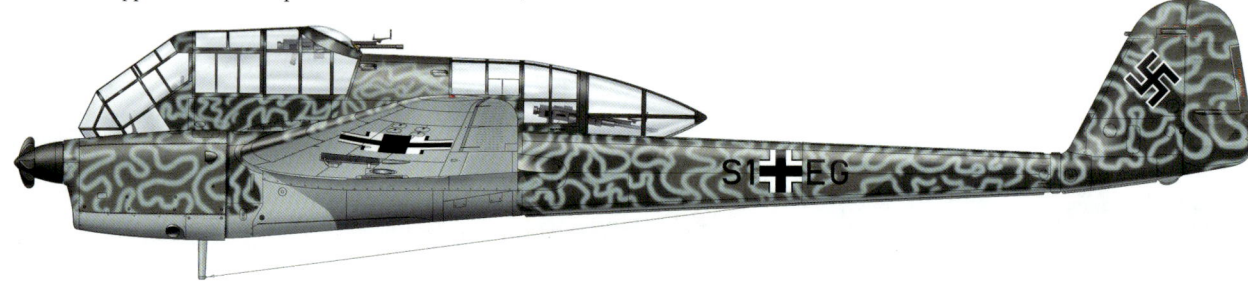

Focke-Wulf Fw 189A-1 Uhu, 4E+GK, 2.(H)/Aufkl. Gr.13 Luftwaffe, Russian Front, late 1942
RLM 70/71 upper surfaces with RLM 65 undersides. Black codes with 'G' in red, outlined in white, the latter repeated in black below each wingtip. RLM 04 Gelb (yellow) bands around tail booms and undersides of wingtips. Unit badge on engine cowlings

©2015 Richard J. Caruana

Camouflage & Markings
Profiles, Side 3

3

97

Focke-Wulf Fw 189A-1 Uhu, 5D+FH, 1.(H)/Aufkl. Gr.31 Luftwaffe, Russian Front, 1942
RLM 70/71 upper surfaces with RLM 65 undersides. RLM 04 Gelb (yellow) underside of wingtips and bands around tail booms. Codes in black, with 'F' thinly outlined in white. Unit badge on engine cowlings

Focke-Wulf Fw 189A-1 Uhu, +HL, 3/NA Gr.1 Luftwaffe, Ukraine, March 1943
RLM 70/71 upper surfaces overpainted with blotches of temporary white; RLM 65 undersides. Yellow undersides of wingtips and bands around rear fuselage. Codes in black (with the first two overpainted), with 'H' in RLM 04 Gelb (yellow), the latter repeated below wingtips in black. Unit badge on engine cowlings

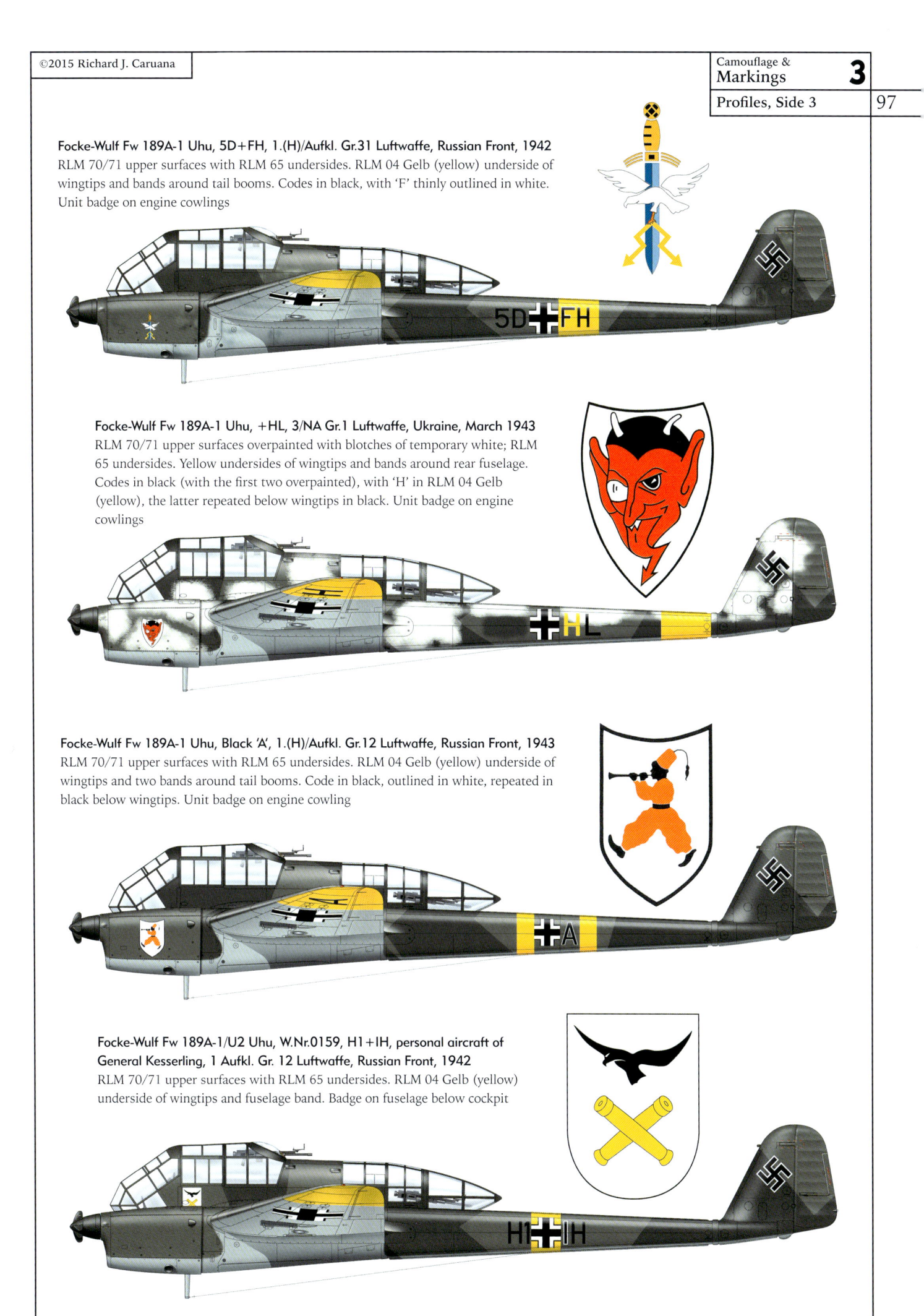

Focke-Wulf Fw 189A-1 Uhu, Black 'A', 1.(H)/Aufkl. Gr.12 Luftwaffe, Russian Front, 1943
RLM 70/71 upper surfaces with RLM 65 undersides. RLM 04 Gelb (yellow) underside of wingtips and two bands around tail booms. Code in black, outlined in white, repeated in black below wingtips. Unit badge on engine cowling

Focke-Wulf Fw 189A-1/U2 Uhu, W.Nr.0159, H1+IH, personal aircraft of General Kesserling, 1 Aufkl. Gr. 12 Luftwaffe, Russian Front, 1942
RLM 70/71 upper surfaces with RLM 65 undersides. RLM 04 Gelb (yellow) underside of wingtips and fuselage band. Badge on fuselage below cockpit

AA06/31/97 · Valiant Wings Publishing · Issued: February 2015

Camouflage & Markings 3
Profiles, Side 4

©2015 Richard J. Caruana

Focke-Wulf Fw189A-2 Uhu, W.Nr.2317, 5D+CK, 2.(H)/ Aufkl. Gr.31 Luftwaffe, 1943
Standard RLM 70/71 upper surfaces overpainted in temporary white; RLM 65 undersides. RLM 04 below wingtips and band on tail booms. Black codes with red 'C', the latter repeated in black below wingtips. Unit badge on engine cowling

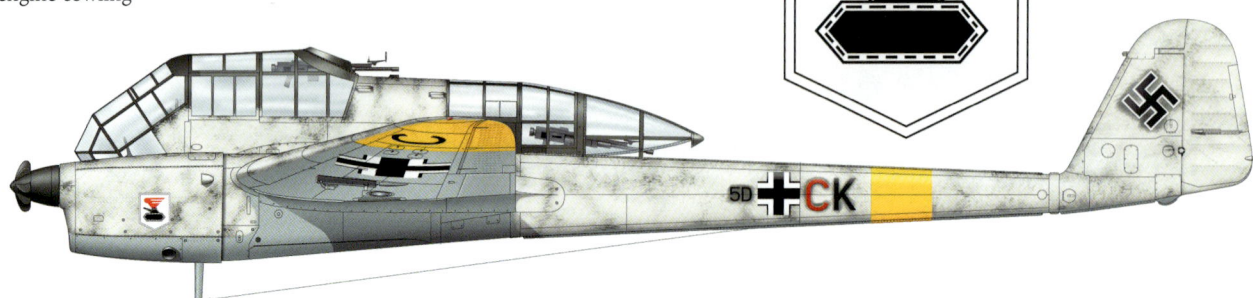

Focke-Wulf Fw189A-2 Uhu, 2./Aukl. Gr.14 Luftwaffe, Salzburgh, 1943
RLM 70/71 upper surfaces with RLM 65 undersides. RLM 04 Gelb (yellow) engine cowling and spinner, rudders and wingtips. Codes in black with RLM 23 Rot (red) 'R', outlined in white

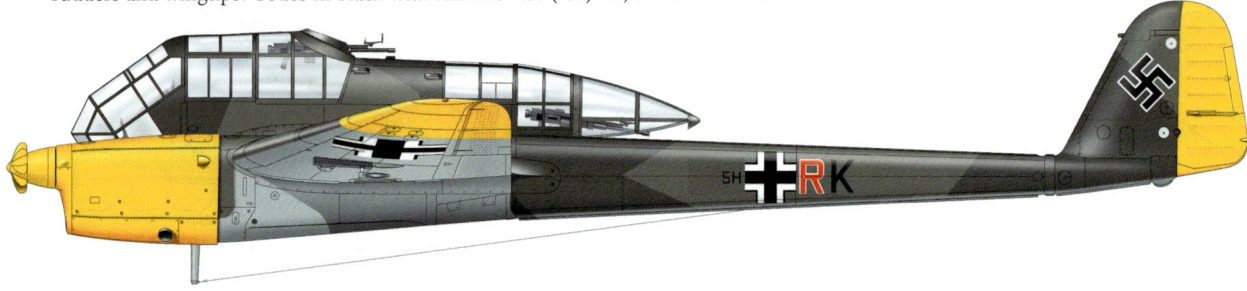

Focke-Wulf Fw 189A-1 Uhu, V7+1E, 1.(H)/Aufkl. Gr.32 Luftwaffe, 1943
RLM 70/71 upper sufaces overpainted in temporary white with RLM 65 undersides. RLM 04 Gelb (yellow) undersides of wingtips and band around lower half of tail booms. Codes in black with white 'E', the latter repeated in black below the wings. 'Bird' motif on engine cowling

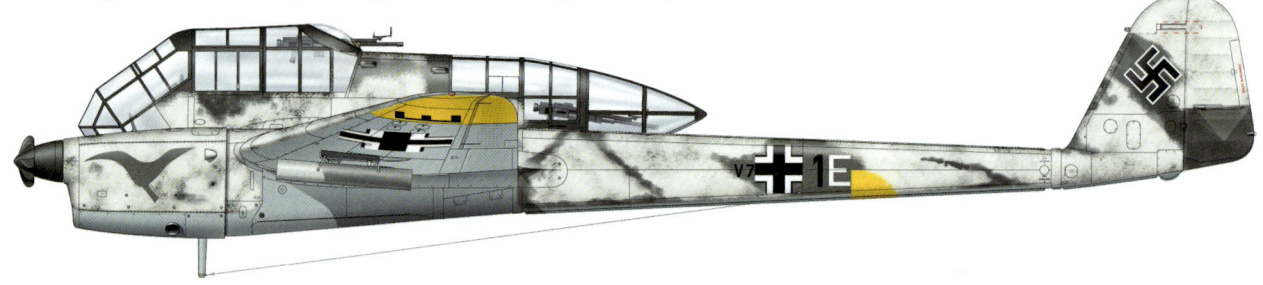

Focke-Wulf Fw-189A-1 Uhu, H1+EN, 5.(H)/Aufkl. Gr.12 Luftwaffe, Southern Russia, 1943
RLM 70/71 upper surfaces with RLM 65 undersides. RLM 04 Gelb (yellow) underside of wingtips and bands around tail booms. Codes in black, with 'E' outlined in white repeated in black only below wingtips. Unit badge on engine cowlings

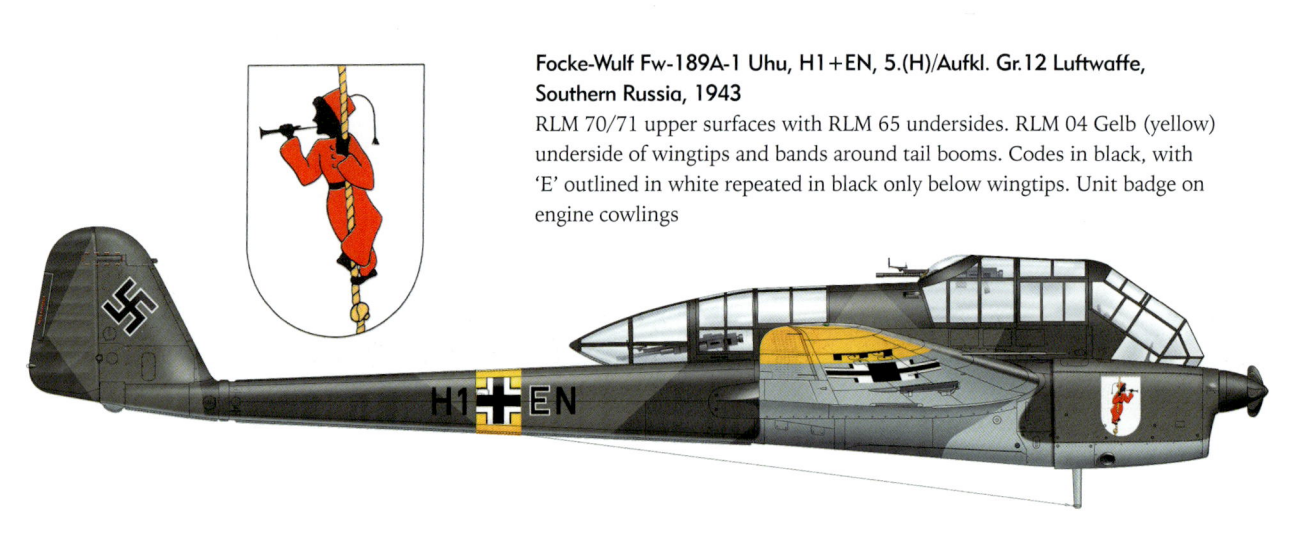

Camouflage & Markings Profiles, Side 5

Focke-Wulf Fw 189A-1 Uhu, White 'F', Luftwaffe, Nachtkette/NaGr 15, 1944
RLM 75 upper surfaces with mottling in RLM 76; RLM 22 Black undersides. All markings in white

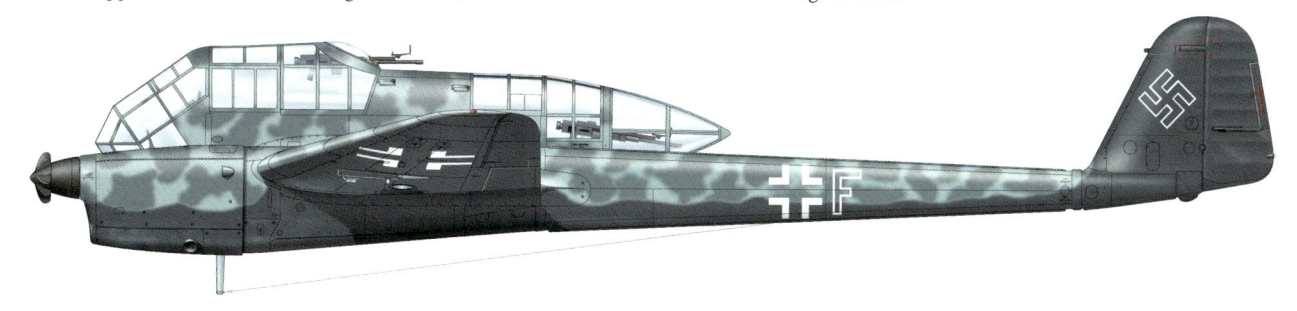

Focke-Wulf Fw 189A-2 Uhu, 17, No 331 Air Squadron, Bulgarian Air Force, Sarafowo, July 1944
RLM 70/71 upper surfaces with RLM 65 undersides. RLM 04 Gelb (yellow) Engine cowlings, spinners, undersides of wingtips, bands around rear of tail booms and rudders. Codes in white. National markings in six positions. 'Eye' motif on engine cowlings

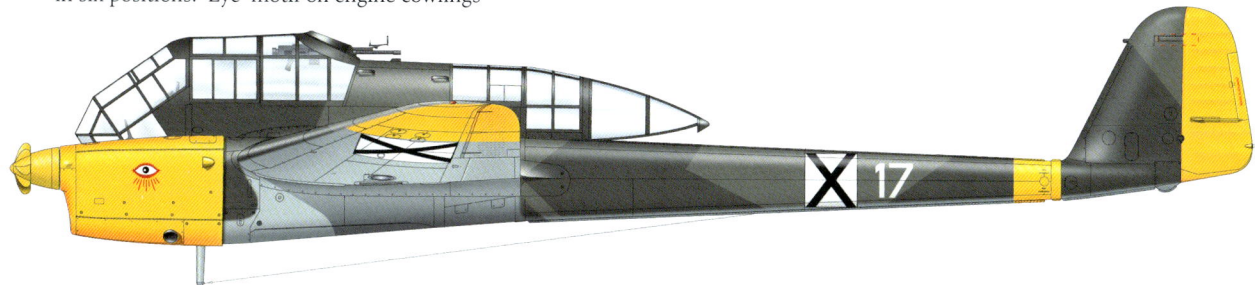

Focke-Wulf Fw 189A-1 Uhu, DI+ZJ, 4/1 Tactical Reconnaissance Squadron, Hungarian Air Force, Balicze, Russian Front, summer 1944
RLM 70/71 upper surfaces with RLM 65 undersides. RLM 04 Gelb (yellow) underside of wingtips and bands around tail booms. National markings in six positions and red/white/green bands around vertical tail surfaces (inner and outer faces). Red spinner on port engine, white spinner on starboard engine which has an unpainted natural metal cowling

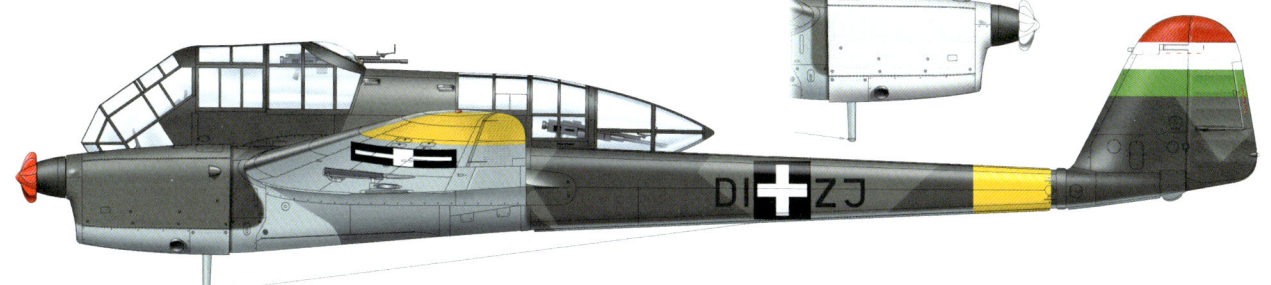

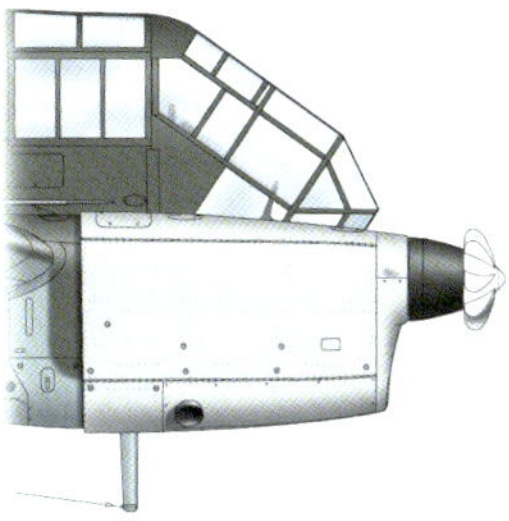

Focke-Wulf Fw 189A-1 Uhu, F0+55, 3/1 Tactical Reconnaissance Squadron, Hungarian Air Force, Russian Front, summer 1943
RLM 70/71 upper surfaces with RLM 65 undersides. RLM 04 Gelb (yellow) underside of wingtips and bands around tail booms. Black codes, national markings in six positions. Red/white/green tail bands on outer faces of vertical tail surfaces. White Pegasus insignia on engine cowling. 'Hableányka' (Sirene), and 'Ica' (Helena) in white on port and starboard tail booms respectively

Focke-Wulf Fw 189A-2 Uhu, Romanian Air Force
RLM 70/71 upper surfaces with RLM 65 undersides. RLM 04 Gelb (yellow) underside of wingtips and bands around rear of tail booms. National markings in six positions an rudder flash in blue/yellow/red

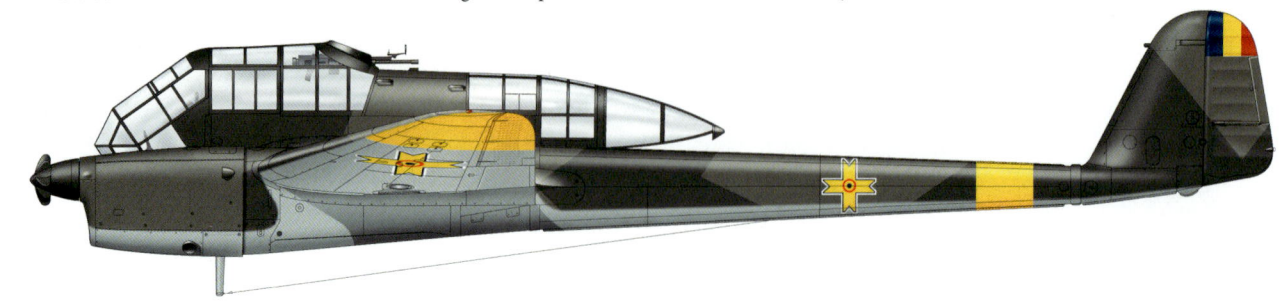

Focke-Wulf Fw 189A-1 Uhu, captured by Soviet forces, previously belonging to Stab NAGr.16 Luftwaffe
RLM 70/71 upper surfaces with RLM 65 undersides. All German markings overpainted. Red Stars on vertical tail surfaces, tail booms and below wings, the latter over a white background. Stab NAGr.16 badge believed to have been carried on starboard engine cowling only

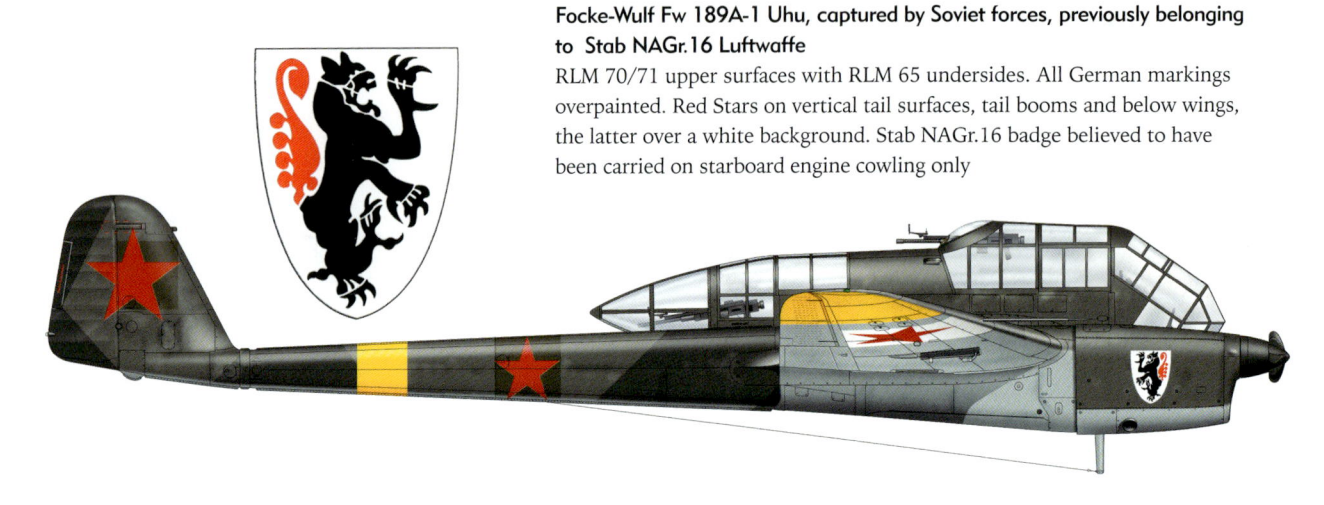

Focke-Wulf Fw 189A-1 Uhu (Air Min 27), W.Nr. 0173, captured and flown to Farnborough from Schleswig, 3 August 1945
RLM 70/71 upper surfaces with RLM 65 undersides. All German markings overpainted with RAF roundels. Yellow/Blue/White/Red roundels above wings

Focke-Wulf Fw 189A-1 Uhu, 'The Green Man', Norwegian Air Force, 1945-46
Dark Green (possibly RLM 70) overall with natural metal propellers and front of spinner. Post-1945 Norwegian national markings in six positions. Name and beer mug in white on engine cowlings, both sides

Camouflage & Markings 3
Profiles, Side 7

©2015 Richard J. Caruana

Focke-Wulf Fw 189A-2 Uhu, W.Nr.2340 in the provisional markings of the insurgent Slovaks, Tri Duby, September 1944
RLM 70/71 upper surfaces with RLM 65 undersides. RLM 04 Gelb (yellow) undersides of wingtips and bands around tail booms. National markings (with white and red reversed) in six positions. This aircraft went to the Soviet Union on 24 October 1944

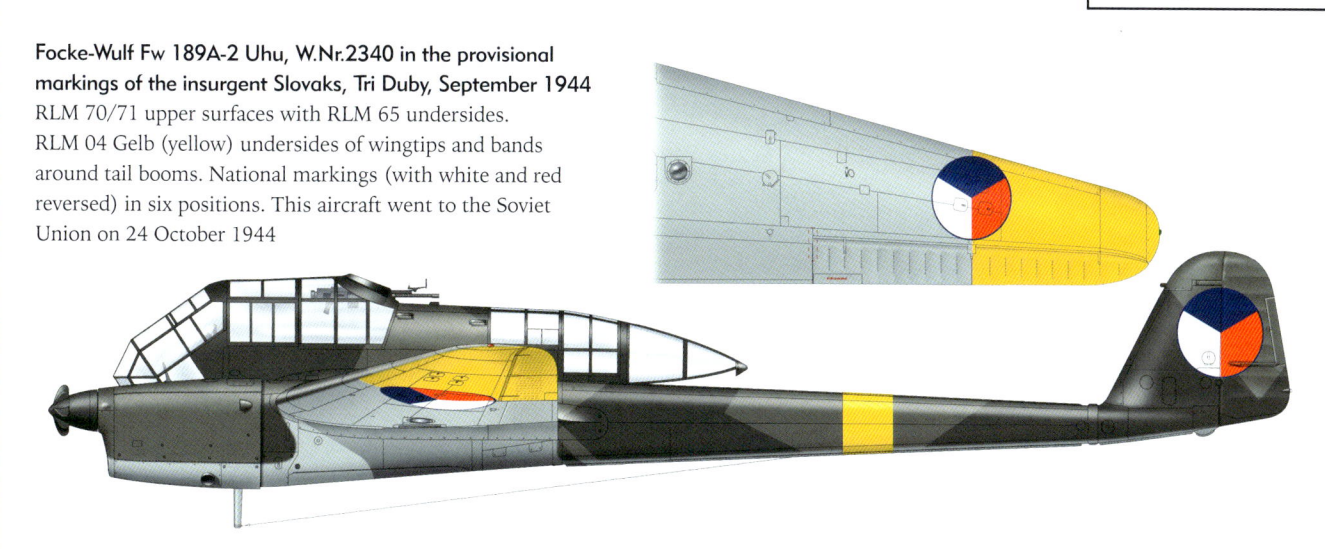

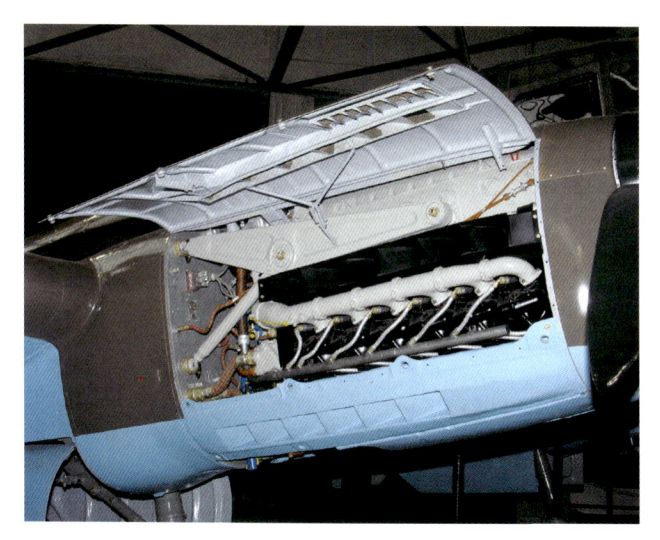

The As 411 was needed for the Si 204 so that is the best way to see one today, as in this view of the right side of that installation at Kbely (©*George Papadimitriou*)

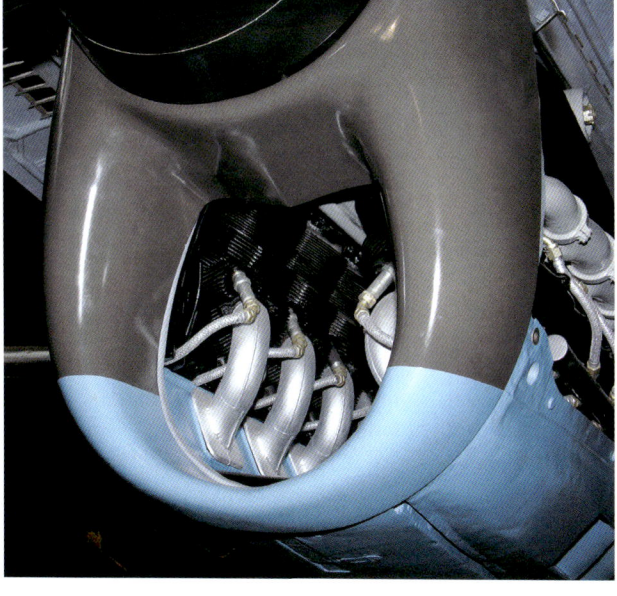

The front of the nacelle for the As 411 was slightly revised from that of the As 410, as seen here on the Si 204 at Kbely (©*George Papadimitriou*)

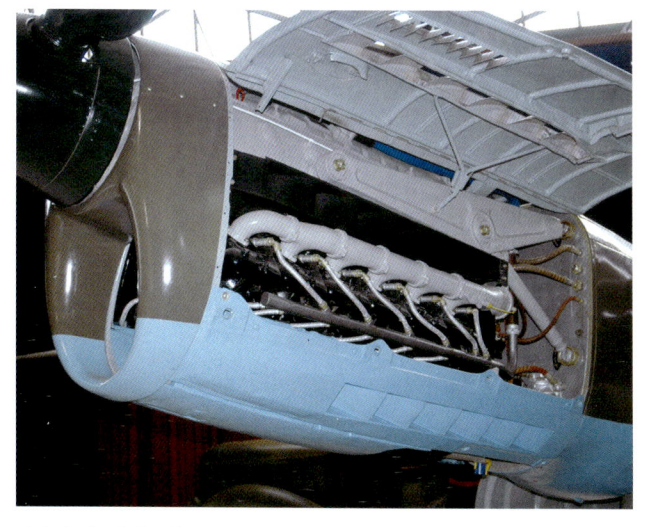

This is the left side of the As 411 in the Si 204 at Kbely
(©*George Papadimitriou*)

Here is a close-up of the Argus air-adjusted propeller as used from the V2 and seen here on the Si 204 (Aero C-3) at Kbely
(©*George Papadimitriou*)

Focke-Wulf Fw 189
Models 4
Fw 189A-1

Not a great many kits of the Fw 189 have been produced over the years, so what follows are superb builds of what we consider the 'best' option in 1/72nd by Libor Jekl and in 1/48th by Steve A. Evans, plus a sneak look at the new resin 1/32nd kit due from HpH in 2015.

Condor 1/72nd
Fw 189A-1
built and upgraded by Libor Jekl

From a modeller's perspective the Fw 189 does not seem to have been a priority for modelling companies over the decades because even those offered in the most popular scales have been quite limited. This situation has recently changed, though, with brand-new kits in 1/48th and 1/32nd thanks to Great Wall Hobby and HPH respectively. But while larger scale fans may enjoy state-of-the-art kits, modellers preferring 1/72nd scale have to rely upon an older, but still a pretty good kit, in the form of that offered by Condor (I exclude Airfix's relic, because it is just too ancient and primitive). The Condor label is used by the MPM group and it was distinguished from their usual production methods by the use of metal moulds and this particular kit is no exception. The base moulds were later modified and released by MPM as the trainer/communication B-version and the prototype ground-attack V6, along with minor modifications to offer the A-1 night fighter and A-2 versions; the basic A-1 has also appeared in Revell and Italeri boxes. Thanks to its nature the kit offers very good quality, even by today's standards, with subtle surface detail, fine engraved panel lines and a decently detailed cockpit and undercarriage. Additionally, CMK released a number of update sets and I eventually opted for the Interior Set (#7042) because it seemed essential if you want to display the canopies open, as well as the Detail Set (#7045) that offers a good mix of exterior details and an open engine bay plus canopy masks

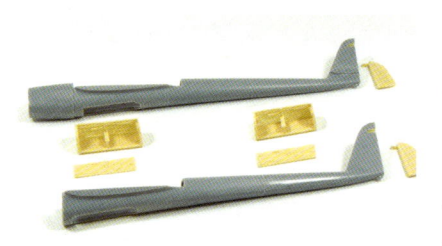

The components of the CMK undercarriage set

The resin wheel wells once they are painted and weathered are vastly superior to the detail offered in the kit

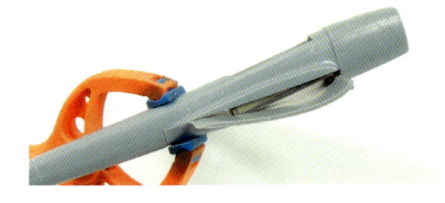

You will need to trim the aft/top of each resin wheel well, as well as the corresponding area inside the upper wing panel to get it all to fit

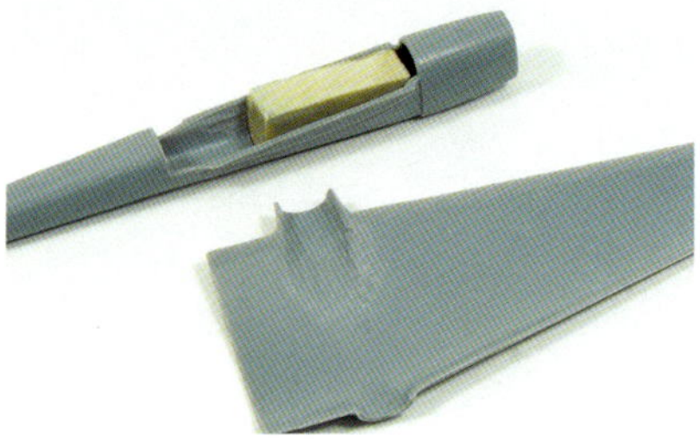

Here you can see the plastic ground off the inside of the upper wing panel to allow the resin wheel well to fit properly

The CMK interior set actually includes a completely new resin nacelle, seen here with the other parts of that set all primed with Mr Finishing Surfacer 1500 Black

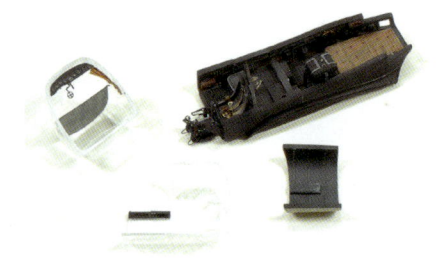

The new resin nacelle centre-section once painted

Focke-Wulf Fw 189
Models
Fw 189A-1

The lower mid-section in place along with the nose and mid-fuselage glazings; note the port front edge of the nose glazing does not match the nacelle

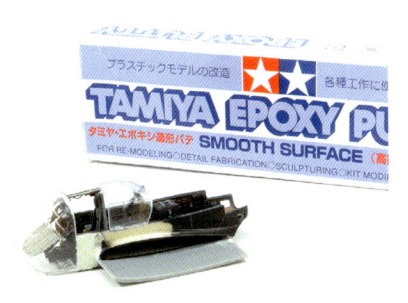

Tamiya epoxy putty is used to level the step between the nacelle and nose glazing on the port side

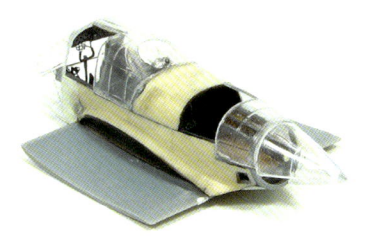

The mid-upper resin section in place, along with the aft glazing and cone; both front and aft sections have already had the opening glazed panels cut out

Assembly of the upper wing sections, tail booms and horizontal tailplane have to be done as one, to ensure all is aligned

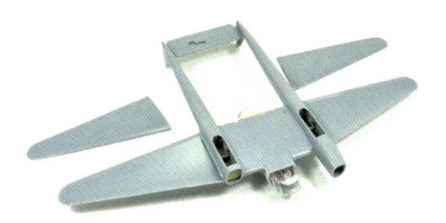

Once all the upper wing panels etc. are properly aligned, you can add the lower/outer wing panels

The Montex masks in place, along with the various raised panels that are missing on the kit and which were added with plasticard

(although I already had in my stash the Montex masks, which are intended for the Italeri reissue).

I commenced the build with modification of the tail booms which was necessary to install the resin wheel wells and engine. I cut off the port engine cowling, rudders and with a motor tool I removed some plastic from the areas around each wheel well. The booms were glued together and after trial-fitting, the painted resin wheel bays were inserted from above; at the same time I checked the fit with the upper wing halves, as these eventually needed some thinning from the inside as well.

I had made the openings for the rudder counterbalances too big, so these were filled with pieces of scrap resin and then sanded smooth.

Now I turned my attention to the fuselage gondola, which is supplied in the CMK set as a single-piece, cast resin replacement item. This part was first sprayed with Mr Surfacer 1500 (black) together with the other resin and etched components, followed by assembly of all the individual interior sub-assemblies. All the parts were then airbrushed with RLM 66 (GSI Creos H416) and the details were brush-painted with Vallejo acrylics. In

Models 4
Fw 189A-1

The openings in the cockpit area are filled with foam, then the canopy framework is sprayed with RLM 66 before the whole model is lightly primed. The engine is then added, so it is easy to check on the joint

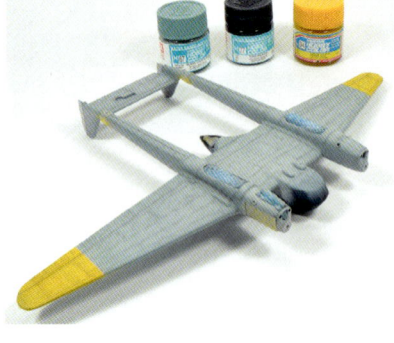

All the underside apertures are blocked with foam, the engine cowlings are temporarily attached with Blu Tack and then the wing tips are first painted yellow, followed by the whole underside being painted RLM 65

Most of the masking on the undersides is confined to the tail booms, tailplane and front and rear of the nacelle

The uppersurface RLM 70/71 scheme is only loosely applied freehand

AK Interactive's 'Worn Effect' is then sprayed onto the upper surfaces

White is applied in irregular patches, then the tail boom band and engine masks are removed

order to give the parts better contrast under the glazing, the edges were accentuated with a mid-grey colour followed by dry-brushing with light grey oil paint. In the front section of the 'greenhouse' I added the pilot's side curtain cut from pieces of cigarette paper, folded to shape and painted with a light beige colour. From the upper canopy parts I removed, with a razor saw, the crew access hatches; the plastic here is brittle so care must be taken during this operation. The removed canopy sections were cleaned up with a fine sanding stick, glued onto a piece of stretched sprue and later used as moulds for making new parts from heated 0.4mm thin clear plastic sheet. The fit of the front and pilot's canopies to the resin gondola and bottom part of the wing was not without problems because on the port side I needed to level the side join with Tamiya epoxy putty. Once this part was sanded and cleaned up I continued with the mid-upper solid part and finished the job with the rear glazing and aft cone, both of which thankfully matched nicely. The small side windows at the gunner's position (these are omitted on the kit parts) were filled with a piece of clear plastic sheet cemented in place with super-thin cyanoacrylate. Now I could attach the wing outer upper parts that were joined with the tail booms and the complete assembly was gradually checked for correct geometry, along with the horizontal stabilizer, which was added at the same time. The wing assembly was finished with the bottom centre and outer parts, which were trimmed and then glued in place. Thanks to this 'step by step' approach to assembly I avoided unnecessary filling and fully controlled the fit and geometry of all the parts.

Now I added some missing surface details on the booms such as the reinforcing strips and raised rims that were cut from 0.12mm Evergreen strips and stretched sprue respectively, then glued in place with MEK. With a small amount of putty I sorted out a slightly deformed area under the rear glazing, and after overall cleaning and smoothing of the surface with fine grade sanding stick and a toothbrush, I added the resin rudders and applied the Montex canopy masks. The resin engine parts were first primed with Mr Surfacer (black) and then the engine was painted gloss black (H2) with the bearers in RLM 02 (H70). While the set contains all the parts necessary for a completely exposed engine, I actually glued the front face in situ and opened just the side panels and ventral oil cooler unit. The rear bulkhead with its oil tank needed a bit of thinning as it fouled the front of the resin wheel well, but after a few passes with a sander

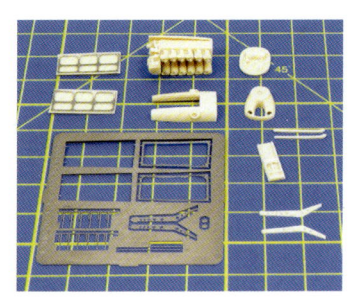

The components of the CMK engine set; the inner etched details for each side cowling have already been attached by this stage

everything fitted just perfectly so that the engine could be glued to the wing. The completed model was then primed with Mr Surfacer 1000 and once any small imperfections were addressed with a few drops of the same, I continued with the painting.

My choice was a machine from 1.(H)32 that was based in 1943 in Finland and wore winter white distemper over the standard dark green and black-green RLM 70/71. First I airbrushed on the yellow (H34) theatre markings under each wing tip and around the booms then continued with RLM 65 (H67) for the undersides. After some masking, mainly on the booms, I sprayed on the upper surface camouflage consisting of RLM 70/71 (H65/H64) with the transition between each colour being done freehand and not very precisely because these colours only form the solid base for the upper white distemper. Once the paints were sufficiently dry I airbrushed the upper surfaces with AK Interactive Worn Effects acrylic fluid and let it dry for about an hour. The upper surface then received an uneven layer of white (H11), which was sprayed with random density to give the upper surfaces a suitable base for the next process. With an old stiff brush dipped in hot water I progressively reproduced paint chips, moving slowly from the heavily weathered wing roots to the leading edges and wing tips as well as the area around the wing crosses; I weathered the tail booms and tailplanes in the same manner. I was trying to not overdo the final effect, and once I was satisfied the surface was fixed with gloss varnish in preparation for the decals. The kit's decals performed nicely and without problems and despite their age they quickly reacted to the hot water without any sign of disintegration, as so often happens with older decals. Next I applied to the panel lines a wash mixed from black and brown oil paints, which was subsequently wiped off the surface with cotton buds.

Between individual painting sessions I assembled the undercarriage, adding the etched detail parts that add a lot to their overall appearance and also provide operating rams that are omitted from the kit, and the resin wheels offer much better tread detail. The mudguard struts were scratchbuilt from 0.4mm wire and then the parts were primed and painted RLM 02. Thanks to the easy and robust design the undercarriage installation into the wheel wells went without trouble, and by using AK Interactive

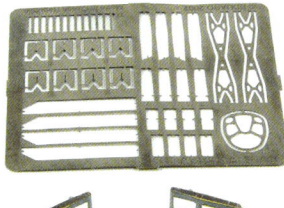

The resin wheels are much better than the kit parts and the etched just adds that little extra realism

With an old brush and warm water, the paint is scrubbed away from the leading edges and other high-wear areas

You can take as little or as much of the white off as you like

The decals behaved very well, regardless of their age, settling down with the help of Mr Mark Setter solution

A dark wash is applied to all the panel lines, then later the excess is wiped away

The DF loop housing is solid, when it should be clear, so this area was first painted with Duraluminium (Alclad 2), then toned down with a coat of Tamiya Smoke (X-19)

Mud and dirt is replicated aft of each wheel well, by blowing pigment and fixer mix on with an airbrush

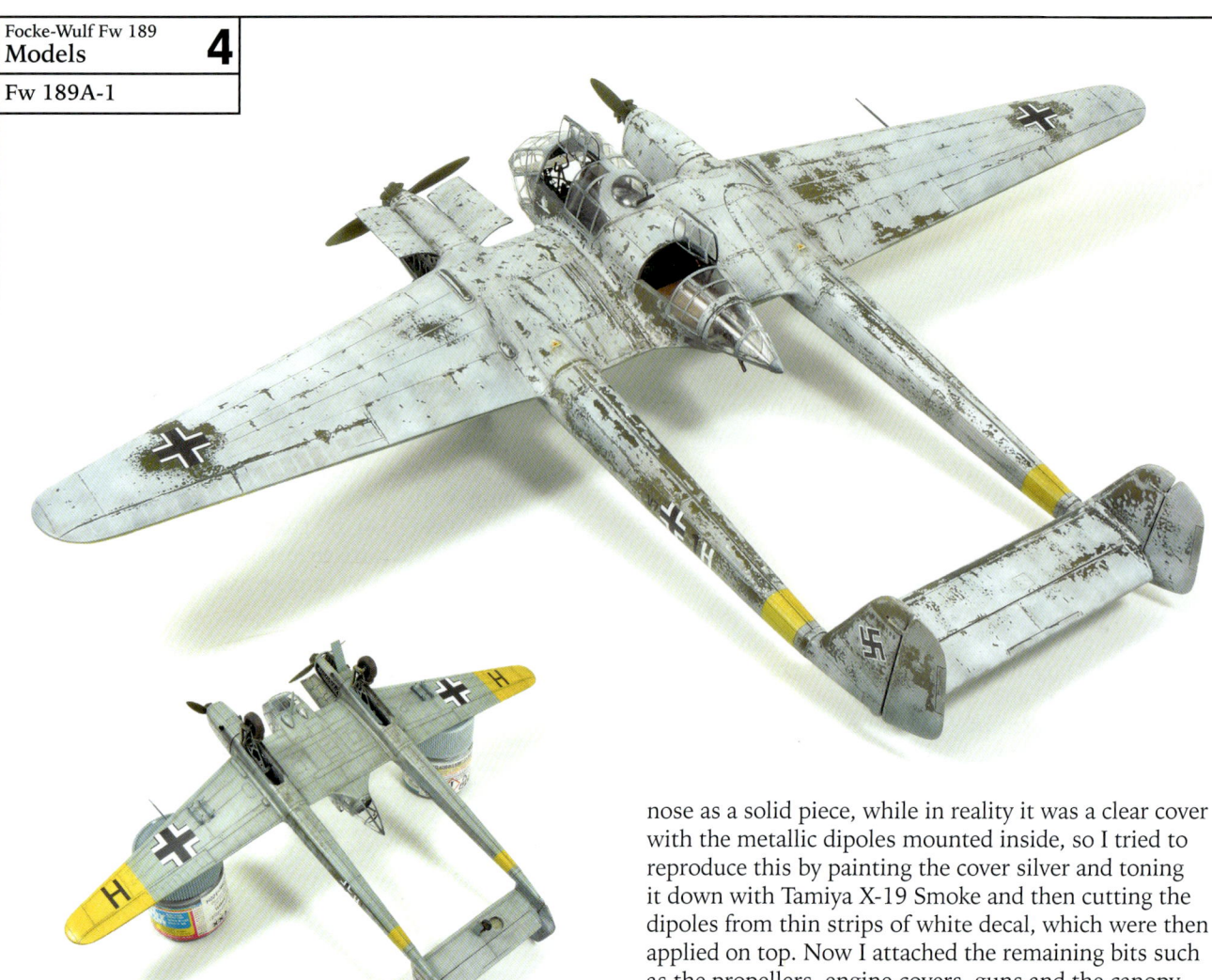

Streaking Grime enamel I reproduced some dirt on each unit. For the mud and water streaks on the undersurfaces, which were unavoidable during winter operation, I used a method known to armour modellers: a small amount of MIG Productions Russian Earth pigment was thinned with blue label thinner of the same brand, then loaded onto a brush and using the airflow from an airbrush streaks and splotches were applied aft of the wheel wells. The kit supplies the RDF antenna cover under the nose as a solid piece, while in reality it was a clear cover with the metallic dipoles mounted inside, so I tried to reproduce this by painting the cover silver and toning it down with Tamiya X-19 Smoke and then cutting the dipoles from thin strips of white decal, which were then applied on top. Now I attached the remaining bits such as the propellers, engine covers, guns and the canopy access hatches, all secured in place with thicker cyanoacrylate. Using Albion Alloys micro tubing I replaced the pitot and then added the bomb racks – job done!

Verdict

As already pointed out this kit represents the only reasonable choice in 1/72nd and offers acceptable standards of detail etc. in comparison with recent kits. It can be built to offer a nice looking replica even without the aftermarket products used here, which are obviously aimed at the more skilled modeller because their incorporation requires substantial modifications to the base kit.

Great Wall Hobby 1/48th
Fw 189A-2

by Steve A. Evans

The Shanghai Lion Roar Art Model Co. Ltd was founded in 2001 to produce aftermarket detail and conversion sets as well as production for other companies. As Great Wall Hobby they have branched out into producing their own fully formed plastic kits, complete with all the lovely photo-etched bits and pieces that we modellers love so much. This Fw 189 was the first of those aircraft back in 2010 and their hi-tech approach to producing it is evident from the very first glance in the box. The parts are beautifully formed on five sprues of light grey-coloured plastic and one of clear bits. There is some great moulded detail and everything is crisp and sharp looking. There is a single photo-etched fret that is very thin and delicate, a single decal sheet and a whole sheet of vinyl masks for the extensive glazed canopies. High points of the box contents are the inclusion of two Argus AS410 engines, complete with ignition harnesses, two engine maintenance platforms and two chocks as well. You even get a single pilot figure if you fancy that kind of thing, how nice. The interior is very neatly moulded and with the addition of the etched parts for the seat-belts and rudder pedals it looks very busy in there. The mouldings are pretty comprehensive; the only additions I made

The box presentation is good and although the art is a bit ropey, the contents look excellent

were the oxygen hoses, throttle and actuator levers for the pilot and the brake lines from the rudder pedals. This makes a very busy looking office and it all fits together in the fuselage halves pretty well, with only the minimum of fettling. The one noticeable absence is the main wing carry-through spar, which runs right across the centre of the interior. To be honest I didn't have enough information in my books about its size and shape so I opted to leave it out, and hopefully the rather gloomy interior colour will hide the fact that it's missing. Apart from that it looks pretty good. Fit of the clear parts is excellent with most of them dropping into place without any kind of adjustment; however, those vinyl masks are just awful. Not only are some of them the incorrect size and shape but they have a tendency to 'spring' back to a flat shape and lift away at the edges. I replaced some of the curved ones with Tamiya tape and to be honest I should have done

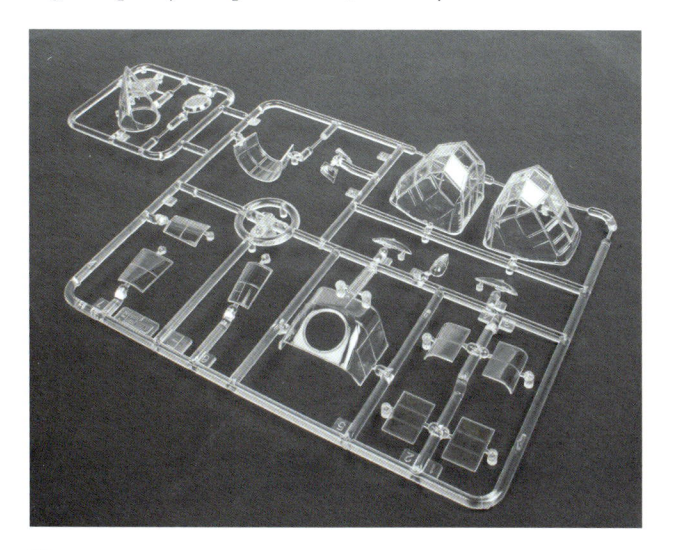

Clear parts

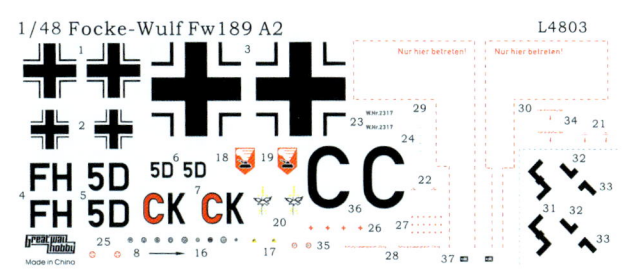

Decal

the whole bunch, as it would have solved a lot of problems a bit later. The long, slender wings of this machine are very well moulded items without a hint of warping but they are made in a multitude of sections. They all fit together very well but you do have to do lots of trial fits to get it right. At least you get fully poseable control surfaces with photo-etched parts for the interior structure of the flaps. You have to build the tail booms as an integral part of the wing structure, which means that you capture the wheels and engines between the two halves of the booms. The engines are glorious bits of moulding work with excellent detail needing only a lick of paint to look good. The ignition harnesses are supplied as PE bits and are a bit tricky as they are very thin but make a huge difference to the engine bays. Fitting the wings to the fuselage could have been a nightmare with a model of this shape but the mouldings are pretty accurate, making the joints trouble free for the most part. You do have to adjust the fit of the gun muzzle inserts but that's a minor point and nothing to worry about. With the tail in place as well, it's time for the paint.

The standard Fw 189A machines don't really have a huge variation in paintwork; it's mostly the usual RLM 70/71/65. In the box you get two options, one in this scheme and the other in a full-on winter distemper. I opted to try my hand at the temporary white finish, knowing that it's pretty tough to get it looking right; if you don't try these things you never know, do you? It all starts out pretty ordinarily with a coat of primer and a flash of White Ensign Colourcoats ACLW03 RLM 65 Hellblau. This was masked off and the upper coat of RLM 70 sprayed on, this time it's Humbrol 91 Black Green. I used the darker green first to get a low contrast scheme, so this was masked off and over-sprayed with the lighter RLM 71 Dunkelgrün, again White Ensign ACLW11 RLM 71. The masking was peeled off and the tail boom identification stripes were applied with a flash of yellow paint before the whole thing was set aside to fully harden off for a minimum of 24 hours.

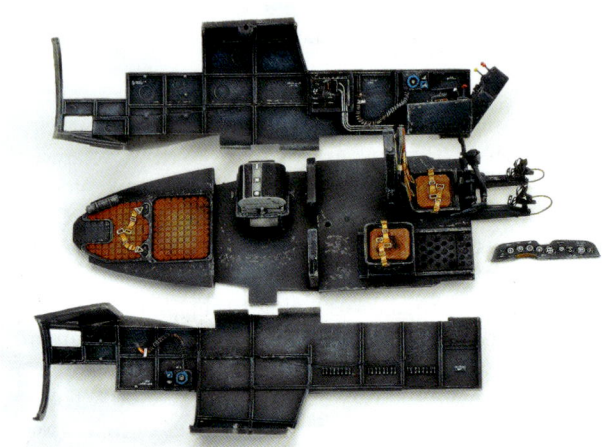

The interior is very nice, even if it is going to be a bit gloomy with the RLM 66 paint

Focke-Wulf Fw 189
Models
Fw 189A-2

What followed were several coats of Johnson's Klear and then the decals. The markings are well printed on the small sheet but are very glossy and a bit on the thick side. They do have great colour density and were easy to move around and position but they took a long time to settle down into the nooks and crannies. A good soaking in Microscale decal solutions helped them along but they were still reluctant. They were sealed in under another couple of coats of Klear and set aside to harden off for a while, in preparation for the next stage.

I used a lot of Klear on this kit, because I needed to isolate the paint from the process that followed, namely spraying the whole thing with Halfords Gloss Appliance White, decanted into the airbrush. I wanted this machine to look pretty scruffy, so I decided to scrub the white paint off using some White Spirit and a short-bristled brush, along with some 3200 grade Micro-mesh cloth. I concentrated along the panel joints and the leading edges as well as any areas that the groundcrew would have been crawling around on. This took off

The undercarriage units display more good moulded detail but they're a bit on the fragile side: handle with care

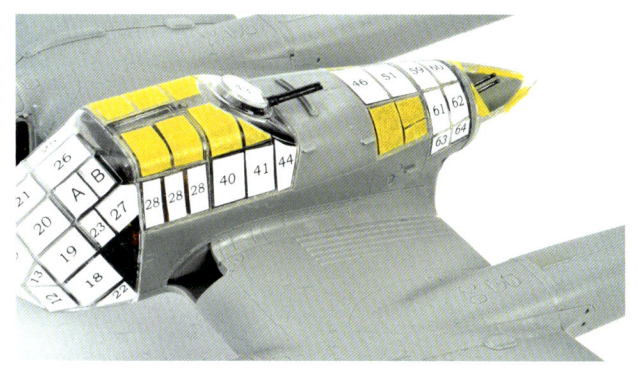

The fit of the wings to the fuselage pod could have been a bit troublesome but it's taken care of with some accurate mould work. Note the wing root inserts for the guns, a quick swap of parts and you could have another version on offer

Halfords Grey Plastic Primer is the first step on the paint ladder

Upper surface RLM 70 is very dark and is applied first so that the following colours will have minimum contrast

Yellow theatre band applied and it's time for the multiple layers of Johnson's Klear to isolate the paintwork

layers of the outer white surface, revealing the greens beneath in varying degrees. It wasn't wholly successful in that the gloss paint dries really hard and tended to come off in patches that were a little too sharp-edged. If I do this again I'll try using a softer white primer paint and see if I can get a more feathered edge to the removed areas. Not to worry, it looks pretty good as it is so I won't try messing around with it too much or I just know I'll wreck the whole thing. I did my usual accentuations of a bit of pastel dust and a very thin dark brown paint sprayed along the panel lines which blended it all in quite nicely, including the bright colours of the decals; the last coats of Xtracolor XDFF flat varnish were applied and all the masking was peeled off.

Remember I mentioned the vinyl masks earlier in the build? Well I was right about not using them as paint had got under just about every single one of them, even the ones that looked like they were sealed down properly. Oh well, a couple of hours cleaning up the canopies with a cocktail stick and some washer fluid had them looking nice and shiny again. Just be warned, the masks don't work!

Verdict

What a great kit! No arguments from me about its quality and the fit and finish of the parts, Great Wall Hobby can be rightly proud of their first aircraft. The only negatives are the useless vinyl masks and the missing detail in the cockpit. Apart from that the subject matter is an inspired choice and they have approached it in a logical and beautifully produced manner. There are even the spare bits in the box to make the nightfighter version, so top marks.

Here we go, full-on white application, if this doesn't work it's going to be tricky to fix

Focke-Wulf Fw 189
Models
1/32 Scale

1/32nd Scale

As we write this in early 2015, there are no kits of the Fw 189 in this scale, however Czech manufacturer HpH have announced a resin kit of the type for release at some stage during 2015. We are delighted to be able, thanks to the generosity of HpH, to include here a number of images of the prototype/master components being test-assembled as well as details of the colour schemes that will be in the kit.

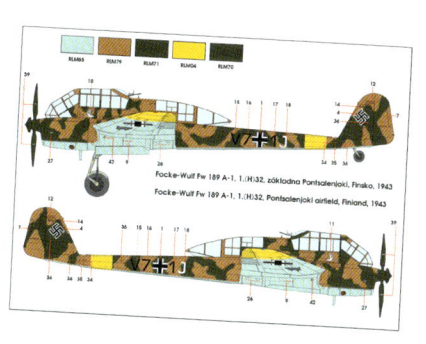

Camouflage option 1 is V7+1J of 1./(H)32 at Pontsalenjoki airfield, Finland in 1943; we doubt the use of actual RLM 79, as period accounts state 'olive brown' and that is most likely a field-mixed colour

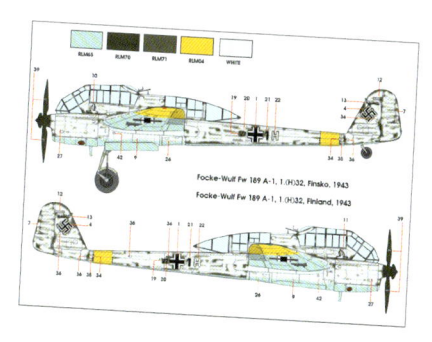

Camouflage option 3 is V7+1H of 1./(H)32, Finland in 43 this time in the winter distemper over RLM 70/71/65 scheme

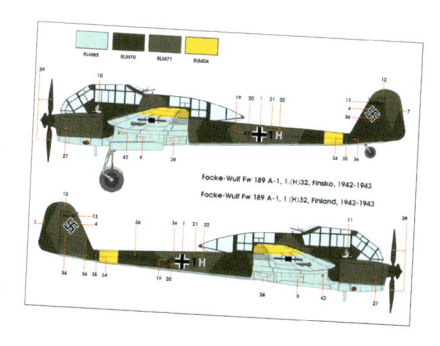

Camouflage option 2 is V7+1H of 1./(H)32, Finland in 1942-43 in the standard RLM 70/71 over 65 scheme

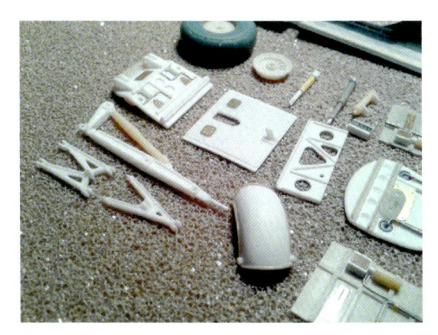

Here you can see some of the parts that go into the undercarriage area

The superb glazings

Here you can see the engine cowling and propeller hub, we presume the vanes will either be etched or resin parts

Close-up of the canopy and framework

Overall shots of the main components assembled, with the glazed access panels in the open position

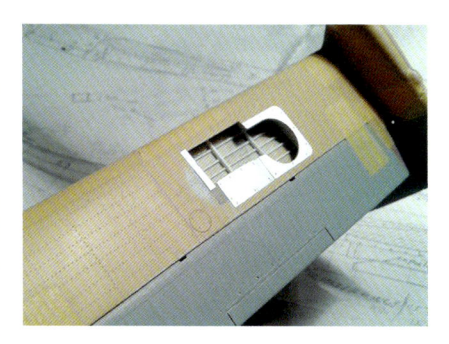

Lovely engraved details on the underside of the tailplane, along with the etched parts used on this master to create the closed-in effect of the wheel well

AA06/40/111 — Valiant Wings Publishing — Issued: February 2015

Focke-Wulf Fw 189 Kits
Appendix I

Below is a list of all static scale construction kits produced to date of the Focke-Wulf Fw 189 series. This list is as comprehensive as possible, but if there are amendments or additions, please contact the author via the Valiant Wings Publishing address shown at the front of this title. All kits listed below are injection-moulded plastic (including limited-run) unless otherwise stated.

1/72nd Scale

- Airfix 1/72nd Focke-Wulf Fw 189 #Patt. No.267 (1970) – Depicted the A-2 – Renumbered #02037-8 in 1973 (Type 4 & 5 box), #903053 in 1985, #03053 in 1986 and 1993, announced for reissue in 2009 as #A03053 but not actually released until 05/2010
- Anigrand Craftworks, Hong Kong [res] 1/144th Focke-Wulf Fw 261 #AA-4026 (2009) – Included bonus kits of the BMW Strahljäger P.III, Arado E.500, BV P.196 and Fw 189 V6
- Aoshima 1/72nd Fw 189A-1 #502 (mid-1960s) – Later renumbered #015230
- Bilek (ex-Airfix) 1/72nd Focke-Wulf Fw 189 #920 (1995)
- Condor 1/72nd Fw 189A-1 #C72005 (2001) – N.B. Originally announced in 1993/4 as an A-2 version, but that version was eventually released by MPM in 2008
- Condor 1/72nd Focke-Wulf Fw 189A-1 'Upgraded' #C72017 (2002)
- Condor 1/72nd Focke-Wulf Fw 189B-1 #C72006 – Announced 1993/4 but never released [produced as a limited-run kit in the MPM range in 2002]
- Czechmaster [res] 1/72nd Focke-Wulf Fw 189B-0 #301 (1997)
- Italeri (ex-MPM/Condor) 1/72nd Fw 189A-1 Uhu #1239 (2003)
- MPC (ex-Airfix) 1/72nd Focke-Wulf Fw 189 #2-2112 (1965-1985)
- MPC (ex-Airfix) 1/72nd Fw 189 Flying Eye including crewmen #72-2112:250 (N/K) – In the 'Air Combat Collection' series
- MPM 1/72nd Fw 189B #72506 (2002)
- MPM 1/72nd Fw 189 V6 #72516 (2002)
- MPM 1/72nd Fw 189A-2 'Night Fighter' #72529 (Announced 2003/4, released 2007) – Same tooling as Condor
- MPM 1/72nd Fw 189A-2 #72550 (2008) – Same tooling as Condor
- Planet Models [res] 1/72nd Fw 189B #053 (N/K)
- Revell 1/72nd (ex-Condor) Focke-Wulf Fw 189A-1 #04294 (2009) – Released with kits & paint as a Model-Set in mid-2010 (#64294)
- RS Models [res] 1/72nd Fw 189 V6 #7227 (1993->)
- Yumtk [vac] 1/72nd Fw 189 Uhu (1992-2000) – Production not confirmed

1/48th Scale

- Airmodel [vac] 1/48th Fw 189 #AM-4819 (1969-2000) – Under Frank Modellbau ownership from 1980s
- Great Wall Hobby 1/48th Focke-Wulf Fw 189A-2 #L4803 (2010)
- Great Wall Hobby 1/48th Focke-Wulf Fw 189A-1 'Nacht Jäger' #L4801 (2011)
- Great Wall Hobby 1/48th Focke-Wulf Fw 189A-1 'Solderaktion Schneekufen' #L4808 (2012) – On skis
- ICM 1/48th Focke-Wulf Fw 189A-1 #48221 – Announced for 2010, not released to date
- ICM 1/48th Focke-Wulf Fw 189A-2 #48222 – Announced for 2010, not released to date
- Karo-As Modellbau [vac/res] 1/48th Fw 189 'Uhu'/'Owl' #Nr.48.19 (1992) – Ceased production in 1996. Decal options: Fw 189A-2, W/Nr.125715, 5H+RK/, NAGr.16, Salzburg, Austria, 1945; Fw 189A-1, 5D+FH, 1/(H)31, Russia; Fw 189A-1, W/Nr.2317, 5D+CK , 2/(H)31, Russia, January 1943
- MPM 1/48th Fw 189A #48030 (1997)
- MPM 1/48nd Fw 189A 'Hi-tech' #48034 (1998) – Included two resin engines, detailed cowlings, injected & vacformed canopies and photo-etched detail parts. Decal options: Fw 189A-1, W/Nr.2100, V7+1H, 1/(H)32, Pontsalenjoki airfield, Finland, May 1943; Fw 189A-1, F0+64, 3/1 Sqn., Magyar Királyi Honvéd Légierõ (Royal Hungarian Air Force), Ukraine, 1943; Fw 189A-1, 1st Reconnaisance Flight, Slovenské vzdušné zbrane, Žilina, 1943
- MPM 1/48nd Fw 189B #48035 (1998)
- R&D Replicas (ex-Karo-As) [vac/res] 1/48th Fw 189 Uhu #48.19 (1994-1999)

1/32nd Scale

- HpH [res] 1/32nd Fw 189A #TBA – Announced in late 2014 for 2015 release

Notes
pe – Photo-etched metal
res – Resin
vac – Vacuum-formed Plastic
(1999) – Denotes date the kit was released
(1994->) – Date/s denote start/finish of firm's activities, the exact date of release of this kit is however unknown
ex- – Denotes the tooling originated with another firm, the original tool maker is noted after the '-'

Focke-Wulf Fw 189
Access. & Decals
Appendix II

As there are only a few accessories and decals for the Focke-Wulf Fw 189 we thought it best to combine these in one Appendix. Below therefore is a list of all accessories and decals for static scale construction kits produced to date for the Fw 189. This list is as comprehensive as possible, but if there are amendments or additions, please contact the author via the Valiant Wings Publishing address shown at the front of this title.

1/72nd Accessories
- Airwaves [pe] Fw 189A-2 Detail Set #AC72141{Airfix} – Later renumbered #AEC72141
- CMK [res/pe] Fw 189A Interior Detail Set #7042 {Condor/MPM}
- CMK [res/pe] Fw 189A Exterior Detail Set #7043 {Condor/MPM}
- CMK [res/pe] Fw 189A Engine Set #7044 {Condor/MPM}
- CMK [res/pe] Fw 189A Detail Set #7045 {Condor/MPM}
- CMK/Quick & Easy [res] Fw 189A/B/V6 Tailplane & Rudders #Q72 155 {Condor/MPM/Italeri/Revell}
- CMK/Quick & Easy [res] Fw 189A/B/V6 Main Undercarriage Bays #Q72 156 {Condor/MPM/Italeri/Revell}
- CMK/Quick & Easy [res] Argus AS410 engine for Ar 96 & Fw 189 #Q72 165 {Condor/MPM/Italeri/Revell}
- Cobra Company [res/vac] Fw 189A Detail Set #72015 {Airfix}
- Cobra Company [res/vac] Fw 189A Detail Set #72016 {Condor/MPM}
- Eduard [ma] Fw 189 Canopy & Wheel Masks #XF168 {Condor/MPM}
- Equipage [res] Fw 189A Wheel Set #72021
- Falcon [vf] Clear-Vax Canopies 'Luftwaffe WWII Part 4' #Set No.21 {Airfix}
- Montex [vma] Fw 189A-1 Nachtjäger Canopy Masks #SM72067 {Condor/Mpm/Italeri/Revell}
- North Star Models [pe] Fw 189A Flaps #NS72001 {Airfix/Condor/MPM/Italeri/Revell}

1/48th Accessories
- Aires [res/vma] Fw 189 Wheels & Paint Masks #4561{Great Wall Hobby}
- Cutting Edge Modelworks [vma] Canopy & Wheel Masks #CEBM48476 {MPM}
- Eduard [pe] Fw 189 Landing Flaps #48-710 {Great Wall Hobby}
- Eduard [pe] Fw 189 Exterior Detail Set #48-712 {Great Wall Hobby}
- Eduard [pe] Fw 189 Surface Panels (SA) #48-714 {Great Wall Hobby}
- Eduard [pe] Fw 189A-2 Interior Detail Set (PP/SA) #49-565 {Great Wall Hobby}
- Eduard [pe] Fw 189A-2 Interior Detail Set – Zoom (PP/SA) #FE565 {Great Wall Hobby}
- Eduard [pe] Fw 189A-1 Interior Detail Set (PP/SA) #49-578 {Great Wall Hobby}
- Eduard [pe] Fw 189A-1 Interior Detail Set – Zoom (PP/SA) #FE578 {Great Wall Hobby}
- Eduard [ma] Fw 189 Canopy & Wheel Masks #EX152 {MPM}
- Eduard [ma] Fw 189 Canopy & Wheel Masks #EX350 {Great Wall Hobby}
- Eduard [pe/ma] Fw 189A-1 'Big ED' Detail Set (PP/SA) #BIG4966 {Great Wall Hobby} – Includes EX350 (masks), 48-710 (flaps), 48-712 (exterior), 48-714 (surface panels) & 49-565 (interior)
- Quickboost [res] Fw 189 Propeller w/tool #QB48393 {Great Wall Hobby}
- Scale Aircraft Conversions [wm] Fw 189 Landing Gear #48124{Great Wall Hobby}
- Montex [vma] Fw 189A-1 Nachtjäger Canopy Masks #SM48350 {Great Wall Hobby}
- North Star Models [pe] Fw 189A Flaps #NS48001 {Great Wall Hobby}
- North Star Models [res/pe] Fw 189A Main Wheels, Tail Wheel and Tailwheel Bay #NS48002 {Great Wall Hobby}
- North Star Models [res] Fw 189A Main Wheels #NS48003 {Great Wall Hobby}
- North Star Models [res/pe] Fw 189A Interior Detail Set #NS48004 {Great Wall Hobby}

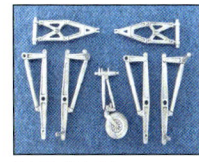

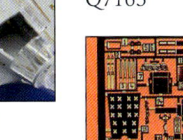

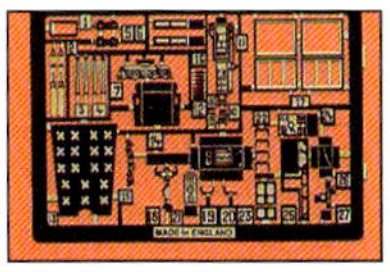

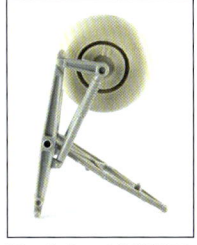

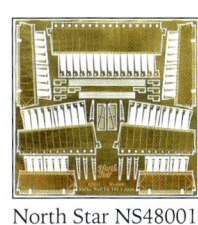

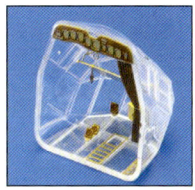

1/72nd Decals – Esci
#55 Fw 189 & BV 141
- Inc: JZ+KC, C2+EH, NI+1H, V7+IS

1/72nd Decals – HAD (HungAeroDecals)
#72133 Fw 189A-1
- Fw 189A-1, FO+55, 3/1 Squadron, Hungarian Air Force, Russia, summer 1943
- Fw 189A-1, +A, 11.(H)12
- Fw 189A-1, H1+BI, 3.(H)Pz/Aufkl 12, Don river area, Russia, summer 1942
- Ex-Rumanian Air Force example captured by the Soviets at Zhukovsky airfield and tested in the USSR
- Unmarked machine of the Solvakian Air Force for operations in the Tatra region

1/48th Decals – Authentic Decals
#48-45 Focke-Wulf Fw 189 Uhu
- Fw 189A-1, W7+DB, 1/NJG100, Russia, 1944
- Fw 189A-2, V7+1K, 1.(H)/32, Petsamo airfield, Finland, 1942
- Fw 189A-2, T1+GM, 4.(H)/10, Kharkow area, Russia, 1942
- Fw 189A-2, 'White 17', 331 Squadron, Bulgarian Air Force, Sarafowo airfield, July 1944
- Fw 189A-1, FO+55, 3/1 Squadron, Hungarian Air Force, Russia, summer 1943
- Fw 189A-1, SI+EG, unknown unit, Russia, 1942
- Fw 189A-2, 5D+KH, 2.(H)/31, Eastern Front, 1942
- Fw 189A-2, 5H+RK, NAGr.16, Germany, 1945
- Fw 189A-1, H1+BI, 3.(H)Pz/Aufkl 12, Don river area, Russia, 1942
- Fw 189A-2, 4E+MK, 2.(H)13, Smolenska, Russia, 1942
- Fw 189A-2, 5D+HH, 2.(H)/31, Eatern Front, 1943

1/48th Decals – HAD (HungAeroDecals)
#48133 Fw 189A-1
Same five options as listed above for 1/72nd version (#72133)

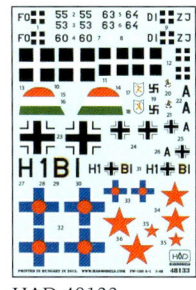

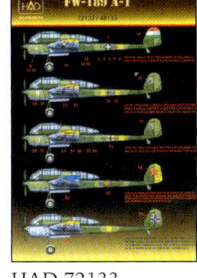

Notes
- ma – Die-cut Self-adhesive Paint Masks [tape]
- pe – Photo-etched Brass
- PP – Pre-painted (photo-etched)
- res – Resin
- SA – Self-adhesive
- vac – Vacuum-formed Plastic
- vma – Vinyl Self-adhesive Paint Masks
- wm – White-metal (including Pewter)
- {Academy} – Denotes the kit for which the set is intended

Bibliography
Appendix III

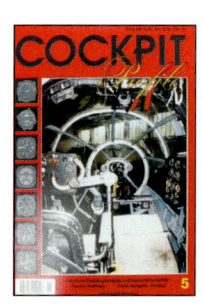

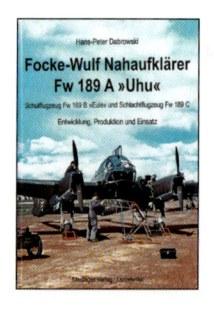

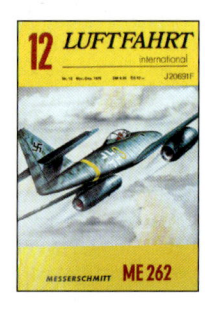

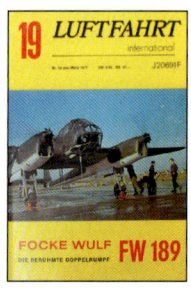

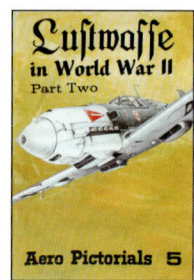

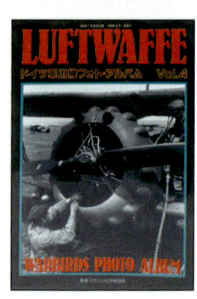

The list of Focke-Wulf Fw 189 related publications below is as comprehensive as possible, but there are bound to be omissions so if you have amendments or additions, please contact the author via the Valiant Wings Publishing address shown at the front of this title.

Official Documents
- Flugzeug-Handbuch, D(Luft)T 2189, dated 1941 (Aircraft Manual)
- Ersatzteilliste, dated 1942-43 (Parts List)
- Bed-Vorschrift-Fl., dated 1943
- Kurz-Betriebsanleitung KBA/Fl, dated 1940 (User's Manual)

Publications
- Aircraft of World War II by C. Chant (Dempsey Parr, 1999)
- Aufklärer: Luftwaffe Reconnaissance Aircraft & Units 1935-1945 by D. Wadman, J. Bradley & B. Ketley (Hikoki Publications 1997 ISBN: 0-9519899-8-7)
- Camouflage & Markings of the Luftwaffe Aircraft Vol.2 Night Fighters, Bombers & Others, Model Art Special No.356 (Model Art Co., Ltd 1990)
- Cockpit Profile No.5 – Deutsche Flugzeugcockpits und Instrumentenbretter by P.W. Cohausz (Flugzeug Publikations GmbH)
- Colours of the Luftwaffe by S.W. Parry & F.L. Martshall (Clifford Frost Ltd 1987 ISBN: 1-8700666-03-0)
- Eagles of the Third Reich: Hitler's Luftwaffe by S.W. Mitcham (Airlife Publishing Ltd 1988/Guild Publishing Ltd 1989)
- Flugzeugtypen Vol 4 Military Aircraft of WWII (Modelsport Verlag GmBh 1999 ISBN: 3-923142-12-9)
- Flugzeug-Typenbuch – Handbuch der deutschen Luftfahrt-und Zubehör-Industrie (Joachim Beyer Verlag 1984, reprint of January 1944 edition)
- Focke-Wulf An Aircraft Album by J. Richard Smith (Ian Allan 1973 ISBN:0-7110-0425-0)
- Focke-Wulf Fw 189 by P. Kucera, D. Benad & S. Androvic (MBI 1989)
- Focke-Wulf Fw 189 In Action No.142 by G. Punka (Squadron/Signal Publications 1995 ISBN: 0-89747-310-8)
- Focke-Wulf Fw 189 Uhu by B. Belcarz, Typy Broni Uzbrojenia No.191
- Fw 189 by Z. Luranc, Skrzydla w miniaturze No.11 (Avia Press 1994)
- German Aircraft of the Second World War by J.R.Smith & A.L. Kay (Putnam, 1972)
- German Short-range Reconnaissance Planes 1930-1945 by M. Griehl & J. Dressel (Schiffer 1989 ISBN: 0-88740-190-2)
- Hungarian Air Force by G. Punka (Squadron/Signal Publications 1994 ISBN: 0-89747-349-3)
- Hungarian Eagles: The Hungarian Air Forces 1920-1945 by G. Sárhidai, G. Punka & V. Kozlik (Hikoki Publications 1996 ISBN: 0-9519899-1-X)
- Luftwaffe in World War II Part 2, Aero Pictorials 5 (Aero Publishers Inc. 1979 ISBN: 8168-0316-1)
- Lufwaffe Warbirds Photo Album Vol.4, Tank Magazine Special Issue (Delta Publishing 1993)
- Photo Archive 1 – Luftwaffe Camouflage & Markings 1933-1945 by K.A. Merrick, E.J. Creek & B. Green (Midland Publishing 2007 ISBN: 1-85780-275-6)
- The Bulgarian Air Force In Action During the Second World War (Air Power of the Kingdom of Bulgaria Part IV) by D. Nedialkov (Air Sofia)
- The Luftwaffe In Camera 1939-1942 by A. Price (Budding Books 2000 ISBN: 1-84015-111-0)
- The Warplanes of the Third Reich by William Green (Macdonald & Co Ltd, 1970)
- Typy Broni Uzbrojenia No.155 (1992 ISBN: 83-11-08278-2)
- Warplanes of the Luftwaffe (Aerospace Publishing 1994)
- War Prizes: The Album by P. Butler (Midland Publishing 2006 ISBN: 1-85780-244-6)
- Wings of Fame Vol.3 (Aerospace Publishing Ltd 1996)
- Wings of the Black Cross Nos.1 & 2 by J. Crandall (Eagle Editions Ltd 2005/2006 ISBN:0-9721-060-3-0 & 0-9721-060-9-X)
- Wings of the Luftwaffe by Capt. Eric Brown (Airlife Publishing Ltd 1987 & 2000 ISBN: 1-85310-413-2)

Periodicals & Part-works
- Luftfahrt International No.12, Nov-Dec 1975, No.19, Jan-March 1977 & No.20 March-April 1977
- Plastic Kit Constructor No.68
- RAF Flying Review, October 1956
- Replic No.79 (March 1998) & No.236 (April 2011)
- Scale Aircraft Modelling Vol.13 No.11 August 1991 & Vol.25 No.11 January 2004
- Skrzydla w miniaturze No.11